0845

6

fixed text lower

SYS

07971012185

in

Meeting 4.15

CW00724224

Building for Self-Sufficiency

Building for Self-Sufficiency

**TOOLS • MATERIALS • BUILDING • HEAT
INSULATION • SOLAR ENERGY • WIND POWER
WATER & PLUMBING • WASTE & COMPOST
METHANE • TRANSPORT • FOOD**

Robin Clarke

UNIVERSE BOOKS

New York

Illustrations by JANINE CLARKE

Published in the United States of America in 1977
by Universe Books
381 Park Avenue South
New York, N.Y. 10016

© Robin Clarke, 1976

Library of Congress Catalog Card Number: 76–5093
Cloth edition: ISBN 0–87663–230–4
Paperback edition: ISBN 0–87663–945–7
Printed in the United States of America

For Peter Bynon, Peter Collis, Nick Tunstall and Frank Ruscoe –
who showed us how.

For John and Maria, Philip, Johanne, Peter, Roger, Mike, little
Robin, Ruth and Ellie – with whom we did it.

For Benson and Eileen, Giles and Kyrle, Hugh and Terry,
both Simons, Geoffrey and Bruce, Tim and Prem, Bret and Julia,
Linda, Ralph, Maryke, George and Suzie, David and Fiona,
Rodney, Chris and many, many others – who helped so much.

And for the International Publishing Corporation, who made me
redundant and so helped to pay for it.

Author's Note

THIS book is written at a time when metrication is still beginning. I have interchanged metric and older units freely, using older where they are still the more familiar, and metric where, as in insulation and heating, they are in any case the more useful. A conversion table is given as an appendix at the back of the book.

Contents

List of Illustrations

Chapter 1

⊷∘⊶

The limits to self-sufficiency

ON 30th March, 1973, I left my centrally heated house in London to join a rural commune in Wales. We had bought a 43-acre hill-farm there a few months previously, and our first job was to convert the small and near-derelict stone cottage on the farm to a house to shelter and succour the community of 16 people which we planned for the site.

We set ourselves up as BRAD – standing for Biotechnic Research and Development. We were certainly not short on theoretical ideas. We were going to turn the place into a research centre to investigate such things as solar heating, wind power, heat pumps, methane generation, composting, highly productive but organic methods of growing food, and new building techniques. We wanted to devise a life-style that would be valid, not for just this generation living off a depleting stock of natural resources, but for generations far into the future. So we planned to be self-sufficient not only in food, but also in energy, water and, eventually, perhaps even materials. We planned to live on a very low income indeed – and to live closely with other people in a way which we thought ought to be far more fulfilling than the various jobs which we had all come from.

Someday, one of us will certainly write a book about that community – but that is not my intention here. Suffice to say that I and my family left 18 months later, and another five a few months after that. Nearly all of us left for the same reason: the struggle to do the things we wanted to do against a background of mounting inertia and community dissent proved too great. Just over three

13

years later the community had been officially disbanded, and the farm sold.

So, in a way, the experiment could justly be called a failure. But I don't think any of us who were there regard it as such. Certainly, I spent some of the most depressing moments of my life at Eithin. But, equally certainly, I experienced some of the highest points I have ever known, and for at least a year revelled in a freedom of spirit which I had never dreamt was possible. But, above all, I learnt. More, I think, in 18 months there than in 15 years of being an editor, journalist and freelance writer. This book is an attempt to put down, in a very practical way, something of what I learnt.

None of us at Eithin were very practical people – we had all come from jobs where we used our heads a lot and our hands but little. Yet I still look at the house we built there with pride. It is certainly one of the most remarkable buildings in the British Isles, and it is built to a standard rarely found in contemporary homes. We had the thing water-tight and habitable within nine months of starting work on the foundations. The building was a success.

So, too, was the solar roof we put on top to heat our hot water. And by the time I left, the 43-acre farm was running quite smoothly, thanks largely to the help of our neighbour Frank Ruscoe, who took it on himself to instruct us in the art of proper farming. We were pretty near being self-sufficient in food. And we made out financially – just. Even before we had killed the first pig for meat, we found we could live on about £2 a head per week – excluding such things as clothes, sweets and tobacco, but including all other bills, food, running the farm and providing ourselves with at least one vehicle in working order at any one time. That is no mean achievement, particularly as we certainly never felt poor, and only rarely were overcome by the need to go to town to spend a couple of crisp fivers. We had more than enough to do, and the temptation to spend money, other than on beer in the local, was virtually non-existent. Technically, we lived far below the poverty line, but we were certainly never deprived.

What, then, have those of us who left carried away which may be of interest, even of help, to others? Certainly not that living in a commune is better than any other kind of life – though it can be. Nor that the world would be a better place if we all strove for self-sufficiency and ecologically valid life-styles. In the four years since I first thought of the idea of Eithin, these things have become less important to me. What I learned at Eithin, perhaps surprisingly, has little to do with the million and one reasons I dreamt up for going there in the first place.

By far the most important was the discovery of my own abilities. This was certainly nothing to do with me, for all my previous attempts at being a handyman ended up with ill-fitting doors, wobbles, squeaks, and a sort of prefabricated finish which now seems to be the hallmark of the do-it-yourselfer. At Eithin, with time, the proper tools, and at least one person around who knew more than I did, I found all this vanished. Concrete-mixing, drain-laying, carpentry, joinery, roofing, plumbing, wiring, guttering, rendering, farming, and even vehicle maintenance soon became part of the daily life. And we did them well.

So, I suspect, can everyone else. Yet in our society there is a mystique attached to such crafts which leads 95 per cent of us to declare ourselves incapable of them. This is profoundly untrue. Within six months of starting work at Eithin I think we had all realized that there was nothing we could not do on that site if we put our minds to it. Apart from time, there was never again any reason for us to call in outside help to do something of which we were not capable.

That is not necessarily a virtue. Human life depends for its lubrication on contact with others, and much of that contact comes about from the need to do certain things. In this sense, self-sufficiency – which means living for yourself – is a deplorable aim. Living for others would be a better credo. ·

At the same time, we have lost something very precious. Our total dependency on others for services of all kinds does nothing to lubricate the wheels of social intercourse in a mass, anonymous society. On the contrary, it becomes a constant source of frustration, because you can never get anyone to do what you want when you want it, and of bankruptcy, because when they do come they charge the earth. For reasons of sanity and economics it makes sense to learn a few skills.

But there are other reasons. Whatever job it is, with a little practice you can certainly learn to do it better than most of those whose business it is to do it for you. I don't blame them. Squeezed as they are between mounting taxes, self-employment contributions, transport costs and all the rest of it, they can make ends meet only by skimping the job and charging you too much. The whole process has gone berserk. There has to be some way out of it, and your two hands are the only solution.

The divorce which modern society has effected between the head and the hands is possibly its greatest evil. It turns us all, in the end, into less than half a person. And anyone who learns again to use them together will, I guarantee, experience a rejuvenation not normally associated with the mundane tasks of laying drains and learning to make a ridge ladder. It is all something to do with bringing your life back under your own control. And of spending your time at a number of highly different jobs. The human being, surely, was never intended to do the same thing for hours on end for most of his waking life. There is more to living.

But, if I read the signs of the times correctly, such philosophizing may turn out to be only a luxury. When we're all on three-day week jobs, we shall, none of us, have the income to pay others to do for us what we convince ourselves we cannot do. Then there will be no choice – but much time, and little money. How shall we use the time? This book, in a way, is an attempt to tell you how to survive the three-day week, and live better at the same time. It could be that the three-day week turns out to be not a disaster but a salvation. Three days a week, surely, is enough of one's life to give to someone else? If we use the other four to enrich our own lives, I suspect we shall end up better off in every sense of the words.

To do that means much more than keeping your own house or flat in good repair, or even than building a new one. It means finding substitutes to expensive fuels, expensive transport, expensive food, and expensive materials. My own experience at Eithin was limited. In some areas we found some solutions, in others we found only improvements, and in yet others we found nothing. I have tried to include everything relevant in this book. Many of the things, though not all, I have done or tried myself – and where I depend on others for information I have tried to make it clear.

No one, even if he worked only a one-day week, could possibly do everything described in the pages to follow. That is not the idea. This is a book to browse through, to pick from, and to borrow from. It is not a recipe for life. There are limits to self-sufficiency which I think should always be respected. The aim is not to turn yourself into an over-worked, half-crazed hermit. The aim is to make do with less, and to live better as a result – either by choice or through necessity. If you make yoghourt for yourself and your neighbour, and he keeps his and your gutters in good repair, you are both better off than if you each did both things for yourself. But, most assuredly, you'll be worse off if you pay someone else to do either; you'll also eat worse yoghourt and probably have leaking gutters.

Chapter 2

⋘○⋙

Tools

EVERYTHING in this book depends on your having a good set of tools, and knowing how to use them well. Without that, you are lost before you start.

You can expect a lot from your tools. First, of course, tools will enable you to do a great many things which the tool-less will regard as totally mysterious. Contrary to popular opinion, a good workman does blame his tools – or at least he would if he didn't already have very good ones. There is all the difference in the world between having the right tool for the job and making do with something not quite right.

Second, you get a great feeling of power using a good tool well. Power is not exactly the right word – it's more a feeling of mastery or control, a sense that the world is not such a hostile place, that you're not such a cretin with your hands as you thought. You begin to realize that the age of specialization was a bit of a nonsense, and that there are few things, short of rebuilding the Severn bridge, that you can't do if you put your mind and tools to it. Incidentally, you do need both; a good tool without a brain behind it is as useless as a good brain with nothing to stimulate it. The whole point is to get the hands and head working together, and that's something no one seems to have thought much about since Adam Smith invented his damn pin factory.

Third, you'll get poetry from using tools well. I won't say much about it because it's a personal thing and this is a practical book. People these days may get sentimental about craftsmanship (by which they usually mean making ugly, coarse bits of pottery and spiky basketry) but with some practice you will discover some strange sensations and curious joys in good tool-using.

Finally, a word of warning. Gadgets are not tools, and before you get into tool-using in a serious way you need to cultivate an impeccable taste for telling the difference. A tiny propeller on a long shaft which you attach to an electric drill for paint stirring is not a tool but a piece of expensive consumer gadgetry. You stir your paint with an odd scrap of wood, and it'll do the job perfectly well. Many of the things you can buy in the do-it-yourself shops are gadgets and you should avoid them like the plague. They won't do the job properly, they'll break after a few weeks, and they'll give you nothing but hassles. For example, almost any tool which has got plastic in it is basically a gadget (there are some exceptions, of which more later). Above all, avoid anything with a plastic handle. Plastic slips in a sweaty hand, and gives you blisters. Wood handles absorb the sweat, don't slip, and are a pleasure to grasp. Tools made of 'special' steel which are said never to need sharpening are gadgets, because they are brittle and will eventually snap. Buy tools that do need sharpening, learn how to sharpen well, and you will have the cutting scene under your control.

This means that one of the first things to do is identify your nearest tool shop. If you have to go a few miles further afield than the local hardware stores so be it. But don't go mad when you get there. Some tools you buy from your tool shop: others can be got more cheaply. In *Buy Lines*, *Mother Earth News*, and some want ad columns you'll find second-hand tools of every description, as well as new tools offered at discount prices. Both are usually good buys. And in addition you can get many tools second-hand in junk shops, still for nearly nothing although the time will come soon enough when old tools will cost as much as useless Bakelite radios and other junk of the Art Deco period. For the moment, just enjoy the antique dealers' perverted sense of value which for once is still working in your favour. Junk shops are good for wrenches, screwdrivers, braces, wooden planes (better than the modern metal ones), hammers and odd bits and pieces. But not for chisels or saws, or any other precision instruments which are easily damaged. If you find old wooden planes, don't worry too much about the state of the blades. They can be ground down again in an hour or so, or you can buy new ones if necessary. But watch the wood for splits and worm. If you have either, forget it. I recently bought a wooden jack plane, a smoothing plane and a moulding plane from a junk shop. The set new would have cost at least four times as much and would not have been so good.

There are tools you need every week, some you need every month, and others you use once a year or once a lifetime. Forget the latter, and reckon instead to borrow or hire it if and when you need it. The rest are about the best investment you're ever likely to make, so be prepared to fork out. And every time you hesitate in the shop between the best and the second best, think of the money you are going to save and always buy the best. If you can't afford the best now, wait till you can, and borrow someone else's meanwhile.

The tool-kit

As to the tools you are going to need, I think you could do nearly everything in this book with those listed below. I haven't included many of the special tools needed for metalwork or car mechanics because I don't know much about them. But again nearly all your mechanics can be done with this set, and the special hub-pullers and expanding reamers and so on which auto-fiends need can be hired, or even borrowed if your garage is friendly enough. Nor is there anything for decorating as this book is more about the basics than the finishes. If you want to get into cabinet-making or inlay techniques (and why not), you need the help of a craftsman, not someone like me who mostly found out for himself.

The basic tool-kit
mallet
16 oz claw hammer
rip saw (four points to the inch)
crosscut saw (8–10 points to the inch)
miter saw (14–16 points to the inch)
coping saw
keyhole saw
hacksaw
14-inch screwdriver; set of smaller screwdrivers
set of bevelled chisels ($\frac{1}{4}$ to $1\frac{1}{4}$ inches)
paring chisel
jack plane (about 14 inches long)
smoothing plane (about 9 inches long)

shoulder plane, moulding plane, combination plane*
mortise gauge
ordinary gauge
miter box
brace and set of auger bits ($\frac{1}{4}$ to 1 inch)
electric drill
high speed bits for wood, masonry and metal (keep well separate)
pliers
vise wrench
crowbar
large adjustable wrench, preferably Stilson
set of open-ended or combination wrenches
set of off-set ratchets
set of socket wrenches
combination square, try square and bevel
two levels (one 9 inches long, one 4 feet long)
cold chisel
bricklayer's or mason's hammer
wood and metal floats
pointing trowel
countersink
nail punch
framing square
wooden rule (3 foot)
measuring tape (at least 30 feet long)
set of C clamps and two pairs of clamp heads
utility knife
pipe cutter and blow-lamp
glass and tile cutter
gimlet/bradawl
saw set and saw file
set of files and hasps
oil stone
plumbline
shovel
wheelbarrow
pick
sledgehammer

* Expensive and rather specialized. But if you are to do a lot of joinery, the combination plane is the best buy for making rebates, drips and channels.

If you go to a tool shop and order the complete set, you'll certainly not have much change from $600. If you shop around, buy some special offers and pick up some tools second-hand, you could probably get nearly all of it together for no more than $400. How long it'll take you to pay that back depends entirely on how much work you do – but an odd-job handyman will charge at least $5 an hour, an average builder nearer $8 an hour and a real craftsman a good deal more. So if you reckon your time at, say, $5 an hour (and with a few months practice you'd certainly be worth that), the break-even point comes at around 80 hours work, if you bought the tools cheaply. So say three months of an hour or so's work every day – and after that every second you put in is sheer profit. Of course, it all depends, the economist would say, on how highly you value your own time, on how much money you could earn doing other things for which you might be more highly trained. But I am assuming you are going to enjoy the work; and if it gives you pleasure, you are profiting right from the time you walk out of the shop with some tools under your arm. If you are not going to enjoy it, then best to forget the whole thing any way.

There is only one way to learn to use your tools: get someone who knows to show you. You can get a certain way with trial and error and a pile of do-it-yourself books at your elbow, but I give fair warning that it can be a frustrating business. No one can pack a lifetime's experience into a few pages of a book, but work with a cabinetmaker for an hour and you'll learn more than you could in a month's reading. Often it's a good idea to have a go at something before working with a professional. That way you'll have already discovered the snags, and be ready to recognize the solutions when the professional gets to them. They make it look so easy that it's not until you try that you realize the skill involved.

If you don't know anyone well enough to give you some basic lessons, then ask the local freelance handyman or builder in to do a couple of jobs for you. Make it clear you want to work along as his mate, and stick to him like a leech. I learnt to lay bricks that way in a couple of days, which not only taught me a new skill but just about halved what I would otherwise have had to pay a pro. Another possibility is to take a course. A night-school in carpentry or cabinetmaking or bricklaying or car mechanics can be quite good. The trouble is that you learn slowly, putting in only a couple of hours a week over a longish period. It goes without saying that once you know what to do and how to do it, you have only just begun. From then on you are going to get better and better at it throughout your life. Practise, practise, practise.

To which there is not much I can add except some tips and priorities which may help keep you on the right road. So the next section is better read *after* you've tried out a few things, by which time you'll know very well what I'm talking about without my having to go into complicated exploded diagrams. And that gets me out of listing a lot of the tedious and obvious things which mar most do-it-yourself books, like which end of the saw you hold and which end cuts the wood.

Saws

People who don't like sawing have never used a properly set and well-sharpened saw. Those who have, have been known to sneak out in the middle of the night to recapture the sing and bite which has replaced the sweaty struggle they used to think sawing involved.

Setting is done first, and is the easier. Adjust the setting tool to the number of points to the inch in the saw to be set, and go down one side pushing out the teeth. Turn the saw over, and do the same to the other side. If you've done it right, you should be able to put a needle between the points at one end and make it slide all the way down the groove between the pushed out points until it falls out at the other.

Next, clamp the saw between two bits of wood in a vise, teeth uppermost and just projecting clear of the wood. Stroke the saw file a couple of times away from you on alternate teeth. Hold the file horizontally and, for a rip saw, almost at right angles to the blade; for all other saws you file at about 60 degrees to the blade, but the exact angle will be obvious when you look at the teeth. When you've done one side, turn the saw round and do the other. When I was building the timber-framed house in Wales, all the saws used to be sharpened every week. Unless you're doing something really intensively, once a month will be often enough – but in any case it'll be obvious when it needs doing. When the pleasure goes out of sawing, it's time to sharpen.

Funnily enough, most amateurs know nothing about rip saws,

which are used for sawing wood down the grain. They're incredibly useful, and a good one works very fast and without much effort. A 10-foot length of 2 × 4 inch wood can be ripped down into two 2 × 2s in about ten minutes. And that's the way to do it unless you've got hundreds of feet to be done, in which case take it all to the sawmill and pay up. These days you'll perhaps be using second-hand timber (see next chapter), so remember if you buy some awful old stuff with one edge split away, the rip saw will save it for you and turn it into a near perfect piece of wood, only slightly smaller. I've seen an expert joiner use a rip saw for ripping down the side of tenons in joinery for doors and windows. It's the quick way to do it, and providing you saw down the away-side of the line, let no one tell you you should be using the much finer miter saw.

To rip wood properly, put it between two saw benches (see p. 33), stand well over the work and saw at an angle only about 30 degrees off vertical. Mark the saw cut with a gauge; if the wood is to be ripped into equal pieces, set the gauge by trial and error, making small marks alternately from either side and adjusting the gauge until the marks coincide exactly (easier than it sounds).

The use of cross-cut, panel and miter saws is mostly a matter of marking out and supporting the wood. Always square round with a square and carpenter's pencil on at least two sides of the wood – the far side and the top. Cut steeply at first to align the cut with the mark down the far side, and when that's done, cut shallowly to take out the mark across the top. After that, you can more or less forget the lines as the saw is in a groove which it is bound to follow until the cut is finished. Two sawing rules: always cut on the away-side of the line on the principle that you can always plane some more off but you can never plane some back; and always cut or exert pressure only on the away-stroke (which applies to all filing and sharpening as well). Your saw won't cut when you're drawing it back because of the way you have sharpened it.

Whenever you can, put the wood to be sawed in a vise. It saves so much trouble and slipping about and nasty vibrations (mental and physical). If it's not practical to use a vise, all cross-cutting should be done with the shorter end of the timber hanging over free space – never with the far end supported and the saw cutting between two supports. If you do that, the timber will bend in the middle and the saw will stick. To cut large panels, put the piece between the benches and climb up on top of the board. If the timber is wet, lubricate the saw frequently either with oil or a candle, and it'll slip through easily.

Screws, nails, dowels

Your 14-inch screwdriver will be one of the nicest discoveries you've ever made. Gone are the days of wrist-breaking hassle with the screwdriver slipping out of the screw notch, the edge of the notch burring, and the screw ending up a quarter of an inch proud of the surface and refusing to budge. The twist from a long screwdriver has to be felt to be believed. Of course, for everything but very short screws, you drill a hole first a bit smaller than the screw itself. If there is a lot of screwing to be done, go round all the holes with the electric drill first. And when screwing two pieces of wood together, make the hole through the first piece big enough for the screw to slip through on its own. You don't want it biting into the wood. Where you need a really strong fix, don't forget the lag bolt – a screw with a square head which fits into your socket set. That's even easier than using a 14-inch screwdriver, and gives a terrific fix. Incidentally, you can get a screwdriver attachment to fit into a brace, and of course the circular movement of the brace then gives an enormous leverage, but I have always found it difficult to keep the thing aligned and prevent the bit slipping out of the screw notch. All wood that is to remain visible should be countersunk, so that the head of the screw sinks down into the wood. A hand countersink is all you need, unless it's a production job when it may be worth getting a gadget for the electric drill (except for bits, nearly all electric drill attachments, in my view, are gadgets best avoided).

When screwing something to a masonry wall, you need to plug the wall. And this is where you use plastic rather than wood. Plastic plugs are incomparably better, for they are so shaped that they really grip when you drive the screw in; the old wooden plugs were very much a hit-and-miss affair with every other plug disappearing irretrievably into the wall or simply turning round and round with the screw.

To fix a wooden batten to a wall, here's what you do. Hold the batten to the wall and, with a masonry bit on the electric drill, go through the wood and the wall to the right depth at one end (you can buy a rubber ring to go on the drill bit to mark the required depth). Then take the plastic plug and just start the screw in it. Place it in the hole in the batten and with a hammer gently tap it through the wood and into the wall until it stops. Tighten the screw until the hold is secure but the batten left swinging. Then hold up the other end and repeat the procedure there. With the batten fixed at both ends, you can now go along the middle putting in as many extra plugs as are required – every three feet or so is usually enough. The only trick is to select a bit size just large enough to allow the plug to go through the wood and yet grip the masonry when the screw is driven home. Experiment until you get it right.

Most people, incidentally, seem to think that hammers and screws don't mix. They do. If you have a lot of screwing to do, the quickest way is to start the screw off with a hammer and drive it into its hole until only $\frac{1}{2}$ or even $\frac{3}{4}$ of an inch is left showing. Then screw in the rest of the way, and you'll get a perfectly good fix.

Screws (and nails) should be bought in boxes (or by the pound). Only idiots buy them in plastic packs because the pack costs more than the contents and you pay two or three times over the odds. When I was helping to build the three-storey timber frame house in Wales, we used to buy 4-inch spikes (nails 4 inches and longer are called spikes) by the half hundredweight. And we found the price varied enormously from shop to shop. Further, with orders of that size, you may be able to get the box cheaper from a building supply house than from a local hardware store.

Hammering nails is a nice job, once you've discovered the feel of the hammer and how best to let its weight work for you. On a good day you'll learn to drive a 4-inch spike home with four, or at most five, blows. And if you bend the nail, use the claw end of the hammer to lever it straight. Don't forget that spikes go easily only in soft wood. If you come across any oak anywhere, you will have to drill a small hole first, otherwise the nail will always bend after the first inch.

Which reminds me of the day one of our amateur builders in Wales looked at the towering timber frame of the house standing some 30 feet high, and was struck by an appalling thought. 'It's only held together with nails,' he muttered, and you could see his mind wrestling with thoughts of metal straps and coachbolts and heavens knows what other concoctions. But it's true that you can build a complete house using only 4-inch nails to hold it together, and it will be there far longer than you. In other words, a nail is a very strong fix, and two nails more than twice as strong if you angle or dovetail them to each other. As a general rule, the nail needs to go into the second piece of wood as far as it went through the first: so use 4-inch spikes when nailing two pieces of 2-inch timber together. If you use a 5-inch spike and bang the end over (called cleating), you've got a fix nearly as good as a bolt.

You remove nails more than 2 inches long by using a crowbar or claw on a hammer (pliers for anything smaller). When you've started the nail, you need to slip a block of wood under the heel of the crowbar to get the right leverage (something which no-one ever seems to work out for himself but cannot understand why he didn't think of it once he's been shown). Bits of wood full of nails are very dangerous and definitely not to be left lying about. And a nail is not a once-only, throw-away product. It can be used again and again; all you have to do is to straighten it roughly with a hammer against some stone or concrete. There's a lot of money to be saved re-using nails.

The art of dowelling is something which seems to have been unjustly forgotten. Which is a pity, for it's a tidy way of giving you a very neat fix. First, buy your dowel (⅜ of an inch is big enough for most jobs), or cut some slender boughs from a tree and start whittling if you want to be really purist. Drill a hole of exactly the same size with the brace and bit, and cut a length of dowel about half an inch longer than the depth of the hole. Dip it in carpenter's glue and simply tap it home with a mallet, having first clamped the two pieces to be joined together. When the glue has dried, saw the end of the dowel off roughly, and then chisel or plane down the stump flush with the surface. The result looks beautiful and is very strong. Dowelling is also the way to repair things like broken chair legs where you simply cannot let a screw or nail show. You should really chisel out a slot down the length of the dowel to let excess glue run out when you drive it home – but it's not always necessary. So, wherever you don't want the surface marred with screws or nails, dowel away and the more you do, the stronger the result will be. Dowels, of course, are often used in gates and outside doors for the simple reason that they can't rust.

Dowels are also good for joining two pieces of wood edge to edge to make a wider board – such as the centre rail of a door. Here you line up the two pieces, mark across, square over and drill in the centre of each edge. Cut your dowels slightly smaller than the combined depth of the two holes so that they don't prevent the two surfaces joining each other flush when clamped together. You need a dowel every 12 inches or so.

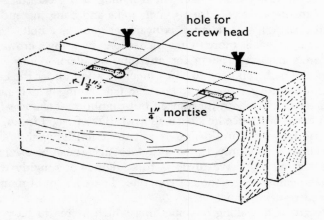

hole for
screw head

$\frac{1}{2}''$

$\frac{1}{4}''$ mortise

SLOT-SCREWING

A better way of joining boards edge to edge is known as slot-screwing. First plane the edges so that the boards fit snugly together at each end, but you can just see daylight between them in the middle (you dish the centres, in other words). Then clamp the boards together and mark across both boards every foot or so. Into the edge of one board screw 2-inch no. 8 screws in the centre of these marks until the thread of the screw has just disappeared. On the other board, mark off points $1\frac{1}{2}$ inches to one side of the original marks and drill holes just large enough for the screw head to fit in without friction. Then chisel out a mortise $\frac{1}{4}$ of an inch wide from the holes back to the original marks, the same depth as the length of screw sticking out of the other board. The $\frac{1}{4}$ inch mortise will just be big enough to take the haft of the screw but not the head. Then place the board with the screws upright in a vise, and drop the other board onto it, so that the screws disappear into their holes and the boards are flush, edge to edge. Take a mallet and tap gently along the top board until the boards are lined up as when originally marked out (you may have to press down while doing this to keep the boards together). The boards have now joined well together, held by the bite of the screw heads into the sides of the mortises too small for them. But you haven't quite finished. Tap the top board back again, and lift it off. Give all the screws one extra turn and repeat the operation with the mallet. Do it once again, but this time add glue to the edges and clamp when finished. After planing you should have a board which it will be hard to tell was once two pieces. And it doesn't take nearly as long as it sounds.

Chisels and planes

The all-function chisel usually has bevelled edges. With that you can do most things. But if you are going to do a lot of joinery, and hence mortises, invest in a mortise chisel – a fat, heavy chisel that will really take the wood out quickly. And buy a paring chisel which will help to tidy up the ragged holes of the mortise fairly easily.

The chisel and the plane (plus a mallet) are the joiner's tools. And joinery is the art of working with planed wood, as distinct from carpentry which is more structural and involves sawn or machined timber left with a rough finish. In carpentry you work to an accuracy of perhaps $\frac{1}{8}$ of an inch, and in good joinery you should be aiming for accuracies of $\frac{1}{64}$ of an inch. Doors and windows are joined, timber stud walls, joists and flooring are all carpentered. It's best to know the difference because you can waste a lot of time working to greater accuracies than are really necessary.

As with saws, so with planes and chisels – you need them sharp. The technique is the same for both, and the sharpening is done with an oilstone or carborundum. This has one smooth side and one slightly rougher. You use the rough one only when taking a nick out of the blade, or when re-grinding. If you do a full day's work with a plane or chisel, you'll need to sharpen them at least twice – but it depends a bit on the type of timber you are working with.

Chisel blades and plane irons have two angles at the end, and sharpening involves only the steeper angle at the very tip. Hold the blade on the stone at that angle and push it firmly forwards and backwards (you sharpen only when pushing away from you). Either make a figure of eight movement across the stone or make sure you push down the sides of the stone as much as the centre – otherwise you'll dish the stone and it'll be useless. When the blade is really sharp, turn it over and lay it flat on the stone. Push it up and down two or three times to remove the burrs of metal left by the sharpening, and you are ready to start. Every time you use the stone, you need a few drops of oil to lubricate the surface.

The plane must then be adjusted. Metal planes are easy, for there is a knurled knob which raises and lowers the blade. Adjust until, when looking down the bottom of the plane, you can just see the edge of the iron sticking out. Test it on a scrap piece of wood, and make finer adjustments if necessary. To make the plane glide easily over the wood, you must rub its bottom with a lump of tallow which the butcher will give you now that no one uses the stuff to make their own candles (but see chapter 15 for other uses of tallow).

A wooden plane is more difficult. To loosen the iron and remove it, you hold the plane with your thumb against the iron and either tap the top front of the plane with a mallet or knock the front of the plane against the work bench. The insides should then fall out. To reassemble, insert the iron in the correct position, place the wedge in and carefully tap it home with a hammer. A hundred to one you'll then find the iron has moved slightly out of position. If it sticks out too far, loosen slightly in the way just described and if necessary tap the wedge again to tighten it all up. If the iron is too shallow, tap it slightly with a hammer. The best way is to play around a bit; but write off a morning to learning the tricks otherwise you'll end up in a sweaty, bad-tempered mess and probably throw the plane through the window.

When you take a plane to pieces, you'll find a metal cap is screwed into the cutting iron. Before sharpening, this must be removed. Its function is simply to break or crease the shavings taken off by the plane, so that they flow easily through the throat and out without jamming up the works. When reassembling, the cap is left short of the edge of the cutting blade – it should trail it by about $\frac{1}{16}$ of an inch for hardwood and nearly $\frac{3}{8}$ of an inch for softwood. Finally, rub your wooden planes – and all other wooden tools – with linseed oil to keep them healthy.

The jack plane, the longer one, is used for taking substantial amounts of wood off a surface, or to level it all. The smoothing plane is a finishing tool which you use after the job is completed or ready for assembly. It simply smooths off all the marks and leaves a velvet surface which some people will ruin by painting, and wiser ones will preserve by oiling or possibly by using a clear polyurethane varnish. If you must have colour, then the best finish is a standard wood preservative. They come in many colours, need two coats and sink deep into the wood. They're better than paint for they not only preserve the wood but leave the grain patterns visible. They also last longer.

If you have trouble holding a plane iron or chisel at the right angle for sharpening, you can buy a device (I'm not sure whether it's a tool or a gadget) which will do it for you. It's basically a clamp which grips the blade and a wheel underneath which runs along the oilstone. I've never seen a joiner use one, and I have not found them very satisfactory. But if it helps, use it.

For the rest, which is basically how to use a chisel and make a mortise and tenon, see chapter 4.

Work-room, bench and saw-horses

There's one thing that you, and your wife or husband, mistress or lover, had better get straight from the start. You can't do all this in the sitting-room. Or the kitchen or the bedroom. You must have a work-room and you'll either have to filch a spare room, use the garage, or construct a lean-to on the side of the house (not a bad first project, incidentally, for it's like building a house in miniature and will bring you up against most of the problems of house-building in a small and controllable way).

And the second thing is that you must have a work bench. I wouldn't give twopence for most of the ones you can buy new (never mind the $100 to $200 which they actually cost). If you can get a second-hand one, either locally or through a want ad, that's your best answer. If not, you'll have to make one. The frame is best made from timber no smaller than 2 × 4, and bigger if you can get it cheaply. Ask the foreman on the nearest demolition site for some scraps, fingering your wallet lovingly while you do so. You'll need four legs and two sets of cross-members for the frame – one about ten inches off the ground, the other flush with the top. End-lap all the joints and then bolt them together (or practise your dowelling). Some bits of plywood or block-board all the way round, say from the top to about halfway to the floor, and screwed or nailed into the legs and cross-pieces, will give the thing enormous strength. For the top, you really need beech, or some other hard wood, and you'll probably have to

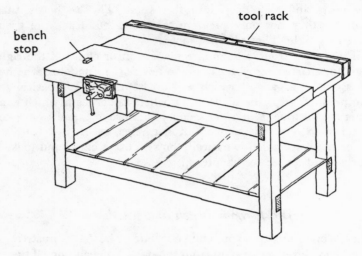

bench stop

tool rack

WORK BENCH

dowel a number of boards together to make up the surface. If you can't find pieces the right size and shape second-hand, then you'll simply have to pay up and buy them new. Fix the top to the frame with countersunk lag bolts. You can add your own refinements such as tool racks, drawers and so on as you wish. But you will need two vises. The first should be a woodworking vise, and you will have to buy that new from your tool shop (they are surprisingly cheap). The second will be a general purpose, but large, vise of the type usually used in metal working. They cost a fortune new, so try for one in the junk shops, and keep an eye open for garages closing down and old workshops being torn apart and turned into gracious homes for the wealthy.

While you're at it, you may as well make a couple of saw-horses at the same time (see drawing). The alternative is to put it off

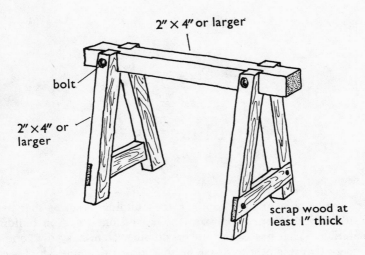

SAW-HORSE

until you really need them, when you'll start cursing and swearing because you have to lose two days in making them when you really want to get on with the job in hand. Also, it's better to make them at the beginning, for the experience will be useful on later and more important jobs. You'll just have to take my word for it that they are well worth the time and trouble.

Chapter 3

❦

Materials

IT used to be a rule of thumb in the building business that two-thirds of your money went on labour, and one-third on building materials. What passes for our economic system has now gone so berserk that it is best to forget all that; it just depends which week you buy your labour and which week you buy your materials. Of course, if you do all your building yourself, you have to pay only for materials – but at today's prices new materials will certainly cost you too much. This chapter is about how to buy what you want at prices you can afford; and how to make use of it once you've got it.

If you're building big, our experience in Wales is a useful guide to costs. We built a house of some 3,300 square feet of floor area for a materials cost of $25,000 – in other words, we paid about $7.50 a square foot, or 90¢ a cubic foot (not counting attic space). I must admit we didn't do very well in picking up cheap materials. All our wood we bought new, though we did do it early in 1973 just before timber prices went through the roof. On the other hand, the cost included a number of extras, such as $2,000 worth of mechanical excavation, a solar roof and a septic tank, and the building was made to last; although done by amateurs, all the professionals who visited us were impressed by the structure, which was obviously better built, and with a more extravagant use of materials, than most houses. But, after allowing for inflation, your building will cost you a lot more than $7.50 a square foot of floor area in materials alone at today's prices.

But it does depend a lot on how you do it – and one disadvantage of being an amateur is that the easier building techniques, which it is a good thing to opt for, usually demand the more expensive materials. Maybe that's all right, in the sense that you are then using your own labour partly to pay for better materials and a higher standard than you could buy off the shelf which is as it should be.

Timber

Britain used to be a forest. The tragedy which turned it into wind-swept areas of rough pasture is another story, but suffice to say that the Forestry Commission's pathetic attempts to replant the worst areas with foreign softwoods is no solution. Of course we need the agricultural land, but a wood can be a supplier of both timber and food as well as a thing of beauty. Forest farming, with cattle, sheep and pigs browsing through adjacent areas of pasture and woodland, is sure to come, and the quicker we work out some really effective ways of doing it the better. But none of that is going to help this generation.

It wasn't very long ago that many British houses – and some in America – were built of hardwood. Forget hardwood. And unless you really have money to burn (in which case you won't be reading this book), I'm afraid you had also better forget the lumber yard. A piece of machine-sawn 2 × 4 softwood will now cost you up-wards of 20¢ a linear foot. So where else to go?

The first place is the demolition site. Wrecking is now a specialist trade (characteristically, perhaps, a booming one). Wreckers get paid for the job, and so their one aim is to reduce an old building to a roughly cleared site as quickly as they can. That means the more wood they can put on their fire the more profit they show. You need only a van or small truck, a crowbar and a wallet full of notes. Visit each demolition site in turn and plead for any wood you can get. Offer to help free it from other building rubble (brandish your crowbar at this point) and of course offer to pay (brandish your wallet). You won't get a good reception every-where, and on many sites you'll be beaten to it by other enterprising builders. But this is now the only way of getting wood at a really cheap price. You may even have to buy a fair amount of useless wood (good for the fire later on) to get a few usable pieces. Don't worry much about sizes – you buy either structural wood (2 × 4, 2 × 10, 6 × 6 and so on) or flooring. With the help of the rip saw you should be able to use it all, and even the damaged bits of flooring you get will saw down into useful and very cheap shelves. While you are at it, look for old doors and windows, particularly doors which can often be bought for $5 or less. If they won't do as doors, at least you can dismember them for the frames which will be useful for something. If by chance you come across old wooden beams (such as 8 × 8s or 4 × 12s), try for them as well. They have two uses: as beams in your new building far cheaper than buying new or metal ones, and just as good; or they can be sawn down into smaller sizes, preferably by the sawmill since ripping up very large beams is a bit of a job even if you have a double-handled rip saw and saw pit (you won't have). Remember you can never have too much timber.

When you have exhausted all the local demolition areas, go to the second-hand building supply scrap yards and second-hand timber dealers. First, of course, visit the sawmill and make a list of all the prices for new softwood. Then, when you find what you want second hand, refuse to pay more than 50 per cent of the new price; you should in fact be able to buy in at less than that. Second-hand timber is now sometimes auctioned, particularly in Britain, where the auction is sometimes held on market day. Be careful at these auctions. Shortage of timber means that some builders may be prepared to pay more for second-hand timber than new, simply because they need it next week and cannot afford to wait until the next delivery. So again, work out 50 per cent of new price, bid up to that, and then stop. If you lose the lot, console yourself with the thought that anyone who pays more for second-hand wood must be heading for bankruptcy anyway. Incidentally, buying second-hand timber ensures that your wood is properly seasoned. These days new timber is very poorly seasoned, and that will give you headaches later on.

If you still haven't bought enough structural timber there remains only one other possibility. You will have to buy trees. This is not so heroic as it sounds, but it is definitely for people who have time on their hands. Most people who want large trees removed from their gardens will be happy to have it done for nothing, using the timber as payment. So set up as a local tree feller (you need a chain-saw, a little practice, and a good deal of confidence) and build up a pile of trees in your garden. The longer you keep them there the better. Eventually, of course, you will have to make a deal with the sawmill to have them ripped down into whatever sizes you need, and probably to have them kiln dried. But all that will cost surprisingly little. You'll end up with cheaper timber than anyone, though it will take you a year or two to accumulate enough. Before you get into this, of course, you have to find out which woods are of any structural use. No good ending up with a few tons of wood that isn't even good to burn.

There's one big problem with second-hand timber: preservation. Except for cedar, which is rot proof, you shouldn't put any softwood in your house without first treating it against both rot and woodworm. Now if you buy new timber from the yard, you can have it pressure treated, or preserved, before delivery. It saves a lot of time and gives your timber superb protection. If you use second-hand timber I suppose you could lug it to the yard if they will agree to treat it, but most people end up by painting on one or two (it should be two) coats of a standard wood preservative such as Cuprinol by hand. It's a tedious and smelly business, and though it will protect your timber, it won't give the same protection as pressure treating, which forces the chemical right down into the wood. But – to repeat – whatever you do, don't put any untreated timber in your house.

There's one other good source of wood which you won't need until the structural work is finished, when you'll have an empty shell of a house and probably nothing much to put in it. A few years ago you would then go to the nearest wood supplier and buy huge quantities of small wood and blockboard to make up fitted shelves, cupboards and wardrobes. Not any longer. Now you go to the junk shop and auction sales and pick up pieces of furniture for as little as you can get them. Then with mallet and crowbar you smash them to pieces – their component pieces, not wood splinters. You'll be amazed at how much wood you can get out of a simple chest of drawers; and we have long since lost count of how many chests we have bought for £1.50 or £2 to this end. Sometimes you'll find that when you have stripped off all the paint and chipped veneer or polish, the piece is good enough to use as it is. Last year we bought a wardrobe, 5 feet wide, with hanging space, a set of shelves and a roomy cupboard, as well as an upright wardrobe and a matching chest of drawers, all in mahogany finish, for £4 the lot. We were going to break them up but found in the cramp end they were too good for that, so we used them as they were.

Bricks, blocks and stone

Unfortunately, there are almost no cheap ways of buying these. Second-hand blocks are useless. Second-hand bricks, if you can get them, are fine and cleaning off the old mortar is not such a big job as it looks. Don't be put off by it. Second-hand stone is as good as new – if you can get it. In the country, you may be converting an old stone building, in which case plan your building to re-use all the old stone you have to pull down. It's a slow way of building, but for an amateur it's actually easier using bricks or blocks: you don't have to align everything perfectly and the irregularities in the stone will hide your worst boobs.

Blocks are awful things. They cut your hands to ribbons when you lay them, and they're ugly as hell. But they are by far the cheapest building material and they give you a good strong wall. I wouldn't blame anyone for succumbing to them – providing they were prepared to plaster the result. This is not so difficult, and with most blocks is essential on external surfaces to keep out the damp. With not more than a day's practice you will be able to plaster a wall and achieve the kind of finish you get with rough plaster in stone cottages. To tell the truth, you can't tell the difference between a stone wall with rough plaster finish, and a block wall plastered by an amateur. So if your conscience can take a little internal deception, you can do far worse than settle for that.

In the United States, there is one basic kind of brick – the modular brick whose nominal dimensions are 8 inches long, 4 inches wide, and $2\frac{2}{3}$ inches thick. (But note that the nominal dimensions include the thickness of the mortar joints, which usually vary from $\frac{1}{4}$ inch to $\frac{1}{2}$ inch.) Its appearance, color, texture, and pattern depend almost entirely on the raw materials used and the method of manufacture. The actual size of bricks also varies because of shrinkage during the manufacturing process. Standard concrete blocks may have two or three cores. Their basic dimensions are $15\frac{5}{8}$ inches long by $7\frac{5}{8}$ inches wide by $7\frac{5}{8}$ inches high. The three basic types are solid load-bearing units, hollow load-bearing blocks, and hollow non-load-bearing blocks.

To cut bricks and blocks and some kinds of stone, you need the cold chisel and the lump hammer. Make a groove all the way round where you want the cut, using only light taps. Carry on deepening the groove until it literally falls into two pieces. You can do it more quickly using a masonry saw disc on an electric drill, but it's noisy and very dirty. I prefer to take a little more time and avoid deafness and suffocation. If the stone you are using is slaty, and cleaves easily, forget about trying to cut it across the grain. Find a smaller piece.

As a guide to speed, the most I have ever done is to lay 44 6-inch concrete blocks in a day. A professional would do far more, and so could you with practice, but building is not a race unless you're in it for profit or speculation. If you are, you are welcome to try for the world speed brick laying record.

There is one way round the problem of buying in masonry. You can make your own. There are plenty of houses in this country, mostly built in the early part of the century, that were made that way, and they have proved to be pretty sound structures. One technique, called rammed earth building, does away with masonry completely. The walls of the house are shuttered up, the forms filled with earth of the right type, and the material pounded and battered until it has been sufficiently compressed to form a structural wall. The walls, of course, are made very thick and are highly insulating. They are raised some 18 to 24 inches at a time and the whole structure goes up slowly but surely, bit by bit.

Or you can make blocks from soil mixed with a little cement, using a small hand-powered compressing machine. If you have clay of the right type, blocks like these can be made without cement and, even in our climate, left to dry in the sun. I have never built using any of these techniques, although we did plan a second house at the Eithin site to be made from clay blocks, the material for which would first be dug out of the site for the house. It seems pretty certain that if building goes on at anything like the present rate, we shall fairly soon have to rediscover such techniques. There is a natural poetry in the idea of building your house out of the material you have excavated to prepare the site. If you want practice in these methods now, before you're forced into them you can do no better than read *Building in Cob, Pisé and Stabilized Earth* by C. Williams-Ellis and J. and E. Eastwickfield (Country Life, 2nd edition, 1947).

And you should be able to get planning permission, if you're determined enough. I know one couple who approached their Planning Authority with trepidation for permission to build an extension to their house out of rammed earth, and the County

Architect, when told the choice of material, simply asked what technique they planned to use, without so much as the bat of an eyelid. Permission was granted – as it probably will have to be all over the country much before this century has run its course.

Wallboard or sheet rock

These are the cheapest building materials. In Wales we bought nearly all our wallboard in 4 × 6 sheets (a very handy size, easier to work than 4 × 8s) at $2–2.50 a sheet, which meant that we could cover the walls and ceiling of a good-sized room for about $50. Two people (and you always need two for wallboarding) can do a room 12 feet × 12 feet × 8 feet high in a morning after some practice. Meanwhile, reckon on a full day for a room that size. Wallboard hasn't increased in cost as much as other materials; allow 10¢ a square foot.*

To cut wallboard, put it up between the two saw-horses, and mark off the length required (always ⅛ of an inch less than the actual measurement, otherwise the rough edges left after cutting will stick in the gap and there'll be an awful mess). Score one side of the paper between the marks using a straight edge and a sharp knife. Break the board sharply along the cut line, stand it up, and score down the other side of the paper. Twist the unwanted piece off. For small cuts or intricate shapes, use a small saw. For holes, use a small-diameter circular rasp.

Wallboard works best when nailed (with galvanized clout nails) to timber stud walls. You can put it up against masonry, but then it's advisable to mount it on wooden battens (treated with preservative) first. This also gives you the chance to fill the space between the battens with insulation. On external walls, incidentally, a layer of very thin aluminium foil stapled up before the wallboard goes up will cut heat loss a good deal, and serve as a moisture barrier. More expensively, you can buy foil-backed wallboard.

Professionally, you finish plasterboard by coating it with a plaster skim (the plasterboard having been put up with the grey side exposed ready to receive the skim). I have never so much as dipped a float into a plaster mix, so it's better that I don't pass on second-hand information about how easy or difficult plastering is for the amateur. One day I shall, for I've learnt enough to know that

* Water-resistant gypsum is recommended for damp areas.

nothing is that difficult. But if you don't want to get into plaster-ing – and it's certainly a wet and messy job – you can dry finish. Mount the plasterboard the other way round (cream side facing into the room), fill the gaps with filler and cover with tape or special linen strip designed for the job. You should also punch the nails and fill the holes. I must confess that, even after papering and painting, the result does leave a little to be desired. But as we are not playing gracious homes, I wouldn't worry too much. Better your house is strong and you can see the joints between the plasterboard than the other way round.

When you've finished plasterboarding, you'll have hundreds of unusable small bits and pieces left over. Leave them out in the rain for a few weeks, pound up the pile as best you can and dig it into the garden if you have an acid soil. The paper will be good for the organic content and the plaster will help correct acidity.

Ceramics and glass

Glass-cutting is not a specialized job. You need a flat table covered with an old blanket and a glass-cutter. Mark out the size needed and score along a straight edge between the marks. Hold the cut line just projecting over the edge of the table and snap off the un-wanted piece. If the glass is large, it's better to put it over a length of wood (something like $1 \times \frac{1}{2}$) and snap it over that. If the un-wanted portion is very thin, you have to tease it off, using the other end of the glass cutter to break off small portions at a time. Before trying this, give the underside of the glass a sharp tap along the incision with a pair of pliers. Use them to trim up the final edge if the breaks are not as clean as they should be.

Most ceramic tiles can be cut the same way but they are best snapped over another tile held vertically. You can also get a special tile-cutting tool in which the cutting edge is forced down onto the tile by a roller which is spring pressured up against the underneath of the tile. Again, tease off unwanted lumps with the pliers if the break is not even.

Glass is bought in many weights of which single and double thickness are the most common. The lighter glass will do only if you have to span small areas, and it is not strong enough to be used as a pane of, say, 2×3 foot. The only cheaper alternative is to buy horticultural glass as used in greenhouses. It is slightly green in hue and suitable only for small panes. In the mild winter of 1973 I lived in a house for which the only glazing was two sheets of plastic stapled to the window frame. If you want to freeze, that's an effective way of doing it, for most nights the temperature of my bedroom stayed around 38°F (3°C) – the temperature of the inside of a domestic refrigerator. Sleeping nude with eight blankets kept me warmest at night, but getting in and out of bed were pretty heroic actions. In short, you do need glass, preferably two panes of it (see chapter 5, on insulation).

Glazing, incidentally, is one area where it doesn't pay much to do it yourself if there's a lot to be done. A large glazing firm will usually supply and fix glazing for not much more than it would cost you to buy just the glass. What's more, they'll do it in a third of the time unless you're a very dab hand with the putty. In the U.S., professional glaziers are expensive, and you should probably do it yourself.

Plastics

You won't need many but now is as good a time as any to list the uses for which plastics are more than mere gadgets. The best example is rainwater guttering where plastic will save you a small fortune and many hours' work. It's easy to fit, light to handle and very cheap Use it. Perhaps the best use of all is styrofoam insulation, and I know no better way of consuming irreplaceable fossil fuel than turning it into heat-saving insulation which never breaks down (styrofoam is made from oil). The rest of the plastics industry, as far as I am concerned, should be declared redundant as soon as possible. I have no tips for those who want to cover the country-side with those excrescent plastic bubbles known as domes. Like Lou Kahn, I find an environment made from substances whose molecules have been tampered with as little as possible by man is the most satisfactory: wood and stone will always be the nicest building materials.

Cement and concrete

To which I must add that cement is by far the most useful. Any-one who wants to recreate the past by muddling about with cow dung and clay is welcome to do so, but my advice is to pay the $30 or so a yard which delivered cement costs in the knowledge that the result will be satisfactory. Twenty bags of cement go a very long way – if it's mixed right – and you always get a good result. The best and cheapest results are obtained by using lime as well. The mixes are very important and vary somewhat with the local nature of the sand and aggregate being used, as well as with the type of stone, brick or block being laid. This means it's always a good idea to ask a local builder for his recipe. Chances are he's been working with local materials for many years and found the best mix by trial and error. And if you are laying stone, this is essential, for different types of stone vary so much.

Guide to Cement Mixes

	cement	lime	sand	coarse aggregate
footings	1		3	6
floor slabs and lintels	1		2	4
paving slabs and steps	1		3	
screed	1		3	
plaster	1	1–2	6–9	
strong mortar	1	½	4½	
ordinary mortar	1	1	6	
internal mortar	1	2	9	

Note that concrete for footings appears to be a softer mix than concrete for slabs and lintels; this is because more water must be used with the latter, making the final result somewhat less strong.

When making mortar or concrete, you are gluing sand particles together with a binder which sets hard on exposure to water. The binder consists either of cement on its own, or of a mixture of cement and hydrated lime. The cement gives hardness and strength and the lime makes the mix more workable, allows you a longer time before it goes off or hardens, and lessens the chance of cracking. As lime is even cheaper than cement, it's a good idea to use the maximum proportions that the job will take. You mix by volume – that is, the measure is a shovelful. And you have to learn yourself how to gauge the correct amount of water. There will always be enough water for the chemical hardening reaction to take place. Indeed, if you buy your cement too soon, and leave it stacked in what you thought was a dry place, you'll find the outside skin of cement in the bag will set as hard as rock within a month. So never buy until you need it. When the time comes to add water, add as little as possible to make the mix the right consistency to work with. First time off, you won't believe the stuff you made could ever set hard. It will. At all costs, and particularly for concrete, avoid making it too wet – the wetter the mix, the weaker the result. In hot weather, dampen masonry before laying the mix, otherwise it will suck the water out of the mortar too quickly. Similarly, dampen dry surfaces before you plaster them.

The week we started work at Eithin, the excavator hit a spring right at the back of the site. In a day, the place where the house was to be was a slurried quagmire of mud and water up to a foot deep. We had to put in a drain to take the water away, and build a concrete wall a foot thick to channel the water seeping through the hillside into the drain. And to build the footing for the wall we had to excavate with picks some very rocky Welsh ground lying under six inches of water. It wasn't that which nearly killed us, but the price of the ready-made concrete we had delivered to pour in the trench the moment it was dug. So only buy ready-mix when in desperate straits; if it doesn't bankrupt you, it may well go off before you've spread it if you're not experienced in handling large quantities of the stuff, and you're then much worse off than before. Concrete, incidentally, sets perfectly well under water.

The next question is how to mix? One way is to heap your solid materials together, thoroughly mix them, make a hole in the middle, pour in some water, mix some more, add more water, and carry on until you've finished. You probably will be, too, by the time you've done enough to make a small concrete slab or a few lintels. Try it. I don't dispute you *can* mix as much concrete or mortar as anyone can use by hand. But if you detest the job with the unspeakable loathing that I do, you'll soon find yourself looking for a concrete mixer. You can hire one for $5–10 a day, but if you've got a job of any size on, don't make the same mistake as we did in Wales. We hired all our mixers, and over a year paid out more than $400 for the privilege. And because the price had got so high we ended up hand-mixing quite a lot of stuff as well. The answer is to buy your mixer, preferably second-hand, for $250 or so. Buy a big one, both because it's more useful and because it'll be easier to sell afterwards. Don't worry about the fuel consumption either: in a year you'll use less fuel than you would in a week of idling in traffic jams trying to commute to work.

Using a mixer well is quite an art. First, you must get it level or the mix will slop out all over the place. Second, you want it right up close to your sand and gravel so that you don't have a ten-yard march holding a shovelful of sand every time you load. Third, you want to be able to swing the bucket over so that you can tip the mix easily into a waiting wheelbarrow on the other side. And fourth, you must clean the thing scrupulously at the end of every day. The bucket itself you clean with a shovelful of sand and fine gravel, plus two stones or half bricks, and some water. Let the mixer turn it for a couple of minutes and it'll be clean as a whistle. Finally, when you mix, you do it in this order: two shovelfuls of sand first, then the water, then the cement, then the lime, then either the sand or the sand and gravel alternately. If you want to know why, try doing it in a different order, and make sure you have a hole ready in which to bury the result.

You move concrete or mortar about the site in a wheelbarrow. As a barrowful of cement mix is very heavy, it's worth spending a bit of time before starting in making barrow runs. Put planks down over muddy areas and make runs up steps or across difficult ground. They must be secure, because if they wobble someone is going to lose the load and end up with barrow and concrete on top of him. You also have to learn to tip. Lift the barrow up a foot or so, and with a flick of the hands, reverse the grip so that the handles lie between thumb and forefinger, with the heel of the wrist underneath the handle. Then up you go, quickly, so that the wheel guard of the barrow digs in the ground and stops it rolling forward. Once the barrow is nearly vertical, you can relax and shake the mix out or get someone to give it a push with a shovel. Be prepared to spill a couple of loads until you get the knack. It's not easy, and it's a good idea to start with barrows only half-full.

If your mix has to be moved to a height, barrow it to the bottom of the site and tip on to a hard, flat surface. If the only access is by ladder, you then fill a bucket for the bloke up the ladder to haul up by rope. If you've a block and tackle you can do it from the bottom more easily. If the journey is upstairs, you and as many helpers as you can get carry the full buckets up one by one. Don't be put off by working out how many journeys you're going to have to make in the day; you can move an awful lot of stuff that way, providing your energies haven't been whittled away by hand-mixing – another reason for the mixer.

Finally, you can't just pour concrete and leave it to settle. To make it solid you have to vibrate, which professionals do with an electric compressed air vibrator. As you won't have one, you have to puddle the stuff with a piece of wood which means vibrating it very thoroughly to get rid of all the air bubbles – horizontal tapping for a slab and vertical prodding for formwork. You can't do it too much and you can't really do it wrong, either. Just keep pounding away at the stuff, and when you take the forms away you'll end up with smooth clean faces. If you haven't done it enough, the stones will have moved to the sides and the cement mix will not have flowed properly between them leaving an effect which we used to call popcorn. Don't worry, you'll know better next time, and it won't fall down.

How much concrete can you lay in a day? In Wales two of us once mixed, laid and levelled a 6-inch deep slab some 20×15 feet in area. We started at nine, finished at six, and didn't stop much in between. With a mixer you should be able to do the same (though not every day); without a mixer you'll be doing very well indeed to do half.

At some point in your building work you're going to need to make concrete castings. There's no point in paying good money to buy them ready-made when you can do it yourself for half the cost, and not have a transport problem either.

The simplest thing to make is a concrete lintel. You simply make a box the same size as your lintel, fill it with concrete and vibrate it like mad to ensure a good finish and no air pockets inside. You'll also need to put reinforcing rods in the concrete – either $\frac{1}{4}$-, $\frac{3}{4}$- or $\frac{1}{2}$-inch – consult your architect. But with all reinforcing there are some golden rules. No rod must come within 2 inches, or $1\frac{1}{2}$ inches at the very least, of any edge of the concrete. When you pour a lintel, then, you pour the first 2 inches of concrete and puddle it well. Then lay your rods on the concrete, pour your next 2 inches, and so on.

Don't be deceived. Concrete is heavy stuff, and when you puddle it in formwork you exert great pressures on the sides. You may think you have built your form solidly, but the chances are that at the very first attempt the sides will spring apart and concrete start oozing out. The more you puddle, the worse it gets. The answer is good fixing, and there are many different methods. Small things like lintels you can do by propping blocks against the sides, nailing the timber together, and wedging a few bits of long wood between the sides and some really solid object a few feet away. Larger items, like concrete beams on top of masonry walls, and solid concrete walls, need better fixes.

At Eithin we built a single skin of stonework from damp course level to a height of 3 feet. The inside of the wall we shuttered up and concreted in to make a finished wall 14 inches thick, concrete on the inside and stone on the outside (we didn't have enough stone to build a proper stone wall). The forms for that job were made from 2 × 9 planks, nailed to 2 × 4 uprights every 3 feet or so. We wedged the bottoms of the form against existing block walls with timber, and wired the tops together by driving nails into the mortar outside on the stonework and to the outside of the wooden uprights. Heavy wire twisted round each nail and secured over the top of the form held it all secure, and only one of our forms moved more than a fraction of an inch. Even so, we poured those walls only a foot at a time, allowing at least half a day between each foot for the last lot to go off somewhat. When you puddle the next foot in, the foot beneath it has then set more or less solid and the puddling doesn't exert any further pressure at that level. A tip worth remembering.

If you've formwork on both sides, you can drill holes through the forms, thread some wire through and fix each end to a nail held tightly against the formwork. Or you can put bolts through from one side to the other, so long as they run inside through a metal tube. When you undo the bolt you can slip it out and take off the forms – but the tube stays forever in the concrete (as does the wire). If you need reinforcing rods in a wall like that you hang the rods in position, suspended by wire, and then pour the concrete over the lot. Once again the wire stays inside.

Removing forms is also an art. You can't just rip them off when you think the concrete is hard, or you may bring half the concrete out as well. You must loosen the fixing and then gently tap the forms all over with a mallet or hammer. As you do so, you'll see minute cracks begin to appear between the forms and the concrete.

Go on tapping until these cracks are all the way round and then gently remove the form. If you've a big job, you can coat your forms with a special oil which will prevent the concrete sticking to them.

The wood you use for formwork can be used again, once you've wire-brushed the muck off (our 2 × 9s were our joists). Or you can buy proper plywood shuttering, but it's expensive, even if you do use it three or four times. And for tanks and things where the look of the internal finish doesn't matter, remember that corrugated iron makes a very good form, providing you can fix it securely.

Sand, gravel and hardcore

Don't buy these in plastic bags but by the truck load (around 8 tons at a time). And whenever you can, by-pass the lumber yard and order straight from an excavation company, saving 10 to 20 per cent every time you do so. For mortar, of course, you need clean, washed sand, and take a good look at it before the truck tips it out. If it's full of muck and odd bits of gravel, don't accept it because you'll never make a decent mortar from it. For concrete, by far the best stuff is all-in aggregate graded $\frac{3}{4}$ to dust. Which means it'll be ready mixed in the right proportions, the largest gravels being $\frac{3}{4}$ of an inch across, decreasing in size down to a fine dust. If you can't get that, order two loads of gravel to one of coarse sand and mix them in the mixer by loading alternately with one, then the other.

You'll need hardcore to go under all concrete slabs and nothing should be bigger than 4 inches across. You can put anything solid under concrete, including old stone, bits of brick and broken up bottles. This is a good chance to get rid of all your rubble. But you must not, on any account, let old plaster, paper or wood get in, for obvious reasons. So first use up whatever scrap materials you have lying around the site and then pound all the rest down with the sledgehammer. If it isn't enough, work out how many more cubic yards of hardcore you need and order it from the quarry. Make very sure before the truck comes that you have a level, hard stand on which it can tip. Getting this right may save you several days of excruciating work. Shovelling hardcore up off something like flat concrete can be very quick and, when you've got the feel of it, actually pleasant. Trying to do it off uneven mud is a worse job even than hand-mixing concrete. You'll lose your temper in half an hour and end up throwing each piece of hardcore individually into the barrow. And as there are well over one thousand pieces of hardcore to the cubic yard, you can reckon on doing it for a long time to come.

After a couple of weeks of deliveries of sand, gravel, hardcore and cement, not to mention timber, blocks and bricks, your site will look pretty much like a battlefield, studded with broken pick handles, old plaster and heavens knows what else. You'll have lost most of your tools and there won't be room to push a barrow anywhere. Now you can either go on like that, or you can aim at keeping what one builder who helped us used to call 'a nice, clean tidy site'. I blush to say we laughed at him and one of us even began to speculate on his anal complexes. We didn't laugh so much after he left and we found we could never get on with the next day's job because of the mess the day before had left. I mention it with hesitation because how you keep your site is very much your own affair. But if you want to save time, stop half an hour earlier every day to clean up and put things away. If you want to end up with a rusty 4-inch spike through the sole of your boot, don't bother.

Chapter 4

◆⊃∘⊂◆

Building

I CAN'T tell you how to build a house in one chapter, and I'm not going to try. But most people find at some time in their lives that they want to build something themselves, either because they have the time to spare or they don't have the money to pay some one else, or both. So I shall assume that you are in that state but that, like me a couple of years ago, you don't have much idea of how to go about it. Like me, you've probably put up a few shelves, made an awful mess in the garden with a plastic bag of ready-mix concrete, and maybe built a working surface in the kitchen or a wardrobe in a bedroom. Hardly enough to qualify you to build a house.

But, with the help of a lot of friends, I did it and there's no reason why you shouldn't either. The house we built in Wales was enormous and we came up there against most of the building problems anyone is likely to meet. We used concrete, bricks, blocks, stone and timber frame, did all our plumbing and wiring, and made up a number of unusual solutions to problems we didn't know the professional answers to. So what I may be able to pass on are some tips you don't find in most do-it-yourself books, some hints on how to get round the snags no one else ever mentions – and some assurance that you *can* do the job if you really want to. And that includes everything from laying the foundations to making your own doors and windows.

If it's a biggish job, the first thing you need is a tame architect – and I mean a tame one, not a $25,000 a year man or woman who specializes in second bathrooms with gold taps. Ours actually turned out to be an architectural student (we didn't know that at the time) and a very fine job he made of it. Your architect should be someone who's freelancing for himself and who will design something you can not only live in but build yourself. You should be able to go and talk to him about how to do things.

The second thing you need is help – preferably both skilled and unskilled. One experienced man on the site for even a third of the time you're building makes a hell of a difference. Not only will he tell you how to do the things you're up against now, but he'll also explain the things you can see looming up next week or next month. It doesn't have to be someone who's been a builder all his life, but it does have to be someone who's done it at least once before. We had a carpenter on the site called Nick who stayed with us six months, in return for £100 a month plus food and lodging (most of the time it was a leaking barn). If you can find a Nick, all your problems are solved. He knew a way round everything, taught us all with a patience beyond credibility and, when our spirits got low, revived us all with beer and *joie de vivre*.

One of the most curious phenomena of the contemporary scene is that there now exists a wandering band of workers – rather like the wandering scholars of medieval times. They're mostly people who hate the lousy economic system we're all caught up in and have instead settled for a nomadic existence helping people who are doing interesting things. Some ask for payment, some for none. All require feeding, lodging and companionship. The house at Eithin was at least half built by such people and we shall always have cause to be grateful to them. I just hope they got as good a deal out of it as we did.

There are now many magazines and publications which act as a kind of information network for this alternative work scene. If you want builders or architects or friendly help, make yourself known in the pages of these journals, and read them yourself. Don't be surprised if you get more than you bargained for. A lot of people read these things and most of them are mobile and ready for almost anything. It's one area where the alternative scene is really working well. Another is the organizations which try to provide people to do anything at the buzz of a telephone. I've used them as well, and very good were the results.

The third thing you'll need is not alternative at all, but very straight – some good books. There are several standard works on building and if I were doing a house again I'd certainly buy one (see bibliography). They're much more detailed than anything you'll ever need, and they do make building look more complicated than it really is. But once you've mastered the language, and got yourself in a position where you really need to know how to do something urgently, it's a great reassurance to be able to turn the pages and be sure of finding the answer. Because we didn't buy a set of these books, we built our septic tank wrong, and its performance was always a bit of an unknown quantity.

Getting off the ground

If you can get your house to the point where it's said to be off the ground (damp proof course level), you've won the main battle. From there on everything else is easier, and much, much quicker. The business of laying out the site, digging the foundation trenches and pouring the footings, laying the first courses of masonry and the first slabs seems to take forever, Partly because it involves a lot of heavy work, partly because all the materials come at once, and partly because you're simply not used to it. It's really the wrong way to work but, as you can't start with the roof first, you don't have much choice.

When you've cleared the site, the first thing to do is set it out. You must have a long tape for this, and you must now establish a datum point – a point from which all your measurements for the building will be made until you've finished. You may need two: one to give all the horizontal measurements and one to give the vertical measurements. Mark out the positions of the external walls using wooden pegs as markers, and then re-check. As with joinery, measure twice and cut once is the golden rule. Don't forget that in any square or rectangular structure the diagonal measurements are just as important as the sides. You must make quite sure that both diagonals are the same length. If they are not, it means that none of your corners are right angles, and you'll have to start again. When you've marked out the external walls, do the internal ones.

Now you have to dig the foundation trenches to the sizes specified on the architect's drawing. There are two choices: either use pick and shovel, or hire a mechanical digger such as a backhoe. These come with a driver and cost $15–20 an hour. Unless you've a really enormous house, a backhoe will dig out the trenches probably in a morning, certainly in a day. And it'll dig any drains that run under the site at the same time (something you mustn't forget).

When the trenches are dug, the procedure is as follows. Take a shovel and clean them up to make sure there are no loose crumbs of soil lying in the bottom. Then drive a set of wooden pegs into the floor to a depth where the tops of the pegs mark the future height of the foundation concrete. Start from your datum, and bridge from there to your first peg using a long straight piece of wood with a level on top, or using a water level which will make the job more accurate. Carry on round the site putting in your pegs so that when you come to tamp down the concrete you can do it with a longish piece of wood with either end resting on top of a peg. Before you start this, you should have rung the building inspector to ask him to inspect the foundation trenches – something which must be done before you pour any concrete, or he can legally insist on your taking it all up again. When he comes he won't take long looking round, particularly if the concrete mixer is already turning when he arrives and he sees a tidy site with everything ready for pouring.

When you've got the OK, you can't relax until your footings are all poured. Now is the time to get a move on, for you want those trenches filled with concrete just as soon as is humanly possible. If you linger now, it may rain, your trenches may fill with water and you'll have to pump them dry, the trench may start to crumble and the trenches to fill up with muck. These are all things you are better off without.

Pouring the footings is probably the first big concrete job you'll have done. Ideally, you want two people on the mixer, two barrowing and two levelling and tamping in the trenches. That's luxury. You can make do with two people doing the mixing and barrowing together, and with one (much better two) at the footings end. Either way, the secret is not to rush but just to keep going steadily. Be prepared for an awful moment when you've made three or four mixes and suddenly realize they've made only a tiny blob in the bottom of one of the footings. Don't worry. If you can keep going at a steady lick they'll soon fill up. It's a help at this stage to know what accuracies you're working to. If you can keep the top of your concrete level to a quarter of an inch you're doing very well indeed. If you get it right to half an inch, that's OK. And if it's more than that, it'll be all right, but you'll waste some time fiddling about with the first layer of masonry you lay directly on to the footings. That has to be absolutely level, and it's better you don't have to bother with fractional slivers of masonry at the bottom to get your levels accurately.

The day after you've poured the footings, you lay the drains while waiting for the footings to harden. Consult the building inspector about what materials you can use. If he insists on ceramic, salt-glazed drain pipe with collars, then you'll just have to learn how to prop them together, fill the joints with packing and finish the seal with well-smoothed, rounded and wetted mortar. It's not easy. But if you can get away with Orangeburg pipe, you can just snap the things together once they're propped into position. As the manhole will be outside the main house, you can either build it now if you've time or leave it till later if you haven't. When the drains are laid the building inspector will want to inspect them too, and possibly run a water test on them to ensure that they don't leak (too much). When they've been inspected, you cover them with concrete, very gently so as not to disturb them.

There are now two jobs left before you're off the ground: one, to build up the first layers of masonry to damp proof course level, which must be at least six inches above the finished ground level outside the house. If you're building a cavity wall, you start off from the foundations building as though it were a cavity wall, but when you've got as high as the DPC you fill the cavity in with concrete to make it all stronger. No point in having a cavity to keep out moisture at levels below the damp proof course. For hints on masonry laying, see below.

Second, you now have the choice of pouring the slabs for the floor of the house or building up the structure and leaving the slabs till later. Curb your impatience to reach for the sky, and pour the slabs now. For one thing, it's much easier to barrow all that concrete into an open site than have to manoeuvre it through doorways. For another, you can use the sides of the masonry walls to DPC level to level the slabs from; place a long timber on the masonry walls at either side, and tamp down on the concrete with it to level the floor – using a length of timber long enough to span from one wall to another, tamping down and 'sawing off' excess concrete with each end of the timber on the wall. And, thirdly, you'll have a nice firm floor from which to work while building the rest of the house. In wet weather that can be a real advantage. In the US, Visqueen polyethylene is put down first, as a moisture barrier. The slab, of course, also needs a DPC, and the best solution is to put that on top of the concrete by painting on two layers of a standard bituminous DPC before laying the floor screed and finish. But that comes later; otherwise your boots will chew the

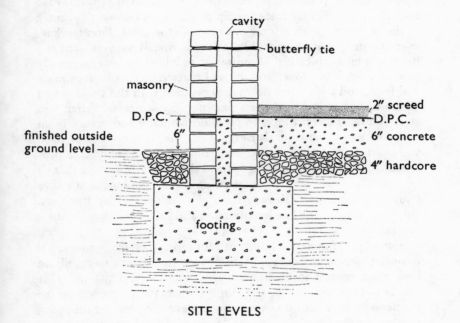

SITE LEVELS

DPC to ribbons before you're ready to screed, that is, lay a final, thin layer over the top.

Laying bricks, blocks and stone

If you've never laid any, don't start practising straight off the foundation, or the DPC. You'll have to invent a bit of garden wall to go somewhere, and stick with it until you know you can do it straight, level and horizontal.

Back on the site itself, you have now reached the DPC. Old buildings with DPCs usually used a layer of slate – and there's no reason why you shouldn't either. But the modern bituminous

DPC you buy in long rolls is very cheap and already cut to the exact width you need. Just roll it out along the wall, preferably on top of a mortar bed, leaving plenty of overlap at the ends, and build your first course off it. To do that, you need a builder's line – and don't settle for ordinary string which will stretch too much and give you a wall with a distinct sag in the middle. The basic technique is to dollop the mortar onto the previous course (in this case the DPC), and lightly trace the tip of the trowel down the centre of the course to push mortar out towards the sides. Don't, whatever you do, pat it all down like a sand castle. What you want is a fluffy and fairly thick bed of mortar on to which you ever so gently place the brick or block. You try and place it so that it sits square and level, and then tap it down into position with the wooden end of the trowel, or a bricklayer's hammer if you prefer. When you start you need a short level to place horizontally and vertically on each block to make sure it's right. When you're more experienced you need do that only on every few blocks; and when you're professional you use only the long level to check once in a while that all is well. The line, of course, you string round two blocks at either end, usually on the side away from you. When you lay the block you bring it up to the line horizontally, and then tap it down until it is level with the line.

Some tips. If there are lumps in your mortar, chuck it out; you'll never lay decent masonry with lumpy mortar. Don't worry about how much mortar spills off the edges – it's cheap stuff and your aim is to lay a good wall, not run a conservation programme for Portland cement. But do worry about preventing mortar dropping inside the cavity – otherwise you'll form a bridge for water to cross. If you don't get the brick right first try, for heaven's sake scrape off the old mortar bed and lay a new one. You can never reposition a piece of masonry on mortar which has already been flattened. Don't let people who've never laid a brick come up and put a few down just to get the feel of it. They'll make a muck of it, and you won't feel like taking it down the next day so for ever after your building will have a few very odd quirks. Show the enthusiastic amateur brickie politely to the garden wall, and let him doodle there to his heart's content.

To get the vertical lines of mortar in place, you butter some mortar onto one end of the brick or block and place it hard up against the previous one when laying. Both vertical and horizontal mortar beds should end up $\frac{3}{8}$ of an inch thick, and you'll soon get the feel of how much mortar that means putting on the course and the side of the brick. When you've done a few courses, or a few lengths, measure the dimension accurately and see if it tallies with the finished brick size. If it doesn't, you'll have to adjust on the next course.

The rest is mostly practice. Discuss with an expert what bond or pattern you're going to use. There are many types, designed to cope with the awkward bits like cornering and closing off cavity walls at window and door frames. These, incidentally, you should build in as you go up. They are normally fastened to the masonry simply by nails left sticking out from the side members and embedded in the mortar joints. Lintels above doors and windows you lay like large bricks, first making sure the overlap is big enough – at least a brick and a half, or a block and a half, on each side.

There is, of course, a lot more to it than that, but the rest is best found out by experience or by learning with someone who knows. The best I can do is give you my own history as a brickie for encouragement. Before going to Wales I had spent only a couple of mornings laying a garden wall with an experienced builder. At Eithin, during the only time we had as few as three people on the site, we had to lay 40 square yards of blocks, measuring 18 inches × 9 inches × 6 inches thick. I laid about two-thirds of them and the job was done inside a week – which is by no means a speed record. Those walls were laid by people with nearly no experience and they are roughly horizontal and vertical and to the correct dimensions. A professional would see imperfections, but they did the job more than adequately. I'm certainly no genius with my hands, and I've been called a bodger often enough. So if I can do it, you certainly can.

A few don't forgets. Don't forget that in a cavity wall you must occasionally bond across from one skin to the other with metal butterfly ties (see drawing on p. 55). Use about one for every square yard of wall, and simply bed them in the mortar between courses. Don't forget that you always lay the next brick or block of stone over the gap between the two bits of masonry in the course below. Don't forget, if your brickwork is to remain exposed, to point up the mortar before it dries too hard. And if you're building in stone, remember you need much thicker mortar beds – an inch or more is fine. A couple of hours after laying rake out all the joints with a stick, as far back as half an inch into the wall. First thing the next morning scrub away like mad at the joints with a wire brush to give a smooth finish to the wide joints, which will now be set back from the stone. The effect is magnificent.

Timber frame

If I had a free choice, I'd always choose to build a timber frame house rather than a masonry one. You'll have to check your own prices but when I did so late in 1974, 4-inch concrete blocks were £2 a square yard, facing bricks were £32.50 per 1,000, and sawn timber was 12p. per linear foot of 2 × 4 inches. At those prices the costs of building a cavity wall measuring 12 feet long by 9 feet high would have been £24 in blocks and £39 in brick. A timber trame of the same size would have cost about £20. But only the brick wall would be a finished job. The blocks would have to be stuccoed and the timber frame covered first with building paper and then either with shiplap or weatherboarding, preferably in Western Red Cedar, which is the only softwood which won't rot if left un-treated. Cedar is expensive, and the final cost of the timber frame plus sheathing would probably be more than £40. The stuccoed blocks would have been by far the cheapest.

But if you can get cheaper timber, or if you really want to enjoy the job and have a little cash to throw about, the timber frame house is the best and by far the quickest solution. You build each wall panel on the ground and then lift it up into position, nailing the bottom down and the sides into adjoining timber frames. Each frame consists of a top and bottom plate, vertical studs at 16- or 24-inch centres, two rows of noggings holding the studs apart at the correct distances, and a brace let into the main frame. Two people can build a large frame in half a day, when they've done one or two. It would take me 3 to 4 days to build the same thing in concrete blocks.

A timber frame house needs careful planning. For example, the studs on each floor should align perfectly with the ones above and below it for maximum strength. The rafters or roof trusses should sit over individual studs, and each frame must be perfectly square, and secured so that its vertical plane is not more than $\frac{1}{8}$ of an inch out of true in every 8 or 9 foot rise. So you plan out the house, drawing in every stud, and then cut all your studs to length. As to what timber to use, we made the external walls at Eithin from 2 × 5 and the internal ones from 2 × 4. We might have got away with 2 × 4 throughout, and as Eithin was exceptionally large and high, you certainly can. But don't go any smaller.

To cut the studs to length, use a pattern – a piece of 1 × 4 cut perfectly square at both ends and to the exact length. Place this on the stud-to-be, mark off both ends, and cut off the two unwanted portions of the stud. You cut both ends because each must be square to do the job properly and you cannot rely on the timber merchant to have cut accurately. You then find two straight timbers to act as top and bottom plates. Placing them side by side, mark off the positions where each stud will sit by squaring over both plates at the same time. Then sit back and think, and check that you've done it right.

You now place all the bits on the ground ready to nail. Put two nails through the plate into the end grain of each stud, and your frame is basically made. The next thing is to take the off-cuts from the stud lengths and turn them into noggings. You do this by holding the off-cut against the studs along the plate nearest to the position of the nogging you are making. Mark off the correct length, cut it and nail it between the studs about one-third the way up. You need two rows of noggings for a good frame, each fastened with two nails into each stud. You'll find one pair of these nails can be driven straight home, the other pair has to be skew nailed.

You must now square up. Do this with a long piece of wood to check the diagonals. If they are not equal (they won't be), secure one corner of the frame somehow, and bash the opposite corner with a sledge hammer in the appropriate direction. When the thing is square, secure each corner so it won't budge. Now lay the brace – probably a piece of 1 × 4 – from corner to corner, tack it in position and mark off with pencilled lines on the studs and noggings where each side of the brace intersects them. Set the gauge to the depth of the brace, and score along both sides of the studs and noggings where the intersection lines are marked. Now saw down each piece as far as the gauge line and then chisel out the slot for the brace to fit in. Knock the brace home with a mallet, and secure with two 3-inch nails into each stud and nogging. You have built a frame.

Now for the variations. If there is a door window to let in, you make the frame as shown in the drawing. If the frame includes a corner to the house, you should use two studs at the corner so

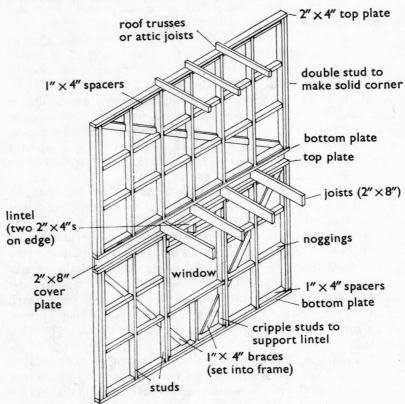

TWO-STOREY TIMBER FRAME CONSTRUCTION

that it can be really well fixed to the adjacent frame. If in doubt, reinforce the corner by screwing a right angle metal strap to the two frames. When ordering the timber, order plates and studs separately, the plates about one foot longer than you need them, and each stud long enough to make the stud and two noggings, with say 6 inches over. That way, you'll waste very little timber. But make sure it's been pressure-treated or you'll have to hand paint each piece of timber with wood preservative which will take a long time and won't be nearly such a good job anyway (though you must do it if you're using second-hand timber).

Finally, the only trouble with the frame you have made is that the studs could pull sideways along the plate – in spite of the two nails holding it there. To prevent that, you must nail in spacers, of say 1 × 4, between each stud and on to the top and bottom plates. Or, better still, install your plywood or other board exterior wall sheathing on the diagonal to impart rigidity to the frame of studs.

And that's about all there is to timber frames. The house we built in Wales must, I suppose, be one of the most ambitious modern timber frame houses in the country. We were well satisfied with it. There were 14 frames to each floor (it's a very big house, with 8 double bedrooms), and it took us two weeks to build each floor, including both frames and joists. We've had no worries about the structure.

The most difficult business was starting off from the masonry. However you build your house, there will be masonry at least to DPC level. We actually then built half a storey of stone wall and on top of that poured a fiendishly complicated concrete sill into which was housed the bottom plate of the first frame. It was complicated because the water running down the sides of the house had to be made to flow down the sill and then drip off clear of the stonework below, which was above DPC height. If you start the timber frame from the DPC you would probably pour a concrete beam all the way round the house directly onto the footings, up to DPC level. In the concrete you set holding-down bolts at about 2 feet centres so that they miss the studs. These have ragged ends which are placed in the wet concrete and hence anchored there. The other end is left protruding and is threaded. The bottom plates to the first frames are then drilled out at the appropriate places and the plate dropped onto the bolts and screwed down to the concrete (which has been covered with DPC). That way there will never be any danger of the bottom of the house moving in any direction. That, incidentally, is also the best way of fixing a wall plate to the top of a masonry wall, so that the roof structure can be nailed down into it. Most builders wouldn't bother with anything so involved – but if you want to be sure, that's the way to do it.

Joists, beams and floors

When you've built a storey of timber frame, and nailed it all together, you're probably going to get very cross. Far from being the strong rigid structure I've been talking about, you'll find it feels fairly flimsy and generally non-house-like. But before you fling me and my book into the footings, remember you haven't yet put the joists (or if it's single-storey, the roof structure) on. When you do, you'll get the effect I promised, for the joists hold the whole thing together at the top, whereas before it was held only at the bottom and sides.

Joisting out a floor in a timber frame building is one of the easiest jobs you'll ever have to do. If the structure has been built of 2 × 4, you cut the joists to give you 2 inches overlap on to each top plate at either end. Fasten the joists to the plate with two skew nails, one from each side. On an internal wall, you can either butt the joist ends against the joists spanning the adjacent room, or lap them the full 4-inch width of the top plate. On an external wall, you mount a joist timber along the length of the plate and nail it both into the joist ends and down into the plate. The job's finished – and it will be just as strong as I said.

When choosing joists, there's a rule of thumb to work out the depth of wood you need (timber spans, of course, are always determined by the depth of the timber, not its width). Divide the length you have to span by two in feet, add three, and you have the depth of wood you need in inches. Thus to span 10 feet, you need joists 8 inches deep. To span 14 feet, you need 10-inch joists (2 × 9 was the joist size we used in Wales). Joists will be expensive but as the only alternative is reinforced concrete floors – which you certainly don't want to get into – you don't have much choice but to pay up.

If you're building another storey, the frames that run across the joists are simply nailed into the top of them. But those that run parallel with the joists are more tricky. You'll have to set your joists out so that you have two joists running side by side, separated by 2 inches, immediately below the next frame. Put a few 2-inch off-cuts between the joists and nail them in position. Then centre your next frame exactly over the gap, so that you have 1 inch of joist to nail into on each side of the plate. Put a few nails into the off-cuts as well.

Two other points to remember. First, each joist should be fastened to the plate below exactly over the stud underneath. That's what gives the structure its strength. Second, the joists will need holding together in the centre of their span, otherwise there'll be a good deal of movement in the finished floor. This is normally done with angled pieces of 1 × 2 arranged in herring-bone fashion. But if your joist off-cuts are long enough, you can use them exactly as you would noggings to fill between the joists in the centre of the span.

If you're joisting out onto a brick or block structure, the easiest way is simply to build the ends of the joists into the wall as it goes up. But it's not the best, because it's never a good idea to hide timber away in masonry where it might be subject to all kinds of rot and other unmentionable afflictions. If you do that, you must ensure that the joist ends don't intrude beyond the first skin and into the cavity. Or you can use metal straps to support the joists individually. These are called joist hangers and are ridiculously expensive – more than $1 each. Finally, you can corbel out two courses of bricks and hang the joists on them, so that the ends never go into the wall but are left proud of it. I don't really fancy that as a solution for the amateur – though if you've a professional around that might be the best solution. In fact, I don't think any of these methods is really satisfactory, which is another reason for using timber frame. If I had to do it, I'd probably build the joists into the wall, first giving their ends an extra coat of preservative and following that up with a thick layer of a standard bituminous paint.

One of the first problems met with by any amateur is that of beams. To make bigger rooms, old houses are knocked about and dividing walls taken out. In new houses usually at least one room is made very large. In both cases one end of the joists is left apparently hanging in mid-air. And to stop the whole house falling about your ears some kind of a beam must be devised to support the joists.

The commonest solution these days is to use a metal I-beam. I don't recommend it. They're very heavy and expensive; furthermore, they're a fire hazard. As the alternative is a wooden beam, this may sound surprising but the fact is that in the fierce heat of a fire a metal beam will start to sag long before a wooden one. The latter, of course, will char on the outside but it will take some time

63

in a very fierce fire for the beam to burn through – if it ever does. So to protect the metal beam some complicated and fiddly work is needed with plasterboard and plaster to give the extra fire protection which Building Regulations demand.

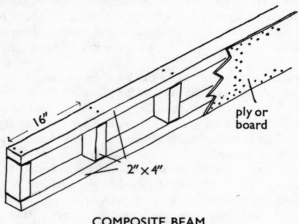

COMPOSITE BEAM

There are four ways of buying timber beams. One is to buy them new – and they may not be quite as expensive as you fear. You don't need hardwood – something like a 6 × 10 in pine will carry your joists over a span of 12 feet or more easily enough. Or you can buy the same thing second-hand much cheaper. At Eithin we once bought three beams of 4 × 12, each over 15 feet long, for £12. You can't do better than that. Or you can make up a beam by nailing, say, three pieces of 2 × 10 together, to make a 6 × 10. I don't recommend this, and it'll never look like much; but it will work. Finally, you can make up a composite beam. Use two long pieces of 2 × 4, on the flat not on edge, and nail them to, say, 6-inch studs, just as though you were making a frame, with the studs at the same separation as in the frame. When that's done, cut two pieces of good quality plywood to the length of the beam and 10 inches deep. These pieces you nail to the sides of the 2 × 4s and to the 'studs' in between – and it is these 'skins' that give the beams their strength. If your beam is long, you won't be able to get plywood in long enough lengths (it's better all in one piece), so use something like ¾ × 10 boarding. Use a lot of 2-inch

64

nails (one every 3 inches) to fix the skins, and you'll end up with a beam that will carry anything you are ever likely to build over 15 feet or more.

If you've got the head-room, of course, you set these beams at such a height that the joists rest on top of them. But if you haven't – and we didn't at Eithin – then roll your sleeves up because you're in for some heavy carpenter's joinery unless you duck the issue

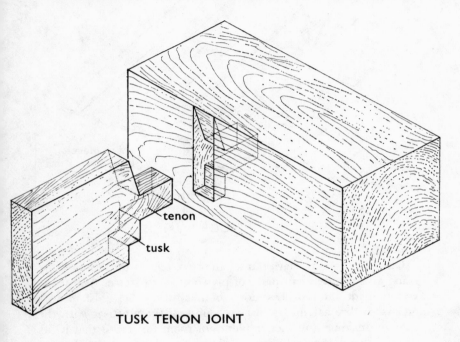

tenon

tusk

TUSK TENON JOINT

and buy joist hangers. If you don't, you have to make tusk tenons on the end of each joist and the appropriate mortise in the beams to receive them. It sounds very heroic. At Eithin we had one long room some 40 feet in length with two 9 × 9 beams carrying the joists which spanned their length in three sections. Using the 44 joist hangers we needed would have cost us more than £25. So with saw, chisel and mallet, we made 44 sets of tusk tenons and their mortises. It took Nick and me two full days going flat out – but the satisfaction when they all fitted together was worth every second of it. I shan't tell you how to do it (but see drawing above) because you need a really detailed book to make sure it's exactly right and doesn't end in disaster. But it's one bit of real building that will give you a hell of a kick if you pull it off.

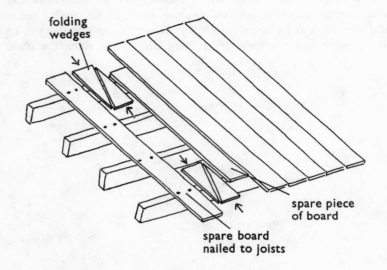

folding wedges

spare piece of board

spare board nailed to joists

CLAMPING FLOOR BOARDS

One tip, though. Mark out all the tusk tenons on the joists by using an accurately cut piece of plywood as a pattern. And when you've made the mortises, don't bother fitting each joist into its mortise before assembly. Just go round all the mortises with the pattern, making sure there's plenty of room for it and that it fits snugly. If it does, all the joists will also fit when you assemble the thing in mid-air. When you've done that, drive 4-inch spikes through the beam and into the tenons to hold it all secure.

About flooring there's not a lot to say except that it'll take you longer than you think and, whatever you do, don't lay until the house and roof are watertight. The quicker flooring is tongue-and-groove chipboard sheets – and they're also cheaper if you don't count the fact that eventually you'll have to cover them with something, whereas a wood floor can be left bare if it's sanded and sealed with polyurethane. Professional builders using tongue-and-groove wooden flooring have a pair of floor clamps several feet long which they use to squeeze the boards together before nailing them down. Chances are there won't be too many pairs of clamps that large lying around your site, so you make a cheap and neat solution by using two pairs of folding wedges as shown in the drawing on page 66. Lay your first 5 or 6 boards down and push them together as far as they'll go. Then nail an old piece of flooring to the joists about 2 inches clear of the last of the loose boards. Insert your folding wedges in the gap and, using a pair of mallets, tap the ends of the wedges together – first one pair, then the other. As you do so, the boards will creak together until you've got as good a fit as any $50 clamp will ever give you. Nail the boards down, take out the wedges and lift up the cramping board. Repeat – and repeat and repeat, until all your flooring is done.

The roof

People who don't know about roofs always wonder why they're made at such impossibly steep angles. Amateurs seem to love flat roofs – at least they do until they've built one and tried to live under it. But roofs are made steep for some very good reasons. The first is that the water drains off much more quickly, and the chances of a leak are therefore less. Waterproofing a flat roof is a devil of a job, and it'll certainly involve you either in pouring hot tar or getting someone in to stick down thin plastic sheet roofing and solder all the edges together with a hot air gun (by far the simplest solution if you must have a flat roof). But a pitched roof gives you a lot of other things as well, such as an attic space for storing junk and apples and other things. An attic is also an insulating air space between you and the outside world – and if you insulate both its floor and its roof, you're going to save a lot of heat in the next 20 years. Finally, a pitched roof is ideal for solar heating – see chapter 7.

The timber frame for a pitched roof is not a difficult thing to build – the books tell you how in great detail. But at Eithin we used ready-made roof trusses, and they cost us less than the timber we'd have had to buy to make up a similar structure. A roof truss is basically a triangle of wood, with the two rafters coming down each side and the chord spanning across the bottom between them (the chord is the equivalent of the joist in the attic space). But the secret lies in the extra bits of wood that are placed between the chord and the rafters to tighten the truss up – they are what enable it to span distances of 30 feet or more. If you do order trusses, make sure to have them pressure-treated before delivery. We forgot, and it took us longer to paint them with preservative than it did to erect the roof.

When your trusses come, you'll find them very light but unwieldy. Looking up at the piece of sky where they're going to sit will give you a bit of a turn because it *is* difficult to visualize how you're going to get them up there and make them stay there when they are. This is what you do. Two people manhandle the trusses and push one end up as far as they can make it go. Someone on top grabs the end and simply pulls it up. It's as easy as that – though you may want to use a rope as well if there are any other difficulties. You then push the bottom of the first truss out to where it will finally sit, and loosely nail a couple of timber props on to the rafters. With someone holding the bottom steady, push the truss up and, when it's exactly vertical, nail the props to whatever you're standing on to hold it secure. Meanwhile someone has prepared two lengths of 2 × 1 batten, marked off at 16- or 18-inch centres, or whatever separation you are using between trusses. The wall plates on which the trusses sit are similarly marked. You now erect the second truss (you may have temporarily to remove the props to the first to do this, and then slip the nails back into their original holes when it's in position). Each truss is fixed to the wall plate by a pair of skew nails, one from each side. Then the battens are fixed near the top of the rafters on each side of each truss, at the exact centres already marked out. Providing your first truss is vertical, you don't have to check any of the others because the batten will ensure they are too. Carry on in this way until all the trusses are up. They are now vertical, fixed down to the floor but held horizontally only by slender battens. These are temporary and you must now hurry to make a final fix using stronger wood, such as 2 × 2, running one length along the ridge inside the trusses and additional lengths from the ridge down across the inside of the rafters to the chord. Nail into each truss and the roof is finished. But hurry – because while your trusses are held only by battens, a strong wind could simply blow the whole thing down like a pack of cards. Once your 2 × 2 is fixed you'll feel the roof stiffen up – and stop fixing 2 × 2 only when it really feels solid. There is, in fact, more strength to come if, as in Britain, you have the roof slated or tiled, for the slaters or tilers will fix battens across all the rafters to hang their roof finish on to. And that will add a lot of strength. Pitching the roof was one of the jobs we feared most at Eithin – and in the event it was one of the easiest and quickest things we had to do, perhaps because we thought about it a lot before we did it.

A word about heights. If you're muttering to yourself that you could never do that because you can't stand steady even on a pair of step-ladders, forget it. I have – or rather had – an appalling head for heights. But somehow, when you build a house, and you get progressively accustomed to working higher and higher, your vertigo will all but disappear. I can't explain it, except that it's something to do with a house being stronger than step-ladders, and there always being something solid to hang on to. I'd now much rather work 40 feet up on a roof than stand upright on a pair of wobbly steps. The same will probably be true for you.

The south or west pitch of your roof I'm going to leave severely alone for the moment, assuming you're sensible enough to want to erect a solar roof to help heat your water or air. The other pitch has to be covered. At Eithin we opted for second-hand slates supplied and fixed by a friendly near-by roofing contractor. It was very cheap, and I doubt we could have bought (or even found) the second-hand slates for less than he charged us for the whole job. But he did make us wait, and with a roof that's not a good thing. Just as you think you can finally keep your house dry, and perhaps start the internal work, you find the promised date cannot be kept, and the slaters have slipped off for a couple of weeks in Majorca. If you do it yourself, you won't save much money but you may save time.

Props and wedges

Particularly if your building involves a part-conversion of an old one, you're going to need to prop up old work at some point. Builders do this with jacks or lolly columns, very tough metal affairs which you can screw round and round to alter the height. As you probably won't want to fork out for hiring them, you make do with timber props. If you are removing a masonry wall, for instance, you first need to hack away all the decorative layers until you get down to the structure and see just what it is supporting. Probably a row of joists, and on top of that some more masonry. In that case, all you have to do is support the rows of joists on either side of the wall by fixing a stout plank to them on their underside. You then prop this plank, using lengths of timber say an inch too long to fit vertically underneath. To fix the prop, present the top end to the plank and with a lump hammer bang the bottom in until it begins to take the weight. Bang away a bit more, but watch the joists and stop just as they begin to rise. You need props like this for every 3 or 4 feet of board you are supporting. You can now begin to take away the masonry – but do it carefully and if there are any signs of movement above, for heaven's sake stop. Get professional advice the moment you get in trouble. There's no point in being so self-sufficient that your house falls down.

And at some point you are going to have to lift very heavy weights – the end of a beam with a load on it, for example, to level it off. All you need is a pair of folding wedges, as used in flooring, but bigger – say 2 inches thick, 10 inches long and 3 inches high. Place them under your timber prop, and slowly knock the two wedges together, hitting both ends simultaneously. The result is miraculous, and you'll find you can lift dead weights of several tons in a couple of minutes with a few blows of the mallet. When you've done this once, phenomena such as Stonehenge become a good deal less mysterious.

The water level

To get your building levels right over distances of say 6 to 8 feet is easy enough with a straight timber and a long level placed on top. But you'll probably need to check levels over much greater distances – up to 30 or 40 feet. For this you can either buy a water level, or make one. You need a long length of plastic hose pipe and two glass cylinders – test-tubes with their ends cut off will do. Fix the tubes in each end of the pipe and fasten them there with twisted wire or a metal clip. Place both tubes lightly but firmly in the vice so that their tops are exactly level, and fill with water until the water level comes half-way up each tube and completely fills the hose pipe. Pop two corks in the tubes and you are ready. One person holds one end to the datum and the other adjusts the level of his glass tube until the meniscus on the first is exactly level with the datum. The meniscus on the other tube will now register the height of the datum at a distance of 30 feet or more away. Remember the thing won't work at all if the hose pipe gets kinked and the water is not free to flow, or the corks have not been removed when the actual measurement is made (they are used only to keep the water slopping out when carrying the level about). And the meniscus may take a few seconds to reach its final level. So always wait a few minutes before announcing that someone will have to pull their wall down because it's 2 inches off the level!

Joinery

As I could fill a book with hints on how to do joinery (and plenty of people already have), I shall deal only with the question of whether you are going to do your own, or buy the stuff ready-made. The arguments are these. As far as building proper is concerned, joinery is door and window frames, window sashes, the doors themselves, and stairs. Now you can buy ready-made windows and frames very much cheaper than it will cost you to buy the timber to make them. The trouble is that almost all of them are totally hideous and completely unliveable with. So if you can afford it, you will learn joinery and make your own windows and frames. Once you've learnt, of course, you'll probably never stop and all the rest of the furniture in your house will be hand-made – and you'll probably start exporting some things to friends who never took the plunge. My advice is do it. Because we had Nick at Eithin we made all our own doors and windows, and several of us learned at least the beginnings of joinery. With surprisingly little practice I found I could turn out two window sashes a day. They may not have been a joiner's delight but they were certainly far better than factory-made stuff. It still takes me three days, however, to make a complete door, with top and bottom rails and a double centre rail.

Doors are a bit different. For one thing, you can buy really elegant second-hand doors and that is your best answer if you can get them. Or you can buy inexpensive flush-doors. You can put them up and resolve to build your own later on when you've more time. We did that too at Eithin, but there's little sign yet of anyone replacing them with the real thing! For internal doors, the frame consists only of simple boarding fixed securely to the walls on to which the door is hung and the appropriate stop beading nailed. For external doors, you need a fully-fledged, properly jointed door frame, complete with hardwood sill. That is something it's well worth learning to make, even if you buy doors to fit it.

Scaffolding

You may as well make up your mind now that you're going to need scaffolding. This book is definitely not for the kind of amateur who tries to lay masonry balancing on the top of a pair of steps. In any case, he will have fallen off and probably broken his neck long before he reaches first-floor level. Now you can hire a kind of aluminium, slot-it-together-yourself tower on wheels which is today held out as the amateur's answer to scaffolding. I give solemn warning to anyone building their house that this is not your answer. I'd be done for libel if I said they were actually dangerous – but I have used one and I could never recommend it to anyone else. If you must hire scaffolding, then hire the traditional clip-together iron tubing. But, best of all, build your own from timber – which is what we did when we'd learnt as much as we wanted to know about aluminium towers.

Wooden scaffold needs 6 or 8 very long uprights – 2 × 4 is ideal – and another 2 or 3 pieces the same length to fix nearly at the top of the uprights at one end, with the bottom ends dug into the ground to act as rakers and to stop any movement in the structure. You also need a lot of gash timber – almost anything will do – to use as cross pieces and diagonal braces. Finally, you need some boards to make the platform – your unused joists will be ideal. The whole thing is held together with 4-inch spikes much as shown in the drawing. The details can be varied as you wish, and of course the more timber you use the stronger it will be. Two of you can make something like that in less than a day – and its only disadvantage will be that you can't carry it from place to place

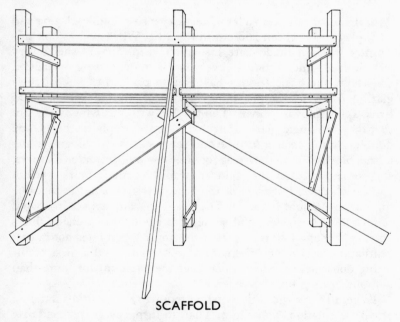

SCAFFOLD

because it will be too heavy. But you can partially dismantle it, and move sections of it around. Scaffold like this you can get really fond of, and it'll be a joy to work from. It'll also be a very nice place just to sit and watch the world go by when you don't feel like working – and on a do-it-yourself building site those days are ones you can value just as much as the others. Which is probably mainly why you are doing it yourself.

Chapter 5

❧◦❧

Insulation

AND that does not mean a lot of very expensive double-glazing and a couple of rolls of felt laid out in the attic. What we waste in this country through inadequate insulation keeps the oil sheiks very rich indeed; and although everyone is now getting insulation conscious, the basic lessons have yet to be learnt. The double-glazing fad, for example, must be one of the quickest ways to bankruptcy known to man. The trouble with our windows is not that they are single-glazed, but that they are simply too big. Good double-glazing costs a fortune and the result is still like installing a large block of ice in the living room. A few well-insulated shutters, and some good draught excluder, would be much more efficient and far cheaper. But most of the heat we waste is not in fact due to poor insulation: it's caused by designing our houses like wind tunnels. We have two, and sometimes even three, outside doors opening directly into the heart of the house; open flues not in use; ventilation bricks here, there, and everywhere; and a mass of ill-fitting doors and windows. Together they account for more than half our heating bills.

To get to grips with this situation requires a good understanding of what insulation is all about. That, in turn, involves some fairly gentle arithmetic. If you can't manage that, you can skip a few paragraphs of this chapter and still emerge with a clear view of where the priorities lie. But to do anything effective about heat loss, you must have a quantitative idea of how much is being lost where, and of how much can be saved by doing what.

The best design for a house I know is one in which the semi-basement level is used for domestic animals, the ground floor for

74

living and sleeping, and the top floor for storing the winter's food, including hay and straw. Farmers used to build like that, and very snug they must have been, warmed by the animals and insulated by the fodder. Hay and straw are very good insulators, but they are a fire risk. In fact, air is the best insulator, provided it is somehow trapped in a matrix of tiny cells so small that convection cannot take place in the air bubbles and sweep the heat away. Modern insulators such as styrofoam and fibreglass work in this way and no traditional material, even hay or cork, is quite as good.

Country people still talk affectionately of those cosy old stone cottages people used to build. There aren't many areas where traditional knowledge is so far off the mark. Those cottages were the world's worst, for stone is probably the most useless insulator ever used in building. Sandstone is the best of a very poor lot, but even a sandstone dwelling would have to have walls a yard thick to compete with just 1 inch of styrofoam. Even a wall consisting only of half an inch of plywood stuck to $\frac{3}{8}$-inch plasterboard insulates better than a yard of sandstone. And if you build in granite – as they do in Aberdeen, that coldest of all places – you would need walls more than 7 feet thick just to insulate as well as 1 inch of styrofoam. What I would call a well-insulated house in granite would need walls nearly 30 feet thick! People in the stone age survived all right – but only by being cold and burning down most of the forests trying to keep warm. We have to be more subtle.

k-values

And that means getting into mathematics. The thermal conductivity of a material is what defines its insulating qualities – the lower the conductivity, or k-value, the better it is as an insulator. A k-value actually measures the number of watts of heat that a one-metre thickness of the material will conduct across an area of one square metre if there is a temperature difference of 1°C between the two sides. The units of a k-value are measured in watts per metre per degree centigrade (W/m °C). But don't worry too much about the theory – how and why you want to use k-values will become clear in a minute.

The table opposite shows the k-values of most of the materials you're likely to come across – and a few you won't, for comparison. It shows that air is about the best insulator and silver the worst.

k-values

(k = conductivity in watts per metre per degree centigrade)

asbestos, loose sprayed	0·034
asbestos cement sheet	
light	0·216
average	0·360
dense	0·576
asphalt	0·576
commons brickwork	
light	0·806
average	0·210
dense	1·470
lightweight bricks	0·374
engineering bricks	1·150
concrete	
ordinary dense	1·440
light aggregate	0·12 to 0·71
stone	
granite	2·012
limestone	1·530
sandstone	1·295
timber	
softwood	0·138
hardwood	0·160
wood chipboard	0·108
wood fibre softboard	0·065
wood wool slab	
light	0·082
dense	0·115
cork	
natural slab	0·046
baked regranulated	0·039
eel grass blanket	0·043
fibreglass	0·032
mineral wool felt	0·037
mineral wool rigid slab	0·049
plasterboard	0·18
gypsum plaster	0·461
vermiculite	0·12 to 0·26
plywood	0·138
strawboard	0·098
sand-cement plaster	1·41
expanded styrofoam	0·033
polyurethane foam	0·023
metals	
cast iron	50
silver	407
air	0·020
water	0·580

All the heavy things, like concrete and stone, are bad. Next come the lighter finishes like asphalt and plasterboard. And finally, best of all, the modern mineral wools and expanded plastics.

How to use k-values? Suppose, to take an easy example, you live in a 2-metre square box of expanded styrofoam which is 25 mm thick (about 1 inch). You keep the inside at 20°C (68°F) and the outside is at freezing point (0°C). Now the k-value of expanded styrofoam is 0·033 W/m °C. The surface area of your box will be 24 m², so you need to multiply the k-value by 24. Your box is not 1 metre thick, but 25 mm (0·025 m) thick, so you need to divide by that as well. And finally the temperature difference is not 1° but 20°, so you also need to multiply by 20. Hence your rate of loss of heat will be:

$$0·033 \times 20 \times 24/0·025 \text{ which equals 634 watts.}$$

Just by being in the room your own body is producing about 110–140 watts, so you need some 500 W or ½ kW to keep your styrofoam room at 20°C when it's freezing outside. Five or six 100-watt electric light bulbs would do very nicely, or the smallest fan heater you can buy. It follows, of course, that if you had not 25 mm of styrofoam but 100 mm (about 4 inches) you could heat your room with one electric light bulb. That, in a nut shell, is the value of insulation.

U-values

As you probably don't live in a styrofoam box, but in something more closely resembling a house, the calculation becomes a little – but not much – more complicated. You need to know what is called the U-value of each external surface of your house. The U-value is measured in W/m²/°C, and if multiplied by the area of your wall, gives the rate of loss of heat for every centigrade-degree difference in temperature between the inside and the outside. The table opposite gives some typical U-values for much used materials in building. To estimate heat loss through a concrete floor, for example, you need to know that the U-value is 1·13 W/m² °C and that the average temperature of the ground underneath a house is 5°C (it's not much affected by changes in the air temperature outside). Then if your floor area is 15 m², and you want to maintain 20°C inside, the floor loss will be 1·13 × 15 × 15, which equals 254 watts. But the problem comes when you want to know the

U-values

(U is air-to-air transmittance in watts per square metre
per degree centigrade)

WALLS

brick solid, unplastered, 114 mm	3·64 W/m² °C
plastered both sides	3·24
plastered both sides, 228 mm	2·44
concrete, dense, 203 mm	3·18
stone, medium porous, 457 mm	2·27
305 mm	2·84
brick, 280 mm cavity, plastered inside	1·70
25 mm corkboard	0·85
13 mm fibreboard	1·19
50 mm woodwool slab	0·85
16 mm vermiculite plaster	1·47
concrete block, 250 mm cavity	1·19
clinker concrete block, 250 mm cavity	1·08

FLOORS

concrete on hardcore fill	1·13
plus woodblock finish	0·85
timber on joists plus underfloor space	1·70
plus parquet or lino	1·42
25 mm corkboard	0·79
50 mm strawboard	0·84

PITCHED ROOFS

corrugated asbestos plus 13 mm timber boarding	2·16
50 mm woodwool	1·25
25 mm quilt	0·85
corrugated iron sheets	8·52
tiles or slates on boarding and felt	1·70

WINDOWS

exposure to south, sheltered single-glaze	3·97
double-glaze (6 mm gap)	2·67
(20 mm gap)	2·67
W, SW, SE sheltered single-glaze	4·48
double-glaze, 20 mm gap	2·50
NW, N, NE, E sheltered single-glaze	5·00
double-glaze, 6 mm gap	3·30
double-glaze, 20 mm gap	2·84
NW severe exposure, single-glaze	6·47
double-glaze, 6 mm gap	3·58
double-glaze, 20 mm gap	3·00

Note: U-values vary somewhat according to wind strength and exposure effect of adding, say, a chipboard surface above 2 inches of styrofoam over the concrete. To do this you must calculate the U-value from a knowledge of the k-values of each material. You add them all up, upside down as it were, and then turn the answer the right way up again. It works like this:

concrete and hardcore U-value = 1·13
50 mm styrofoam k-value = 0·033
18 mm chipboard k-value = 0·108
Then 1/U = 1/1·13 + 0·050/0·033 + 0·018/0·108 = 2·567
hence U = 0·39 W/m²°C.

Therefore, the new heat loss will be 0·39 × 15 × 15 = 88 watts. In other words, the insulation will be saving some 166 watts, or over 24 hours, about 4 kWh. If your heat costs you, say, 5¢ per kWh, you will be saving 20¢ a day or $1.40 a week, just by insulating the floor. And if you know the cost of insulation, you can then work out how long it will take to pay off the cost of the styrofoam.

You can now (almost) pronounce yourself a fully-qualified insulation engineer. Almost, because there is just one more trick you need to know. For reasons which need not bother us, you have to add terms to the above calculation to allow for the conductivity of the inside and outside surfaces of the wall. I'll give the values first and explain how to use them afterwards. For all internal surfaces you must add a U-value of 8·12 W/m² °C. For external surfaces you must add a further value – 18·9 W/m² °C for north and east walls, 13·18 W/m² °C for a west wall, 7·78 W/m² °C for a south wall and 22·7 W/m² °C for a roof. To show how this works, imagine the previous calculation was not for a floor but for a north wall. The new sum would be:

1/U = 1/8·12 + 1/18·9 + 1/1·13 + 0·050/0·033 +
0·018/0·108 = 2·743
hence U = 0·365 W/m² °C.

Not much different, I must admit, from the previous result. But with that extra piece of information you can now work out the thermodynamics of your building to great accuracy.

The whole house

What follows is a worked example for a whole house. If you are doing the same sum, you'll find it very useful but, if not, skip to the end of the calculation and remember, it's there any time you want to come back to it.

The house I've designed is a bit of a bastard – with a flat roof for convenience, and with four different walls of totally different materials to give variety. As you know how to calculate U-values I haven't included my own calculations, just the results of them.

The kind of calculation done on page 81 is worth doing for any house. It packs a lot of information. For instance, the totals excluding air changes are 538·9 for the uninsulated house and 177·2 for the insulated one – which means that the insulation is cutting heat loss down to one-third of its original value. Note, too, that the loss from the windows is only slightly more than one-tenth of the total for the uninsulated house, and just over 20 per cent for the insulated house – which shows neither that the windows are a very important part of the sum, nor that fixing of double-glazing does nearly as much to improve the situation as insulation elsewhere. It saves, in fact, only about 30 W/°C, whereas insulating any of the other surfaces saves nearly twice that.

Next, of course, the sum shows just how huge losses from air changes can be. I've included a figure for just one air change an hour, and try as you may, you're not likely to produce a stuffier house than that. If you had 3 air changes an hour, that would cost you as much heat as leaving the house uninsulated – or it would give you 3 times the heat loss of the insulated house. Put it another way. Insulating the house very well saves you roughly the same amount of heat as cutting down the number of air changes from 3 to 1. As eliminating draughts is much cheaper than insulating, that at least tells you where your priorities should lie.

The final figures of this calculation also tell you how much power is going to be needed to heat your house. But it does depend, of course, on how hot you want to keep it. In England you can ignore temperatures much below freezing point – they do occur, of course, but only rarely do we get conditions of more than two or three degrees of frost. So it is quite reasonable to ignore them, and suffer slightly a few nights a year. Now for the internal temperature. No one wants a house hotter than 20°C (remember that's the average for the house, bedrooms and bathrooms included). On the other hand, anything colder than 15°C (59°F) does get a bit chilly. So if you multiply the final figure for the insulated house by the average temperature differential you want to sustain, you get the

Face and materials	Area (m²)	Uninsulated U-value (W/m²°C)	Uninsulated heat loss (W/°C)	Insulated U-value (W/m²°C)	Insulated heat loss (W/°C)
North wall: timber frame with 12 mm external weatherboard and 8 mm internal plasterboard; insulation is 100 mm expanded styrofoam between studs	42·0	1·30	54·5	0·24	10·2
East wall: brick/50 mm cavity/insulating block; insulation is U-foam in cavity	58·8	1·10	64·5	0·41	24·0
East windows: insulation is double-glazing	7·2	5·00	36·0	2·84	20·5
South wall: brick/50 mm cavity/brick; insulation is U-foam in cavity	42·0	1·70	71·4	0·45	19·5
West wall: 40 cm sandstone plus 8 mm plasterboard; insulation is plasterboard laminated to 25 mm polyurethane foam	58·8	1·78	98·8	0·61	35·6
West windows: insulation is double-glazing	7·2	4·48	32·2	2·50	18·0
Floor: concrete and hardcore; insulation is 12 mm chipboard over 50 mm styrofoam	77·0	1·13	87·0	0·40	30·8
Flat roof: 35 mm asphalt on 12 mm chipboard and 8 mm plasterboard; insulation is 100 mm styrofoam between joists	77·0	1·23	94·5	0·24	18·6
Air changes: assume one per hour; volume of house 462 m³, specific heat of air 0·36 Wh/m³ °C loss = 462 × 0·36			168·0		168·0
TOTALS			706·9 W/°C		345·2 W/°C

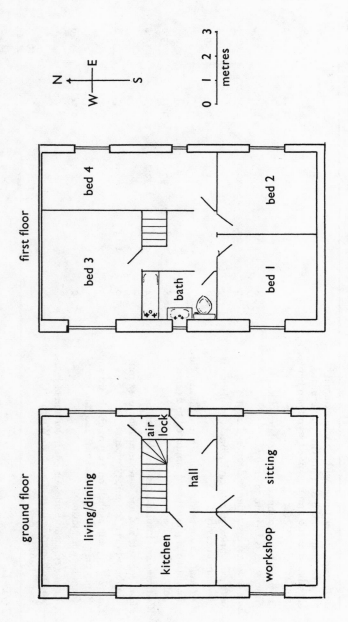

HOUSE INSULATION PLANS

total power needed – for 20°C, about 6·9 kW, for 17·5°C about 6·0 kW, and for 15°C about 5·1 kW. Now those figures are really quite small for heating a house that big – 5 kW is the equivalent of 5 small electric heaters (not that you will choose that way of heating). But you can, for instance, buy for about $300 a scientifically designed timber-burning stove from Norway that will give off some 7 kW. That would do the job admirably, although, unless the house were open plan, the heat would not circulate evenly. But a modern solid-fuel stove, with a back boiler to provide hot water and a few radiators, would supply more than enough heat. More about that in the next chapter.

Month	Average temperature (°C)	Degree days to		
		15°C	17·5°C	20°C
January	3·4	360	437	515
February	3·9	311	381	451
March	6·1	276	353	431
April	8·8	185	261	336
May	11·9	96	174	251
October	10·4	143	220	298
November	6·7	249	324	399
December	4·5	325	403	480
		1,945	2,553	3,161

Heat used in season
  (degree days $\times$ 345·2 $\times$ 24/1,000) = 16, 110 kWh at 15°C;
  21,150 kWh at 17·5°C; and 26,190 kWh at 20°C

The final thing you can do with your sum is to work out how much heat you are going to use over the winter, and what it will cost you. To do this you need to consult the local meteorological office, and obtain from it a record of average temperatures for each winter month over the past 20 years or so. You'll find it falls below 15°C in every month except June to September – which means you have an eight-month heating season. Suppose the average for January is 3°C (it won't be far off). You then have to heat the house by 12°C throughout January to maintain 15°C in the house. In other words, you have 31 $\times$ 12 = 372 'degree days' in January. Above are the sums for the season worked out according to the average figures for Cambridge, England, with a choice of three operating temperatures in the house.

The first thing that must be said about these figures is that they are over-estimates. You won't have to provide quite as much heat as they suggest. For one thing, you'll be cooking, and that gives off some heat. And then your lighting provides a bit more, your own body another 100 watts or so all the time you're in the house, and finally the sun will heat up the house a good bit when it does shine (even though the outside temperature may be below freezing point).

But what is accurate is the difference between these figures. Every $2\frac{1}{2}$°C you turn up the thermostat costs you a further 5,000 kWh each winter. In round figures that means nearly an extra ton of coal, or nearly 200 therms of gas, or 125 gallons of oil, or another two tons of dry timber if you're a wood burner. Another sweater would be a better investment.

With this in mind, we can now deal in a more practical way with the three things you can actually manipulate in your house: air changes and draughts, the windows, and insulating materials.

Air changes

If I were insulating a house, I'd start by looking at its air leakiness. The example above shows that even with just one change an hour, half the heat used in an insulated house goes in warming up cold air leaking in from the outside, and the other half in compensating for heat loss through the external surfaces. Believe it or not, many houses undergo as many as 3 air changes an hour. In the house above, that would cost you 500 W/°C, or 10 kW if there were a 20°C temperature differential. And at maximum rate, 10 kW costs you around 20p. an hour to run.

How can you cut down on the leaks? The worst offenders are outside doors, and houses today are still designed with at least two outside doors which, except in the case of terraced houses, is simply a relic of the Victorian age when servants and tradesmen were required to use one door and the nobs the other. So one possibility is to close off one or the other – almost certainly the front door, because you will need the back door leading from the kitchen to the kitchen garden most of all. Take the door and frame out, brick up the entrance and treat it henceforth as part of the front wall of the house. It may sound an odd thing to do, but it'll save you a lot of money and once you're used to it you'll find it quite a sensible idea. I've seen it done, in an architect's house, with brilliant effect – not only less heat loss, but more usable room in the house.

But you haven't finished with the other door yet. No outside door should ever open directly from the outside world to the inside of the house. If it does you'll let huge volumes of cold air in every time it opens and shuts. So you must have an airlock. Either build a small cubicle with another door inside the house, so that you open the outside door first, enter the air lock, close the outside door, and then open the inner one; or build an air lock outside the house. Providing the door is not in the north wall, the thing to do is to build a conservatory or glass lean-to on to that wall of the house so that you enter the house all the time through the conservatory. That will not only save most of your air leaks, but the conservatory will contribute a good deal of solar heat to the house – see chapter 7 on solar heating.

Next you need to check draughts in all the windows. Use draught-excluding strip wherever possible – the plastic, self-adhesive strip is the easiest to use – and remember that in any room where there is more than one window there is no point in having them all able to open. You can either replace the opening sash with a fixed one, or, if you are double-glazing, fix your second pane over the complete window. If you've cut out the draughts fairly well, you'll find the inner surfaces of the glass hardly ever need cleaning.

Next, you'll probably find that every room of your house has some extra means of ventilation in addition to the window. This always used to be the fireplace. If your fireplace is in use, devise some means of blocking off the flue opening when the fire is not actually lit. Thereafter you have to use common sense. If the house, or some rooms in it, are definitely stuffy or smelly, then let a little more draught in. How much ventilation you need is a matter of personal taste – but it will certainly be a good deal less than you think. Remember that, in a normal room, 0·7 air changes an hour are quite sufficient for good health.

Finally, if your house is on the larger side, you can close some of it off for the winter season. Live in a smaller, central area of the house. Some people seem to think this is a waste of heat, but they are wrong. An unheated room between you and the outside world is a good insulator, particularly if the insulation between the heated and the unheated room is fairly good. And if you have barns, extensions, conservatories and the like to build, always build them on to one side of the house, for they will increase your insulation as well.

Windows

One school of thought believes that houses should be made almost entirely out of window, with just enough supporting structure round the edges to hang the roof on. The idea seems to be that the inhabitants then sit inside and watch the seasons slowly fade into one another until death finally intervenes to stop the picture show. In spite of all our modern technology, I very much doubt that we can even now afford to treat nature as a spectator sport in this way. And when you're in a house, I think it should feel like being in a home, not a kind of superheated extension to the garden or golf course, or whatever you look on to.

I once spent two years in Paris working in one of these glass menageries, and it was insufferable. Even if your windows are double-glazed, you freeze in the winter and roast in the summer. It is high time we reduced this fashion for double-glazing to proper proportions. The myth is abroad that you can now virtually eliminate heat loss, even from huge picture windows, by double-glazing. It isn't true. Double-glazing – if well done, and that means very expensively done – will reduce the heat loss through a window by at most one-half. The other half will still leave you with the biggest U-values in the house – you lose heat through a double-glazed window, for example, twice as fast as you do through an uninsulated concrete floor. The answer does not lie in double-glazing.

The other problem with double-glazing is that it costs too much. For maximum efficiency you have to use what are called sealed panes – units in which the two panes of glass have been made into a hermetically-sealed sandwich with specially dried air between them. They are efficient, but they cost a fortune and you can't make them yourself without a lot of special equipment. The other way of making double-glazed windows is simply to fit them yourself – fitting two panes of glass into the rebate of the sash and fixing them there with additional beading. If you don't get a good seal between the glass and the beading, you won't get condensation between the panes, but you won't be saving so much heat loss either. If you do get a good seal, every winter your windows will mist up, and the only way of stopping that is to drill a number of small holes out through the sash from the space between the panes to give moist air a chance to escape. That may or may not cure the condensation, but it will certainly reduce the efficiency of the double-glazing. In other words, you can't win.

Not with double-glazing, that is. But you can with insulated shutters. Consider: The U-value of a single-glazed window is around 5·00. Double-glazing may reduce that to 2·5. But an insulated shutter will reduce it to 0·8 W/m² °C. The Victorians, of course, always had shutters rather than double-glazing, and thermodynamically they were quite right. Now shutters are something you can make well and cheaply yourself, particularly if you take into account the fact that you don't really need curtains as well as shutters.

Here, then, is what I would do about windows. If you're designing a new building, Building Regulations lay down that your windows must be at least equal in area to $\frac{1}{10}$ of the floor area in every habitable room (and $\frac{1}{20}$ of the area must be a window that can open). Stick to those minima. They'll give you enough light, but will be small enough to cut down excessive heat loss. In rooms that aren't used much in the day, such as bedrooms, I wouldn't bother with double-glazing; fit insulated shutters and keep them closed whenever you can in the winter. In the living rooms I would either make double-glazed windows or buy the most reasonable ones you can get.

In an old house, I think I would fit double-glazing on all really big windows, as well as on any that are in rooms much used during the daytime. And I'd certainly also fit insulated shutters on all windows in rooms which are used mainly at night. If in doubt, you'll find it easier, cheaper, and probably more efficient in terms of heat loss to fit an insulated shutter than double-glazing.

Insulating materials

We insulated the house in Wales with expanded styrofoam slab, and that's the insulator I know most about. If you've got a big job on, as we had, don't buy it from a builder's merchant but from one of the manufacturers direct.

Styrofoam is nice stuff to handle and ideal for timber frame buildings. It cuts easily with a saw; you simply cut off each square to fit snugly between the studs and noggings of a frame, or between

the rafters in the roof. Every time you cut, of course, you manufacture a lot of styrofoam droppings. If you don't sweep these
up and put them in a sack, they'll linger round your house and
garden for years because they are virtually indestructible (unless,
that is, you have a goat with a gastronomic preference for styrofoam which we did). Keep the sacks of droppings. And when
you install the hot water cylinder, make a box round it with hard-
board at least 6 inches away from the tank, and fill the box with the
droppings. That'll give you far better insulation than one of those
expensive and rather inefficient insulating jackets you can buy
ready-made.

The alternative is fibreglass or mineral wool, both of which
come in rolls and simply have to be tucked into the space. No need
for saws or accurate cutting. These have about the same U-values
as styrofoam but are now a lot cheaper. But, be warned, fibreglass
is ghastly to handle. You need gloves on all the time, and it's much
better not to breathe whenever the stuff is about. What it would
have done to our goat I dare not think.

Then you have also to decide what thickness of insulation to use.
If you do your sums you'll see that the first inch of insulation saves
a huge amount of heat, the second inch a good deal less, and each
additional inch even less. As each extra inch costs you the same
amount of money, it's obvious that at some point you reach a
degree of insulation where the extra is simply costing you more
than the amount of heat it's going to save. That point depends on
how much the insulation is costing, how much the heat will cost
and, if you're a capitalist, at what rate of interest you could invest
the money which you're otherwise spending on insulation. So I
can't give you the answer more accurately than to say it's somewhere between 3 and 6 inches thick. As the cost of heat is obviously
going to go on going up, I'd aim nearer 6 inches than 3.

If your walls are not timber frame, you have a problem with
insulation. Cavity walls, I'm afraid, will just have to be professionally filled with polyurethane foam by one of the big companies. Actually, it doesn't cost that much, and is quickly and
easily done. If you have solid brick or stone walls, then you have
two choices. Either build on to them a timber frame into which
you can stuff the insulation and on to which you can nail your
wall finish, be it plasterboard or pine boarding or whatever. Or
you can buy various brands of insulation boards, which come as

plasterboard/polyurethane foam laminates and can be fitted directly on to the wall (if they are smooth you can glue them, if they are rough you will have to nail them to battens). The trouble with these boards is that they will only give you really good insulation if the outer wall is also insulated – as in a cavity wall filled with foam. But half an inch of foam on to solid brick or stone is simply insufficient, and if you are going to insulate properly you will have to build an expensive timber frame out from the wall, and fill it with insulation.

The best solution to a concrete floor, in my view, is to lay, say, 2 inches of styrofoam and place tongue-and-groove chipboard sheets directly on top of it. Although you would think that might give you a spongy floor, it doesn't, providing the sheets are well fitted to the walls so that there is no movement. And that produces a really warm floor to walk on, quite suitable for bare feet. (For this you must use heavy duty styrofoam; consult your supply house or the manufacturer.)

Finally, buy a lot of aluminium foil as thin as you can get it. Very useful indeed, both as a moisture barrier before you put up your plasterboard or whatever and, of course, as an insulator of a different kind. The foil reflects heat back into the room (and cold back to the outside) and will improve your insulation quite a lot for only a tiny cost.

Condensation, ventilation and insulation

One reason why houses used to be made so draughty was that otherwise all the windows and cold walls ran with moisture every time it got cold outside and someone cooked cabbage or had a bath inside. Now the choice between saving heat by insulation and by cutting down on ventilation is not really as simple as I have made out. If you were to cut out all the draughts, and forget the insulation you would save heat, but you'd also be living in a kind of cold Turkish bath. In fact you have to do both – and when you have insulated well, you can afford to cut down the ventilation without risk of condensation because the outside walls will be much warmer on the inside. The exception is, once again, those damned windows; you may find that some single-glazed windows still run with water, and of course the shutters won't do anything to help. In that case, some do-it-yourself double-glazing is called for, and it will solve the problem.

Chapter 6

❧ ⚬ ❧

Heat

FORTY years ago very few houses in Great Britain had either insulation or central heating. They were as cold as hell, which doesn't really matter, and very, very damp, which does. But in the 1950s the central heating craze got underway, and all manner of over-powerful devices were installed, in the houses of both the rich and the poor, to raise the temperature in every room to baking point.

The combined effect of strikes, the Arabs and inflation has proved this to be a mixed blessing. So now the very people who were wheedling us into buying their central heating 10 or 20 years ago are peddling a new commodity: insulation. This, of course, is a good thing – except that when the last of us has installed really good insulation to save money, we shall find that we didn't really need the central heating in the first place. Our climate may be wet but it is not cold – and that means that a properly insulated house can be heated much more cheaply and simply. Which is just as well, for the days of unlimited cheap fuel have certainly gone for ever. Doubtless the colour magazines will soon be cajoling us into investing in alternative heating systems; the next few chapters are an attempt to pre-empt them.

The extensive sums of the last chapter boil down to this: a larger than average, well-insulated house needs only between 5 and 7 kW to cope with the most adverse weather conditions. At least, that was the theory. In practice, you need less. For example, throughout the winter there'll probably be an average of 2 or 3 people in the house at any one time. That provides about 300 watts. Then you'll be burning, say, three or four 100-watt light bulbs for 6 hours a day through the winter. That's another 100 watts. Then there's cooking – and nearly all the heat used here ends up by warming the house. For a family of 4 you can count another 150 watts. Finally, there's solar energy. Even the windows give some gain – you can reckon on an average of around 1·5 kW from 15 square metres of south-facing windows, or nearer 0·75kW if the windows are to the east or west (north-facing windows are a total loss to everyone except artists). That, of course, is the gain over the winter months on average. You might expect to get nearly all that in April and October, and none in December and January. You'd be wrong – for nature has kindly devised a compensating system. The sun is weaker in mid-winter because it gets lower in the sky which means it strikes vertical windows more nearly at right angles. And that means the solar input through a south-facing window is only a little less in mid-winter than it is in early spring or late autumn. But you get more than the average on a sunny day, and virtually none when it's really cloudy.

I reckon that with a solar wall or a really good conservatory (but see next chapter) you should be able to get another one-third at least of your winter space-heating from the sun. At this point you can throw out your gas or oil-fired central heating boiler – the smallest domestic units rate about 10 kW and the largest over 30 kW. Small wonder we are running out of energy.

But make no mistake, with it you are going to throw out a certain amount of convenience. Central heating systems had the virtues of cleanliness and more or less completely automatic control. All you really had to do was adjust the thermostat from time to time. Yet I have seen otherwise more or less sane couples argue quite heatedly about whose turn it is to get up from their chair, walk across the room and adjust the thermostat. In other words, anything is a drag if you want to see it that way. Personally I reckon the chance to live more cheaply, and with less risk of a heart attack, is well worth the loss of some automation.

Fireplaces and chimneys

If you live in an old house, you'll have plenty of chimneys and fireplaces. If you live in a new one, without any, I'd put it on the market straight away. And with the money you get either build something new, or buy something older (both of which will be cheaper) and use what money you have over to provide a sensible heating and insulation scheme. A house without chimneys is like a garden without vegetables.

But of course the Victorian grate was a monstrosity. It only ever warmed part of one room and you could reckon (though I don't suppose the Victorians bothered) that at least three-quarters of the heat went straight up the chimney to produce Victorian smog. Don't despair. There is much you can do with a good fireplace and chimney.

The first thing is to re-arrange the draught. When you burn fuel, the fire sucks in air, heats it up and the chimney acts as an exhaust pipe. In other words, the fire constantly tries to create a vacuum in the room. As nature doesn't like that, cold draughts are drawn in through cracks round the windows and doors – which is why you can toast your front half in front of an open fire but your back always feels cold. The answer is very easy – and it is not to stop up those draughts with 100 per cent efficiency. If you do, the fire won't draw. It is simply to run a supply of air from the outside directly to the foot of the grate in a tube or pipe of some sort. As it's carrying only cold air you can use plastic pipe – a $1\frac{1}{4}$-inch waste pipe is very cheap and does the job well. If the chimney is on an outside wall, simply pass the pipe through the brickwork to one side and vent the open end in front of the fire somewhere (if your grate is so arranged that the pipe has to end very near the fire, you'll have to join on a short length of copper pipe for the last foot or so). If the chimney is on an internal wall (which it should be) you must run the pipe wherever reason dictates. Once you've done it, you're half-way to having an effective open fire.

The other half consists in devising some means of recovering the waste heat in the flue. With ingenuity you can make your fireplace serve as a source of warm air for another room and deliver hot water to the hot cylinder. But at this point you've got to make a decision: if you're rich, that will probably be to play it straight and consult what in this country is called the Solid Fuel Advisory Service. They'll recommend a new fireplace, probably of the Smoke-eater variety. They may be expensive but they are certainly excellent. They're designed to burn up all the fuel much more efficiently than the old-style grate, and they come with a back boiler which will power both radiators and hot water system. They'll almost certainly give you more heat than you want, though. And they'll restrict you to only one or two special smokeless fuels.

If you don't fancy those restrictions too much, or if you're poor, you'll have to opt for the alternative. Here's what you can do. Aim at making your open fire heat at least one other room in the house. In France you can actually buy a heat exchanger to fit in a chimney which will vent a great amount of warm air out of a duct set in the chimney breast above the fire. You can of course equally well duct that air to another room, particularly an upstairs one. You can duct it to a downstairs one if you are prepared to install a small electric fan in the duct to push the air along a bit.

As far as I know, you can't buy anything like that in this country. But you may be able to pick up a heat exchanger second-hand which will fit in the chimney somewhere. The exchanger itself needs to be made from some metal which will withstand the high temperatures, and which has as large a surface area as possible so that it picks up the maximum heat. Basically, that means a long, winding pipe with plenty of metal fins stuck to it. One end should be connected to a cold air source (the great outside will do well enough, or a larder which needs ventilation, or at a pinch the room in which the fire is, providing the intake is at ground level and away from the fire). The other end you duct to wherever you want the heat. If it's a huge room, it won't do any harm to duct it there – but otherwise I'd recommend the master (or mistress) bedroom.

But there is a cheaper, and perhaps even more efficient, way of doing the same thing yourself. For this you need to make your own heat exchanger out of ½-inch (15-mm) copper pipe and use it to heat hot water radiators. For most flues you'll need a copper spiral of 6 to 9 inches diameter, and the easiest way is to ask a plumber to make it for you. But if you want some fun, and can stand the thought of possibly wrecking a length or two of copper pipe, you can do it yourself. First, fill the pipe with sand, and hammer each end completely closed. You then need something like a 6-inch diameter telegraph pole or drain pipe (metal, not plastic) round which to coil the copper. It'll bend easily enough if one person holds one end and another twists it slowly – very slowly – round the drain pipe. The sand, of course, prevents the pipe buckling as you bend it, but even so you have to watch out that it doesn't: the harder you've packed the sand in, the less chance there is of buckling. How many turns you need depends, of course, on how much room there is in the flue. The more there are, the better it'll work.

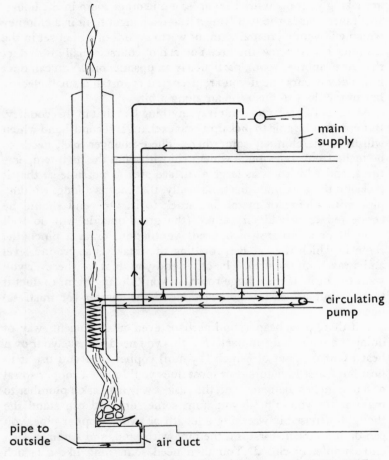

HEAT EXCHANGER AND AIR DUCT FOR OPEN FIRE

The plumbing circuit is easy enough. Connect the cold water tank to the bottom of the spiral, and connect its top to the radiator. Run the return from the radiator back into the supply pipe somewhere well below the tank (which must, of course, be above all radiators). Finally, you must – absolutely must, on pain of great explosion – take a T off the hot end before it joins the first radiator and run it up and down over the cold tank. This is called the vent or expansion pipe; you leave the vent open-ended above the tank so that if the water boils, the boiling water and steam will fizzle harmlessly away into the cold tank. If it does, put the fire out.

How many radiators such a device will power depends on so many things that you'll have to experiment to find the answer. Start with one, and go on adding extras until they lose their effectiveness. Remember, too, that you are going to get very high temperatures round your copper spiral and that if it is ever deprived of water, the copper will simply disintegrate. The only other thing that may go wrong is that the flow of water will not be sufficient if you depend on 'gravity flow' – the effect caused by hot water rising – and nothing else. If you don't have enough flow, it's much cheaper to put in a small circulating pump, which will consume hardly any power, than to use 1½-inch copper pipe and old-fashioned large bore radiators. Consult your plumbing supplier about the best pump to use. Incidentally, if you're worried by the thought of doing plumbing, better turn to chapter 9 now for reassurance.

With that installed you've got the foundations of some pretty good house heating – and you've got what the glossy colour brochures call a living fire. Colour brochures apart, I reckon that's an essential to any house. And if you've got a real fire which you can sit in front of without freezing your backside, and know that you're heating upstairs as well, then you've got the best of both worlds. Why settle for anything less?

Stoves

The only improvement you can make on an open fireplace is to turn it into a closed one. Which means installing a stove of some kind. I became converted to stoves in Wales where we used to heat a huge volume of air with two wood-burning stoves made in Norway, called Jøtuls. Made in cast iron and finished in dark green enamelling, they are spectacularly handsome and almost unbelievably efficient. If you are going to burn wood (see next section for a vigorous defence of that practice) Jøtul is your answer. It gives out enormous heat and yet burns wood very slowly – being designed to make it smoulder from one end only, just like a cigar burning up. One, or at most two, fillings an evening will give you

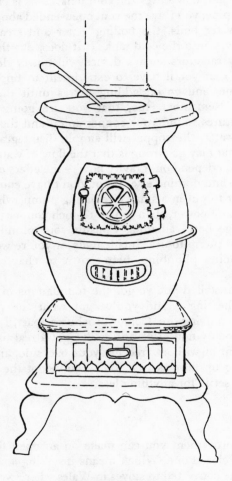

POT-BELLIED STOVE

all you want. There are a number of different models selling from $200 to $800. Before I met Jøtul I thought sitting in front of stoves would be about as exciting as clustering round a central heating boiler. Not at all; they have a life all their own. And they will keep in all night if you want them to. More information from Kristia Associates, Box 1118, Portland, Maine 04104.

It's said that the American Ashley stove is even better because it has a thermostatically controlled draught regulator. I've never seen one unfortunately. But there are at least three other alternatives. You can buy a modern solid-fuel type stove, some with glass doors, from the showrooms, which are excellent but won't burn wood. Or you can buy one of those old-fashioned pot-bellied stoves, fuelled from the top, which used to be used for heating workmen's huts and the like. They're still made and they are just as good as ever.

Last of all, you can make your own stove if you're really poor. Start with a heavy duty 55-gallon oil drum – which you used to be able to pick up for nothing but now cost around $5 each from rubbish dumps. Cut a hole in the back near the top for the flue, making metal tabs round the cut into which to fit self-tapping screws into the flue. Make a hinged door at the bottom and form a grate, either with $\frac{1}{4}$-inch mild steel rods or with 1-inch iron water piping leading to a radiator (as in the copper spiral). Finally fit fireclay round the sides and seal all joints with fire cement – something you get from a building supply store for all work to do with fires and stoves and which is much easier to work than you might think. I've never made a stove like this and the idea is borrowed from the *Survival Scrapbook on Energy*. It is also described in *Energy Primer*.

Cookers *

Though we've almost forgotten it now, it's not that long since the living/cooking/washing up division in a house was arranged quite differently. If you can find an old house, particularly in the country, which hasn't been touched for 50 years or so, you'll find most of life went on in two rooms. In the larger of the two, people lived round a cast-iron cooking range of some kind. The food was cooked and eaten there, and the room served as the main living area. (Posh houses also had a front parlour used on Sundays for entertaining the vicar.) And off the main room was a scullery,

* This section on cookers applies only to Great Britain and not to the US where, unfortunately, such cookers are not available.

usually much smaller, in which there was a stone sink with (for the wealthy) a cold water tap. The food was prepared in the scullery, and the dishes washed up there.

I'm sure we are soon going to return to something similar – except that the scullery will be integrated into the living/cooking room. It'll certainly have to be the largest room in the house because a small kitchen is no good to anyone who's seriously into baking bread and cooking real food as distinct from heating up convenience foods. Today, it's said that no one can afford to cook that way because it consumes too much fuel. But that's because we usually use cookers designed principally to heat up frozen veg. and tinned steak pies. A real cooker goes all the time, and it produces heat for the kitchen and the insulated house, as well as hot water for the bath.

When I was a boy my father was a boarding-house master at a minor public school. My mother often used to cook three meals a day for 60 people without apparently thinking anything of it. The house was huge, without either central heating or insulation, and must, I suppose, have been as cold as a morgue. Being only a boy I don't remember – but I do remember well enough the two Agas on which all the cooking was done. For a child that kitchen was definitely the place to be – good smells, a chance to lick the cake bowl, a lot of activity and a great deal of warmth. Most of us harbour secret fantasies about kitchens like that, and I don't see why even the mighty 20th century should make us suppress them. Why not bring back the proper kitchen?

If you do, the cooker can be the central and main heating element in your house. If you're buying something new, that means an Aga, a Rayburn or an Esse cooker. But first consider a second-hand job. Most models of cookers can be obtained, particularly in the country, for at most £40 if you are prepared to lug the thing away yourself. In Wales we bought an old cooker called a Sofono which had an open fire in the cooker and gave the kitchen real warmth, living flames and good cooking. Be warned: if you buy second-hand, you need at least 3 people and a strong van or Land-Rover to move it. And check very carefully whether or not the thing is meant to have a back boiler to heat hot water. If it does, it must be in perfect condition or you'll have to buy a new one. We ran into trouble with our Sofono because we needed to use the cooker during our first winter before the plumbing was installed. The cooker worked all right but the back boiler was reduced to a pile of copper smelting, and a new one turned out to cost £40.

Don't be intimidated by the thought of moving a cast-iron

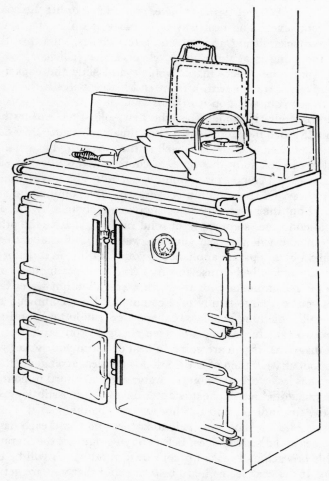

RAYBURN COOKER

cooker – even though some of them weigh over half a ton and most of us aren't used to dealing with weights like that. You need rollers and levers. A crowbar will do quite well for the latter, particularly if you extend its length with a piece of pipe. The rollers should either be iron pipe, steel rod or short lengths of broom handle. Lever the cooker up, slide the rollers under and then push away, with someone whipping round from back to front changing the rollers. When you get to the vehicle, you'll have to lift the cooker up to door level. The best way is to block it up in stages with concrete blocks, lifting first one end a few inches, then the other. When the thing is at the right level, back the vehicle up to the cooker, place the rollers in the vehicle and slide the cooker in. Alternatively a tractor with a front end loader will lift the whole thing up for you, and pop it in your van.

Unfortunately, in some ways, the new solid-fuel cookers have been made much more efficient. Unfortunately, because they don't warm the kitchen and house as well as they used to. The gas-fired and oil-fired cookers of this type, of course, are even worse – but for reasons we'll come to in a minute you won't be buying one of those anyway. Of the common cookers, the Aga is much the most expensive but the best in my view. It gives out about 1 kW of room heat and consumes some 22 lb of solid fuel a day. Like the others in the range, it will also heat your hot water but, officially at least, you must buy a separate appliance if you want to run radiators as well. I say officially because the Aga (the smallest model, to be precise) is recommended for use with a 40-gallon hot water tank. Unless you're a large family or a commune, I'd recommend that you install something smaller, perhaps a 20-gallon tank, and take one or two radiators off as well (see chapter 9 on plumbing for circuit diagram). If you are going to heat or warm your water with a solar roof as well, then of course that is an ideal arrangement, for the Aga has less work to do on the water and can afford to do more for the radiators. See the next chapter for this rather subtle way of using the sun indirectly to run hot water radiators.

All the solid-fuel cookers made today are good, and each has its advantages and disadvantages. Before buying one, get the literature available on each and make up your own mind which will be best for you. If the cost seems high, bear in mind that you are getting something which should last at least two generations, if not more. And also that you are buying what will be for quite long periods of time the only heating you need in your house. Of course, one of these cookers will not suffice in mid-winter when the snow is thick on the ground. But for a lot of the winter the temperature will be mild, and if your kitchen is warm, then you should find additional heating unnecessary. In October and November, and certainly from March on, your cooker will do nearly all the work for you.

Fuel

One of the things which will dictate which cooker to buy is what fuel you are going to use. So far, I've given the impression that solid fuel of some sort is the best answer. The time has come to say why.

The most ridiculous of all fuels is electricity. No one should be allowed to heat their house electrically (with one exception I'll come to in a minute). The first reason is expense. Electricity is not only the most expensive fuel, it is far and away the most expensive – more than double the cost of the other choices. In most countries, you can now make an arrangement with the electricity people to use power only at certain times in the night, for which inconvenience you are usually charged only half price. Even so, your power is still expensive.

The second reason is efficiency. Electricity showrooms will be quick to point out that it is the only fuel you can use in your home with almost no waste. Electrical appliances are pretty near 100 per cent efficient. True enough. But what they won't talk about are their own inefficiencies. The best generating stations are only 40 per cent efficient, which means that for every 2 kWh of energy you use, 3 kWh have already been wasted as surplus heat at the generating station. Further, transmission losses between you and the generating station are also huge – sometimes as much as 50 per cent. In the country, particularly, the overall result is that electricity supply is little more than 20 per cent efficient – every unit you use is matched by 4 wasted ones.

Thirdly, the construction of a generating station is a very energy-intensive business. Much of the energy a power station produces simply goes to pay back all the energy used to manufacture the materials needed to build it. Only after five years or so of its life does a power station actually produce an energy gain.

And, fourthly, more and more power stations are going nuclear (and are even less efficient, by the way). Personally, I believe we would be better off without nuclear technology, and certainly without the promised breeder reactors soon to come into being. My reservation is not concerned so much with safety, disposal of radioactive wastes, and atmospheric pollution, as with weapons. The new breeder reactors will actually manufacture plutonium, the stuff of which nuclear weapons are made. The less of it there is about the happier I shall be.

Not that I am against electricity as such. It is marvellous stuff for lighting, running small pumps, powering refrigerators and deep freezes, and turning the electric drill. But these uses consume almost no power; electricity for heating is quite another matter.

The one exception I would make is the occasional use of small fan heaters in little-used rooms during cold weather. There are rooms in every house which are either used only occasionally or for a very short time every day. Probably the best way to heat those rooms to a reasonable temperature is to switch on a fan heater for a few minutes. Nothing longer is required, and in a well-insulated house the heat will linger around for an hour or two. In the same way, it will cost you only £3 or £4 to install an electric immersion heater in the hot water cylinder. If you use solar-heated water, that immersion heater will actually save you energy, in that it will top up the temperature of the water on cloudy days which would otherwise be too cold to be of any use and would be wasted. In such matters the art of compromise is all important.

Gas, either bottled or piped, is the next fuel. Somewhat cheaper and much more efficiently produced. But, North Sea gas bubbles apart, the supplies look pretty limited and are being mined at a fearful rate. Piped gas, of course, is very convenient but dependence on it has on the whole been a crippling affliction. It has dictated that human beings live mainly in places where it is economical to lay the pipes – which means towns and cities. Now that there are so many ways in which we could live elsewhere, more evenly distributed over the Earth's surface, it seems a pity to remain tied to a system which depends on underground pipes. But there is quite a lot to be said for bottled gas, which is still relatively cheap and will now do anything that piped gas can.

But solid fuel is the most flexible and still the cheapest of all. What's more, the world's coal reserves are going to last a great deal longer than our supplies of oil or gas. I would never recommend anyone to use oil for heating simply because its supply is so questionable. You don't know when that supply is going to dry up, either temporarily or permanently. You do know that it is going to go on getting more and more expensive the nearer we get to the bottom of the barrel. And if I have to pay anyone for supplying me with fuel, then I would rather use that money to give the miners a decent wage than to line the pockets of the oil sheiks who are already quite rich enough.

One of the keys to solid-fuel burning is to have an appliance that will burn anything. Unfortunately, the manufacturers are going the other way, and producing appliances which will work with one fuel and one fuel only. Try to avoid these specialist devices. Something which will take timber, coal, coke or anthracite, plus household scraps which cannot be composted, is a much better bet. You'll always be able to fuel something like that, while a one-fuel appliance may well find you taken short in times of crisis.

In this respect, the Aga is a bad buy, for you are meant to burn only Phurnacite in it. I do know people who burn timber as well, but they are certainly acting against the advice of the manufacturers. The Rayburn is better, in that you are allowed the 'occasional' use of timber with it. I also know people who have run Rayburns for years on nothing but timber, and they and their cooker have survived well enough. Pretty soon someone is going to tumble to this fact and produce a good cooker or stove that will burn anything. When they do, buy it.

And so to timber. City people are passionately united in their insistence that it is a sin to burn wood, particularly in a country where woodland is in such short supply. Rubbish. People who live in the country know very well that timber is a free fuel and not only can, but must, be burnt. Every year millions of trees die natural deaths. Hundreds of millions of branches are blown off. More than 99 per cent of that wood is totally useless for anything except fuel.

Furthermore, timber – unlike coal, gas or oil – is a renewable fuel. You can grow it in a flash compared to the time needed to make the other fuels. If you have land, of course, and are burning timber off it, you should plant at least two trees for every one you burn. In a properly managed country, we would be planting huge areas of land to hazel coppice, in which could graze all manner of domestic animals, feeding partially off leaves, debris and nuts. Some of the nuts would be gathered commercially to produce a marvellous protein-rich supplement. And the coppice would be cropped every ten years to provide nearly 10 tons of excellent timber fuel to the acre.

Of the other woods, ash is about the best fuel for it will burn as well green as seasoned. Apple smells nice and oak, beech, elm and birch are all good. Elder, holly and hawthorn should never be burnt and there are ancient country traditions and superstitions which suggest it is wise not to bring them in the house. Use soft-woods only as kindling for they produce no lasting heat. Finally, preparing timber as fuel with the axe and bow saw is as good a way of keeping warm as burning the stuff.

But, once again, those who compromise best will win in the end. There is no better fire than mixed coal and logs, and both your fuels will last much longer if used that way. If you can add an occasional paper log as well, so much the better. You make paper logs by wrapping a thick wad of unwanted papers round a broom handle, and twisting a couple of pieces of wire round to hold it together. Slide the log off the broom handle and chuck it on the fire. It will burn well and long.

A word of warning to sawdust enthusiasts. Sawdust is available cheaply and in large quantities from timber mills. It can burn well either loose or compressed into sawdust bricks, and quite a few people are convinced that this is going to solve their fuel problem for them. It is more likely, in fact, to kill them, for unless the burning appliance is exactly regulated, you can get a gas build-up in a sawdust fire which will produce a very nasty explosion indeed.

The final advantage of solid-fuel fires is that they are a way of composting non-compostible materials. Inorganic household rubbish, together with organic materials which are difficult to compost like newspaper, can be burnt along with everything else. The ash can then be used on the garden where it will help correct an acid soil. Chimney soot also has a few spectacular garden uses. Both must be stored perfectly dry before being dug into the garden, or the most useful chemicals will be leached away and lost down the drain. Wood ash can also be used to make soap (see chapter 15).

Chapter 7

❧

Solar energy

It is mid-November, the rain is pouring down outside my study window and the sky is half-way between dark grey and dirty black. Where I live, at a latitude of 52° N, the sun next month will not climb more than 12° above the horizon, even at noon. Perhaps only the British would be stupid enough to try to turn that bleak and fairly typical scene into anything to do with solar heating.

Most people who write about solar energy bubble with enthusiasm over Israeli water heaters, solar-heated houses in the Pyrenees and daring solar energy experiments in the deserts of New Mexico. I promise not to. I know well enough that such devices have a very limited use in more northerly climes, particularly in the British Isles where sunshine in winter is as heavily rationed as jam in the last war.

My only practical experience with solar heating is in Wales, well-known as the wettest part of an extremely wet country. Strangely enough, that experience stands me in good stead to talk about solar energy elsewhere. After all, if you can do it in Wales, you can do it almost anywhere short of the Arctic circle. And the trouble with most solar energy research is that its proponents have been so keen to prove their point that they rush off to the sunniest of places where their experiments can hardly fail (they often do, though). In this chapter I'm going to concentrate almost exclusively on forms of solar heating designed for very un-sunny places. Typically, in Britain, we get 1,300–1,400 hours of sunshine every year. Most other places in Europe are both sunnier and further south, which means of course that the sun is stronger. In most places in the United States, there is a great deal more sun than this, and the proportion available in the winter is larger as well. So I shall indulge in what strategists would call 'worst case analysis'. The chances are that you'll be able to do better than I suggest.

There is one building in England which is entirely heated by the sun, winter and summer. This is the solar-heated school at Wallasey in Cheshire where the sun, body warmth and electric lighting are sufficient to keep the building at a reasonable temperature throughout the year. The back-up heating system originally installed has been thrown out for it was found never to be required. The secret is nothing more than large banks of double-glazed windows on the south side, minimum ventilation, and massive walls with large heat-storing capacity which are insulated on the *outside*. As a result, it takes a week for changes in external climate to make much impact on what is happening inside the building. The one drawback of the place is that the large numbers of bodies present during school hours provide quite a large proportion of the heat which, because of low ventilation and good insulation, cannot escape. But those bodies tend to make for a pretty ripe atmosphere, and the low ventilation seals in the fug. Unfortunately, the principle would not work so well in a small house where there would be fewer bodies, less smell, but insufficient heat.

At Eithin, I helped design, build and operate a solar roof for hot water heating. As this is something which will work well in most places in the world, I shall deal with it first. And most of the rest of this chapter will be given over to describing two devices – the solar wall and the solar conservatory – which will also work in miserable climates. They're also cheap and extremely simple – unlike most of the solar-heating systems described in the technical literature. Finally, I'll say something – but not much – about the more grandiose solar-heating systems which are on the drawing board, even though they owe more to the technocracy that gave us the machine age than they do to the pressing need to find simple economic and ecological alternatives.

The solar roof

At Eithin we covered the whole south-west pitch of our roof with a solar collector which was used to heat the water in the hot water cylinder. One fine day in June 1973, when all the fittings and plumbing were complete, Philip Brachi and I went up to the attic, switched on the pump and waited nervously. Till then we had only read about solar roofs, had convinced ourselves they must work but secretly, I suspect, neither of us really believed it. Kneeling on the attic floor we peered anxiously up the return pipe to see if the first trickle of solar-heated water had yet run down the roof to return to the pump. The first sign of success was an unexpected puff of steam. And then a tiny trickle, building up to a steady flow of water falling back into the top-up tank. It looked hot and I confess we yelped with joy when we dipped our hands in. It was too hot for comfort, and later measurements showed that on a hot day we got up to 52°C (125°F) which was too hot to shower under without adding cold. Up to October that roof provided all the hot water a community of ten people could use – and on good days we had to waste most of it because we couldn't use it fast enough. Altogether there were 60 square metres of solar roof, and at their best, on a clear day in July around noon, they were giving us more than 21 kW of heat. As the standard electric immersion heater provides only 3 kW it's obvious we were getting a lot of free energy.

If you want to build a solar roof of that type, the plans are available from CTT, 143 Maple Road, Surbiton, Surrey. But I hope also to include enough information here for you to build either that or something similar – and there is no earthly reason why you shouldn't incorporate variations of your own. In fact, I'll suggest a few in a minute.

First, forget all the complicated calculations of the solar energy enthusiasts and concentrate on one thing: area. You need your roof just as big as you can possibly get it, and other factors like its angle to the sun, its efficiency and so on, are of very minor importance beside that. As much is fairly obvious. Sophisticated design will give you improvements of a few per cent in efficiency. Doubling the area of your roof will double the amount of heat you can collect. This means that it's best you don't simply strap onto your roof a few ready-made solar panels. Take the roof off and put on a new one which will double both as a solar collector and a conventional roof. You may or may not need planning permission, but the precedent has certainly been established by now. If you don't for any reason get planning permission, create one hell of a stink because solar roofs are here to stay and planning authorities have got to be taught sense. Just go on and on till you do get planning permission, and exploit the media unmercifully in your crusade to get it – which means calling in the local newspapers and radio people, both of whom will take an interest in a fight as good as that for a cause as good as that.

So if you are building a new house, or if you live in an old one where the more southerly roof will obviously have to be renewed in the foreseeable future, you start again. If your existing roof is in good repair the choice is more difficult. Do some sums to see whether it will be more expensive to replace the roof or to make up strap-on panels to cover nearly the whole area. You'll find that a new roof will be cheaper. At Eithin ours cost just over £8 a square metre, including all the plumbing but excluding labour.

When the old roof is removed, your next job is to cover it with corrugated aluminium, preferably already anodized black or some dark colour. You can buy untreated aluminium and paint it black, but the hot water trickling down the corrugations will strip the paint off in time. The aluminium you buy either from a builder's merchant or from a manufacturer (ours was 0.5 mm thick with each sheet covering 90 cm; it comes cut to the length of your roof). To support the aluminium you nail 2 × 2 runners across the rafters at intervals of 4 or 5 feet, or board it out with chipboard (more expensive). The aluminium is fixed to these with aluminium nails or screws through the ridge of the aluminium and into the runners or chipboard. You must use aluminium fixings, otherwise there'll be electrolytic action and an awful mess. Buy plastic washers and pop-seal caps to go with each nail. Don't forget to leave every ninth corrugation free of nails so that you can fit the glazing bar onto it. Preferably, drill the aluminium for the nail holes to avoid squashing it by hammering the nail through.

From this point on you'll have to work on the outside of the roof and you'll need a ridge ladder. Don't buy one – make it as shown on page 109. It will take you one hour and cost much less, and will be perfectly safe, providing you've got a decent ridge to hook it over.

Next comes the glazing, and you'll have to decide whether to single-glaze or double-glaze. The professionals reckon on double-glazing, but at Eithin we used one layer and it worked perfectly well. The answer will depend on whether you are using the roof mainly for the summer or the winter. If it's for the summer, then single-glazing is quite adequate. If you want it for the winter as well, then double-glazing will give you a better result, but of course the cost will be more than double because double-glazing bars are

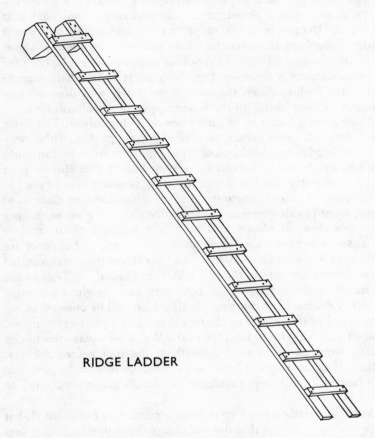

RIDGE LADDER

much more expensive. I reckon the best scheme is to optimize your solar roof for summer heating. You know that it'll work well in the summer, but if you optimize for the winter you'll only ever get mediocre results if you have only a mediocre winter sun. Further, if you plumb the thing in in such a way that your cooker or stove heats the water mainly in the winter, you'll save all round; in the summer, when you don't use the cooker, the sun will take over the job of heating the water. In the winter, the solar roof will provide some warmed water for the stove which will therefore have to do less work. See below for plumbing details. And while on this subject, it helps to know the optimum angles. At a latitude of 52°, you'll get the best performance from the roof in June/July if it's at an angle of about 30° to the horizontal; you'll get best results in December if it's at 78° to the horizontal; and you'll optimize performance over the whole year with an angle of about 67° to the horizontal. Again I'd opt for the summer angle, both for the reasons already mentioned and because at such a shallow angle the water trickles down the roof more slowly and does a more efficient job in picking up the heat trapped in the aluminium.

Your glazing bars can be either wood or aluminium. The latter are better but more expensive – so suit your pocket. Either way they are fixed along the ridges of the aluminium and held down into the runners below with bolts or screws. Finally you clip on your glazing, or putty it down if you are using timber glazing bars.

Glazing, of course, suggests glass which is cheaper than most transparent plastic sheeting. That is, one sheet of glass is cheaper than one sheet of plastic. But at Eithin we used plastic mainly because we were working some 30 to 40 feet up, and chances are we'd have broken a lot of glass by the time it had been manhandled up and fixed in position. Glass is very heavy and if you're not used to handling large areas while balancing at a height on a ridge ladder, I'd advise substituting plastic which will be cheaper in the long run. But it will only be cheaper if you buy a plastic guaranteed against yellowing for at least ten years. We chose a glass-reinforced plastic and had it cut to the length of the roof before delivery. Glass, of course, would have to be used in shorter lengths and overlapped, producing problems of dirt, algal growth and so on.

With the glazing fixed your basic structure is complete. What happens, of course, is that the sun passes through the glazing, hits the blackened aluminium which it heats to a wickedly high temperature (far too hot to grasp with the naked hand). The aluminium then begins to radiate off its heat in the form of infra-red radiation, to which the glazing is more or less opaque. Result: the heat gets trapped between the glazing and the aluminium and can't radiate out backwards because you have insulated the aluminium with at least 4 inches of styrofoam or fibreglass. At Eithin we used only 3 inches and it wasn't enough, judging by the temperature of the attic on a hot day. All this trapped heat is then removed by trickling water down the aluminium, which brings us to the plumbing.

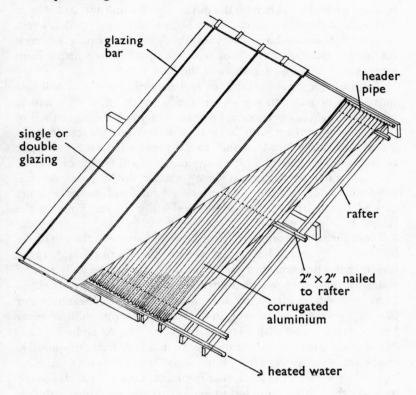

SOLAR ROOF

The drawing on page 172 shows you all you need to know – but again if you're worried about plumbing, there is no cause to be and best turn to that chapter now. To go through the circuit, the water comes out of a $\frac{3}{4}$-inch copper pipe – the header pipe – fixed to the ridge above the aluminium. You need to drill a $\frac{3}{16}$-inch diameter hole in the pipe above every corrugation and to seal the ends of the pipe with a threaded stop plug in a compression fitting. You must be able to remove these ends, because if the pipe or the holes get bunged up with dirt you'll need to be able to haul a bottle brush through with wire to clean it out. The water then runs down the aluminium valleys and is collected in the bottom in a plastic gutter. If you possibly can, make sure this gutter is outside the house – initially we had trouble with the gutter overflowing and had it been inside the house there would have been a very soggy mess. From the gutter the now hot water flows back into the house where it discharges into the storage tank which is supplied by a fitting from either the public water system or the cold water tank.

You need this storage tank for two reasons. First, you will lose quite a lot of water through evaporation on the roof – we had to make up a gallon or two on a hot day, and you'll soon get tired of filling the system up with buckets of water. A ballcock does the job automatically. And second, at the point where the hot water pours back into this tank, it's easy to install a filter of some kind. We used a fine-mesh kitchen sieve – almost anything will do. But filter the water you must, otherwise all kinds of debris will get carried round through the pump and bung up the holes in the header pipe.

From the storage tank the water flows out and into the top of the indirect coil in your hot water system. This is important, for it means that when you turn on a hot tap, you never actually run off water that has been warmed on the roof, but only water that has been warmed in a tank by the effect of the solar-heated water passing through a copper coil in it. This indirect method of water heating is now used with all types of boiler – gas, oil and solid fuel. It's a good idea because it means that, apart from evaporative losses, the water going through the solar circuit is always the same water. If your water is hard, that means that once it has deposited its scale, there is no more left to deposit. If you used new water all the time, scale would quickly build up to the point where the system bunged itself up.

Having passed through the hot water heater, the solar water flows out and into your pump. Actually, you don't need a pump but what is called a circulator – a device used in central heating circuits to push the water round the system. We used a SMC Commander S circulator which will lift 2·4 gallons a minute through a 14-foot head. Your roof may well be smaller, so a smaller version of that circulator will be sufficient. But do check the head carefully – the vertical distance between the lowest part of the solar circuit and the header pipe. Whatever circulator you buy must be capable of lifting the water (or rather pushing it) by that amount. You need a water flow of at least 2 gallons a minute for a 650 square foot solar roof – proportionally less for smaller roofs.

From the pump the solar water, now cooled by passing through the coil or heat exchanger in the hot water heater, flows back up to the header pipe. It's a good idea to split the return into two near the ridge, and provide it with T connections to the header at two points, a quarter of the way along the header from either end. This ensures a more even pressure throughout the header pipe, and the water will flow down the roof evenly. If you just run the return into the centre of the header pipe, water will gush from the holes near the centre, trickle from ones further away, and probably never reach the holes near the end of the pipe at all.

The water then runs down the roof, gets heated again, collected in the gutter and runs back to the storage tank. The connection between the gutter and storage tank can be a problem. We relied on gravity and were able to place the storage tank a few inches below the level of the collecting gutter. That means you have to turn the water through nearly 90° as it leaves the gutter, and down-pipe connections to do that are not available. We used a 45° connector and then sealed into that a flexible 1-inch plastic pipe with plastic padding (you must roughen the surface of the pipe first or the plastic will not grip). The gutter connectors must also be sealed with something or they will leak. The 1-inch pipe we used was only just big enough to carry the water away as fast as it dripped down into the gutter (hence our early problems with overflowing). Remember you'll have only a few inches head between the gutter and tank, so any obstruction will make the gutter overflow. Something bigger than 1-inch diameter would be better.

The drawing shows the complete system as it would be plumbed in if an Aga or something similar were also available. The system looks complicated and is in fact more so than the one we used at Eithin. It is based on a system Robert and Brenda Vale designed for their house in Cambridgeshire. But to give encouragement, two of us bought all the fittings and plumbed the whole system up in three days flat. The secret of it lies in using two indirect hot water heaters. In the first the solar water warms up water in the heater which is supplied from the supply main or a cold tank. The hot water output (or warm water, if it's cloudy) from the first heater then runs to the input of the second heater, the output from that runs to the hot taps, but the indirect coil in the second heater is heated by the cooker. Thus the cooker is only heating up already solar-warmed water and this saves fuel, or provides extra energy for the cooker to power a couple of radiators. Finally, fit an electric immersion heater into the top of the second heater for use when you must have hot water, when the cooker is not running and the sky is heavily overcast.

That is a three-way water heating system, which current heating engineers would deem grossly extravagant on capital. But it is the way to use solar energy in cloudy northern latitudes. You must design the system so that when the sun shines you can use every calorie of extra heat, but when it doesn't you have other things to fall back on. Note, too, that if you do run in a couple of radiators you are doing something very subtle. You are making use of the low-grade heat from the sun to help the cooker optimize its output of high-grade heat and run the extra radiators. It's a way of doing something which experts say is impossible.

But one word of warning. Although there are solar systems running in Britain, and running well, which are hooked up to cookers such as an Aga or Rayburn, this is not an ideal arrangement. The reason is that the Aga is thermostatically controlled, but the thermostat is governed by the temperature of the cooker, not the hot water it is heating. Which means that, even if you do provide solar-heated water to the boiler, the Aga will go on pumping heat out to the hot water heater at the same rate. What you really need is a device which has a thermostat in the boiler, so that the warmer the water that flows into the heater, the less fuel will the device consume.

You can't buy a cooker controlled in that way. But you can buy a solid-fuel stove with a glass door. Either a Rayburn Rhapsody 301 (smaller models do not have a water-way thermostat) or a Parkray 88Q or 99Q. I am currently installing a solar roof with such a Parkray stove, and the more the sun shines, the more often will the stove's damper close down to slow the rate of burning. This should be the most efficient way of using solar energy yet devised.

Incidentally, whatever you do, you must not put the immersion heater in the solar water heater. If you do, then you can only run the solar system or the immersion heater when the other is switched off – otherwise your immersion heater will be heating the solar water, and that heat will be lost from the solar roof. A very expensive way, in other words, of heating the sky!

The final problem will come when the system is working and the sun starts to shine. Off you go to switch on the pump. The water heats up. Clouds come along and you begin to wonder whether the hot water is now warmer than the water coming off the solar roof.

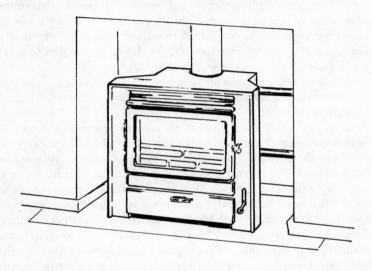

PARKRAY STOVE

If it is, once again you are working a system designed to heat the sky. In any case, arguments about automation apart, you'll soon get tired of rushing round the house switching the pump on and off, even if you did know exactly when it should be done. The answer is a black box of magic electronics which will compare the temperature of the solar roof with the temperature of the hot water, and switch on when the roof is hotter than the water and switch off when the water is hotter than the roof. A black box like this will consume a really tiny amount of electricity and save you kilowatts in heating the water. The same, incidentally, applies to the circulator which won't take more than 180 watts at the most – which means it's worth running even if the solar roof is warming the hot water by only two or three degrees. Our black box was made for us by John Wood, 899 Kingsway, Manchester 20. The components cost £5–£10, and the details are included in the information available from CTT which I mentioned earlier.

Finally, a few tips. If you use metal glazing bars, put some insulation between them and the aluminium roof or they will act like radiator fins and cool the roof down. We used thin strips of DPC which seemed to work well enough; roofing felt should do it too. If you are building a new roof, you can dispense with runners across the rafters or trusses if you space the latter at exactly half the dimension of the width of the aluminium. Simply nail the aluminium down into alternate rafters. Use foam rubber to seal off open ends of the system at the ridge and gutter – just stuff the foam between the glazing and aluminium wherever it'll go in (only, of course, above or below the area of roof which actually carries running solar water).

As to use, you'll soon work it out. On a hot day everyone gets a bath or shower or both – and if your work schedule allows you to take it in the afternoon, so much the better. Early morning bathers have to be discouraged because the water is usually hotter in the evening. And during those cloudy spells, don't just give up and switch the immersion heater on. You don't need a bath every day, and free hot water is worth waiting for. In a bad British summer at Eithin we found that every time it got cloudy for a longish period, we just got to the point where we said tomorrow we have to take a bath when the sun came out again. You need only two hours of good sunshine to heat the water, and even between April and October it's surprising how short are the periods between two-hour spells of good sunshine. Of course, for dishwashing in cloudy weather you boil a kettle, which is much cheaper than heating up 40 gallons with the immersion heater.

There are plenty of variations you can work on the Eithin roof. The first would be to replace the first, solar hot water cylinder by a much bigger one. We used a 39-gallon size, but if you could install, say, a 250-gallon tank and insulate it with at least 6 inches of fibreglass, you should have enough hot water to last you through cloudy spells. That way you'll use much more of the free solar heat and your hot water will always be at least warm. With a small tank you waste most of the free heat during hot weather because you can't store it, or use it fast enough.

A very useful addition to a solar roof is a small electric water heater mounted near the kitchen hot tap – the kind that has a rubber hose which you place over the tap to fill it; the hot water then comes out of a spout in the heater and discharges into the sink.

With that you can use solar-heated water for dishwashing even in cloudy weather. You fill the thing from the 'hot' tap and as the water is already warm, you use less electricity to produce the really hot water you need for dishwashing. No need for that in the bathroom, though; in the summer you can wash and bathe in warmish water quite happily.

The Eithin roof is known technically as an open system. That is, the water flows down the roof in the open and not in pipes. A closed system will work better. For instance, you could use old radiators as the solar panels, painted black, of course, with glazing above and insulation below. Or you could mount copper pipes on a black metal surface and glaze and insulate that. With such a closed system you won't get condensation forming on the underside of the glazing, as we do at Eithin (not that it seems to matter much). A closed system, however, must be more expensive than an open one, unless you have free access to pipe or radiators (in which case use them). And our experience suggests that the extra cost is not worthwhile. Measurements showed that at its hottest, our solar roof was something like 40 per cent efficient – that is, it converted 40 per cent of the incoming solar radiation into useful heat for the hot water. None of the sophisticated solar-heating systems described in the technical literature do much better than that, and some do worse. So why bother with the sophistications?

There is one reason. If your house is so designed that you can use a section of lower level roof for the solar roof, then you can mount your hot water cylinder above the top of the solar roof. If you do that, and if you use a closed system, then you can do without the circulator, because the effect of the hot water rising will move the water round the closed circuit for you (as in gas- or oil-fired boiler systems). If you don't have electricity, or don't want to use it, that is your answer – but you'll have to turn a stopcock on and off manually when you want the roof to work. Remember, too, that a solar roof does not have to be a roof – you can make a solar heater in the garden and plumb it into the house. Personally I'd rather grow vegetables in the garden.

The solar wall

If you want to heat your house as well as your hot water with solar energy you need another system. Keep the solar roof for the hot water, and then add either a solar wall or a solar conservatory (see next section).

The solar wall was developed in France by a French scientist, Felix Trombe, and a French architect, Jacques Michel. When I was living in France I visited them both on a number of occasions, and came away convinced that theirs is the most effective method of solar space-heating yet devised. It is simplicity itself.

The basic requirement is a large and massively-built south wall. It needs to be made of those worst insulators, stone or concrete,

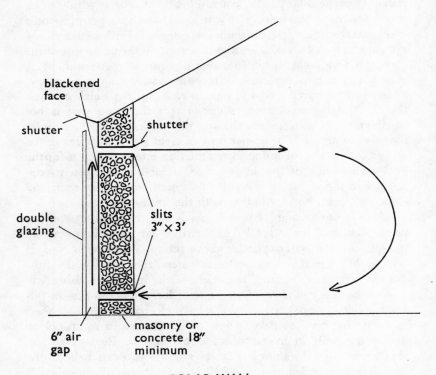

SOLAR WALL

because they have the largest thermal capacity – that is, if heated by the sun during the day, they will store an enormous amount of heat and release it slowly into the house during the night. The outside of this wall is painted black and a system of double or even triple glazing is mounted outside the wall and about 6 inches away from it. The gaps between the glazing and the wall must be sealed off at the sides, and along the top is mounted a shutter which can be opened and closed.

A series of slits is made right through the solar wall, joining the rooms inside to the space between the glass and the wall. You need slits about 3 feet long and 3 inches deep, one near the top and one near the bottom of the wall, at intervals of every 6 feet or so. Mount simple wooden shutters, with draught excluder round the edges, so that the shutter can be lowered to seal off the slit when you don't need it. And that is all there is to it.

So what happens? The sun goes through the glass and is turned into heat by the black wall. As in a greenhouse, it cannot escape and so it begins to heat up the wall. The air space between the glass and wall then gets very hot – temperatures of over 80°C have been recorded in houses built this way. This hot air rises and, because it cannot escape outwards, enters the house through the upper slits. Inside, this hot air warms the room up, and cold air near the floor is driven out through the bottom slit into the space between glass and wall. There it is again heated, and the cycle repeated.

At sunset, of course, this process stops. But if there's been a decent amount of sun during the day, the massive concrete wall will itself have stored up a large amount of heat. During the colder night it then slowly releases this into the room by radiation. The sun keeps you warm night and day, and the wall acts as a heat store which experience shows lasts at least 24 hours. Solar night storage.

With such a system you might expect to get baked during the summer and enjoy little extra comfort during the winter. Not a bit of it. Because your solar wall is vertical, it actually collects more heat in the winter (when you need it) than it does in the summer (when you don't). This is because in the winter the sun is lower in the sky and strikes the glass more nearly at right angles. Further, it rises in the south-east and sets in the south-west, so that in the winter it strikes the glass for a greater proportion of its day-time life than in the summer. In the Pyrenees, for example, the solar energy striking a vertical surface in the winter amounts to some 7 kWh per square metre of surface per day. In the summer, it is only 1·7 kWh per square metre per day. A similar effect prevails in more northerly climes, except that both figures are somewhat lower.

In the summer it is easy to avoid any heating effect from the solar wall. You close off the top slits and open the outside shutter so that air can escape from the space between glass and wall into the great outside. What's more, if you want some summer cooling, you leave open the bottom slits and a north window or door. What then happens is that the air in the space gets heated, rises and escapes out through the top shutter. It must be replaced by something, so air is sucked out of the adjacent room through the bottom slit and into the air space. And that air in turn is replaced by cold air drawn in from the open north window or door. Solar air conditioning.

The beauty of this scheme is that there are no mechanical toys – just a few wooden flaps which you operate at most once a day – no more difficult than adjusting the thermostat. As far as I know, no solar walls of this kind have been built outside France – but bungalows in north-eastern France have been heated in this way, and the information available on them gives a good idea of what could be expected elsewhere.

In the Meuse, where these houses were built, there are some 1,700 to 1,800 hours of sunshine a year – compared to about 1,300 to 1,400 hours more typically in Britain. The houses were 106 square metres in floor area and had a volume of 275 cubic metres. The area of glazed solar wall was 45 square metres and the back-up heating system was electrical. During a typical winter, the house was kept at 68°F inside, and the total heat loss was 32,000 kWh. Of this 20,000 kWh were provided by the solar wall, and only 12,000 kWh by the electrical heating system. In other words, two-thirds of the heat came from the sun.

In foggy Britain you could not expect to do quite as well. But I see no reason why you shouldn't get more than one-third of your heat from the sun. Put it another way. The French houses collect 20,000 kWh with 45 square metres of solar wall each winter; that is, 450 kWh for 1 square metre of solar wall averaged over the winter, or 2·1 kWh for 1 square metre per average winter day. In Britain you should be able to get say two-thirds of that, or 300 kWh for 1 square metre of solar wall over the winter. Measured solar inputs on a vertical surface in Britain amount to about 700 kWh for 1 square metre per winter, so that would mean the solar wall was converting about 43 per cent of the solar radiation into useful heat – which seems reasonable enough.

If the south wall of the house we designed in chapter 4 were a solar wall, you would have, excluding windows, 45 square metres of solar wall which would then give you 13,000 kWh over the winter – about half of the total. If you reckon on a half, and count on a third, you won't go far wrong. In sunnier places such as the United States, you should do considerably better.

Now for the variations. If you are building a solar wall from scratch, you'll probably do it in concrete and there's no reason at all why you shouldn't thread through the upper half of the wall some loops of $\frac{1}{2}$-inch copper pipe. You could use them just as a solar roof and plumb them into the hot water system. Or you could run the pipes to hot water radiators on the north side of the house. Whether the water would heat to a temperature high enough to be of use in radiator heating depends mainly on how much sun you get. Try it and see. If the temperature is not hot enough, nothing is lost for you can re-plumb the pipes into the hot water system, and give your other water-heating systems less work to do.

You don't, in fact, have to build the wall in concrete. In New Mexico (which I mention with hesitation, because I promised I wouldn't), Steve Baer has built a solar wall using 55-gallon oil drums stacked one above the other and filled with water. Water, of course, has a higher heat-carrying capacity than anything, so his is a good idea. At night Baer pulls up a large insulated shutter which seals the barrels off from the outside world; it is lined with aluminium so the heat they give off is reflected back into the house. It's a brilliant idea, but don't ask me for guidance with planning permission; what most local authorities would say of a house wall being made from disused oil drums I dare not think.

If you do use concrete, or stone, how thick should the wall be? There's no real answer to that one – the thicker the better, obviously. I'd say at least 18 inches thick, better 2 feet. The more concrete there is, the more heat you'll store, but the more expensive it'll be.

Finally, we did plan a solar wall at Eithin but eventually abandoned it. The reason was that our house was to be basically timber frame and three storeys high. It turns out that you cannot build a three-storey solid concrete wall which is free-standing – in the sense that a timber frame structure could not be relied on to give any support from the two gable ends. You could probably manage two storeys all right, and certainly one storey would be perfectly sound. But there is a case for using the same structure for all four walls, and you'd certainly have a more solid job at the end. About all this, it is not sufficient to read between these rather vague lines: consult your architect.

The solar conservatory

An alternative to the solar wall is to build a long conservatory or greenhouse along the most southerly wall of your house. It won't give you as much heat gain as a solar wall, but it will do a number of other things. It'll give you a good place to raise seedlings, tomatoes and other necessities which may survive badly out of doors. It'll improve the insulation of your south wall. And you can use it as an air-lock between the house and the outside world if you have one door connecting it to the house and another to the garden (keep them as far apart as possible).

It's also the best solution if your house is already built and its south wall cannot for one reason or another be made into a proper solar wall. In a way, the solar conservatory is just a development of the solar wall, except that you make the air space much bigger and you cannot rely on natural air circulation to do the heating for you. As in a solar wall, paint the outside of the house wall black where it falls inside the conservatory – but insulate it. You'll lose more than you gain if you have low insulation and just let heat from the conservatory drift through the wall into the house. At night your conservatory may get very cold and so will the adjacent rooms if you don't do something about it.

So how does the heat get from the conservatory into the house? The best way is to install one or two (more if your conservatory is very long) extractor fans which will pump air from the conservatory into the house. They're not expensive, and you need only a cheap one. Connect the fan to a simple central heating thermostat (from the plumber's) and set the thermostat to turn it on every time the temperature in the conservatory rises to about 60° to 70°F. You'll get quite a lot of heat into the house that way whenever the sun shines. Of course you turn the fan off in the summer. The one thing you don't get with a solar conservatory, though, is the overnight heat storage of a solar wall. You must just aim to keep the day-time heat in with lousy ventilation and superb insulation.

When she was at the Cambridge School of Architecture, Brenda Vale made a hideously complicated calculation of how well solar conservatories might perform in Britain over the winter. She allowed for all kinds of things like the amount of heat absorbed by the average amount of plant tissue in a well-kept greenhouse and, of course, the heat needed to warm the air in the conservatory itself. After all that, the gist of the calculation was this: if the glass (double-glazed) of the greenhouse was inclined at 60° to the horizontal, 43·7 square metres of glass would provide 8,333 kWh of heat to the house during an average British winter (October to April). That is, 190 kWh for 1 square metre over the winter.

In fact, that doesn't compare too badly with the 200 to 300 kWh per square metre we reckoned on getting from the solar wall. The conservatory will be cheaper to build and, as I've said, has other uses as well. There are a few simple tricks which make building the conservatory easier and cheaper.

First, of course, a greenhouse doesn't need to be two storeys high unless you're going to grow bananas or coconuts. So fix a stout batten, say 2 × 4 to the outside wall of the house with bolts just below the windowsill of the upstairs rooms. Then incline your structural members (which will carry the glass) from the batten down to the ground at an angle of 60°. In most houses that will give you a thin, tapering greenhouse wide enough at ground level to walk along, with a layer of plants on the outside, and high enough not to have to duck. Make a drawing and adjust the angle a bit if necessary to give you sufficient room.

You'll need a footing of some kind into which should be set the bottom timber plate. Nail one end of the timber glazing bars into this and the other end into the batten on the house wall. Your timber glazing bars should be made from something like 3 × 2, with rebates on all four edges to receive the glass. You then fix one skin of glass on the outside and the other skin on the inside, if you can afford it. If not, batten transparent plastic to the inside. It'll be almost as good and will cost much less – but you will have to renew it every other winter or so. If you use plastic on the inside, then of course you need glazing rebated on only two edges. Incidentally, at Eithin we built glasshouses using only a single sheet of plastic, and they reached extremely high temperatures when the sun was out. We had to renew the plastic every year, though, for the wind tore even heavy-duty plastic to shreds in the winter.

At one end of the greenhouse you'll need a door, and you must make a concrete floor sloping down to a drain, so that you can brush the place out. The door end of the conservatory is a good place to store boots and coats. Turn the cloakroom inside the house, if you have one, into a pantry or a darkroom, or a place for showing blue movies if you prefer.

Finally, you'll need some flashing to stop water running down the wall of the house and into the conservatory between the glass and the wall. A few years ago you'd have done that with lead strip. Now you can buy stick-on aluminium flashing in tape form which will do the job much more simply – but I doubt that it'll last as long.

You will need some kind of ventilation for the summer, otherwise all your plants will die from heat death. Don't risk it – I've lost a whole crop like that and it's a tragic end to much endeavour. Half an hour of too much heat and too little water and you'll lose every plant in the greenhouse. The best solution of all is to rig up some kind of external roll-down shutter which you can partially close on hot summer days. The great advantage of that is that you can also let it down on cold winter nights, and reduce heat loss from both the house and the conservatory.

Finally, above all, do build it big. Run it along the whole length of the south wall, and if you can turn the ends at least a little way round the east and west gables as well, then do it. If finance is a problem, better to have a larger greenhouse with plastic on the inside than a smaller one with good double-glazing. As with solar roofs, size is the one factor where you can make the most gain. At 190 kWh per square metre of extra glass, you'll save more every winter for each extra square metre of glass than if you were heating electrically. You know it makes sense.

Solar heating on a grand scale

The trouble with all the solar schemes I've described so far is that they don't store heat long enough. The solar conservatory doesn't store it at all, and depends on you keeping in during the night what you collected in the day. The solar wall gives you 24-hour storage, which is better. And the solar roof, if you use a large enough storage tank and insulate it well enough, will give you warm water at least over a week of cloudy weather, which is even better.

But to do the job properly, you really need to be able to store your house heat for at least a week. And if we are ever to depend completely on solar heating we shall have to find a way of storing the summer sunshine for winter use. That, incidentally, is not really a novel idea; farmers who make hay for winter feed for their cattle are doing exactly that, and have been for millennia.

Since the last war a score or so of really serious solar houses have been built. Most of them provided between one-half and two-thirds of the total heat needed, and without exception the biggest problem they came up against was how to store heat. (Most of them were also judged uneconomic, by the standards of their day. With mounting fuel costs, that restriction is fast on the way out.)

I can't tell you how to build a house which will store the summer's heat for winter use. If you want to do that, it is going to cost you a good deal of money, and you are going to have to make a serious study of the literature on solar energy. You can find almost everything you need to know in the Book List, and if I were you I'd start with the chapter on solar energy in Brenda and Robert Vale's book *The Autonomous House* (Universe Books). It gives the best summary I know.

In the 1950s and 1960s Harry Thomason built a number of solar houses in the United States which worked pretty well. His basic solution to the storage problem was to dump 50 tons of rocks in the cellar. He collected hot water with a solar roof, converted it with a heat exchanger to warm air, and blew that through the rocks which acted as the heat store. When the sun was hidden, he blew cold air through the rocks, which warmed the air up, and then used it to heat the house. There was also a very large hot water tank, and a lot of complicated control equipment.

Thomason's schemes have probably worked as well as anyone's. But even the 50 tons of rocks gave him only a week's heat storage. Other people have tried using a chemical known as Glauber's salts; they have the property of absorbing heat chemically, and can be made to release that heat when needed. Again, a workable system can be devised to give a week or so's storage, but the chemical is expensive, and the number of heating/cooling cycles it will go through is limited. No easy answer there.

A more promising, though even more complicated idea, is to

link a solar roof to what is known as a heat pump. Heat pumps merit a section of their own (chapter 15) but the principle is simply that you use a refrigerator to heat you up instead of cool you down. A normal refrigerator works by taking heat out of the cold box, thus cooling the box down, and throwing out the heat removed through the coil to be found at the back of the refrigerator. You could do that on a bigger scale, of course, by cooling something down outside the house, and directing the heat taken out into the house in the form of warm air or hot water. The question is: what to cool down?

If a babbling brook runs by the side of your house, your problems are solved – you can simply cool the stream water down two or three degrees (without freezing it) and end up with plenty of heat for the house. Most people don't have streams running by the side of their house, so to use a heat pump they would have to remove heat either from the soil or from the air. The trouble with the soil is that you must then sink a lot of pipes deep into the ground to carry the heat away, and that is expensive. The trouble with the air is that, in a damp climate, the water vapour in the air freezes round the pipes as ice, and cuts down the efficiency of the heat pump.

To understand all this properly means getting to grips with the concept of heat as something different from temperature. A stream, for instance, stores a lot of heat but at a low temperature; this is called low-grade heat. What a heat pump does, in effect, is to turn low-grade heat into high-grade heat – heat at a higher temperature. No good running the stream itself through your house – but if you use a heat pump to turn that low-grade heat into really hot water, you can indeed use the stream to heat your house.

Most of the time a solar roof acts as a source of low-grade heat. In cloudy weather, the roof perhaps heats through a few degrees to produce an effect which is normally not worth using. But if a heat pump could convert that low-temperature heat into high-temperature heat, the situation changes. You then have an almost constant source of heat, and the need to provide long-term heat storage vanishes. You can use and get some heating effect from a solar roof/heat pump combination on any day of the year. On the very worst day, or at night, you are simply using the outside air as the heat source. But whenever there is a trickle of radiation from the sky – and there always is except at night – your heat pump will pick it up and provide you with something extra.

People have built solar roof/heat pump installations and they do work. The trouble used to be that the expense involved meant that, allowing for interest on the capital, you came away with heat that cost you more than burning oil or gas. But that can't last for long now. Soon the solar roof/heat pump combination will be truly economic, and I believe it can be engineered to provide most houses with most of their heat most of the time.

Yet, in a way, I also resist the idea. Mainly because such a device is likely to fall once again into the hands of specialists. A heat pump is not a simple thing to build or operate, and to operate it well in conjunction with a solar roof will demand sophisticated controls. Further, heat pumps consume a certain amount – admittedly fairly small in relation to the heat gained – of wasteful electricity. More about that in chapter 15.

How, then, does all this affect you? There is a case for leaving these more experimental and ambitious solar schemes to await developments. Install a solar roof, and either a solar wall or conservatory as well, and make up the rest of your heating some other way. You can add more advanced systems later, if you want, when the technology is better developed.

But maybe there is an experimental twist to your character, and a bit of ready money to put towards some good cause. If that is the case, you can do no more valuable job than design and erect an untried solar system. If it works, fine. Even if it doesn't, what you'll have done will certainly provide a lot of useful information. For instance, Brenda Vale has designed, on paper, an under-house heat storage system which could well provide at least some summer or autumn heating for winter use. The basic element is a large area of sand underneath the house interlaced with air ducts. The sand is surrounded by an incredibly well-insulated box to stop the heat escaping. And then all excess heat – from the house, the solar roof and the solar conservatory – is pumped down into the sand bed where it is stored. When heat is needed, cold air is blown through the bed and used to warm the house.

Calculations indicate such an idea might well work – but we don't really know as yet because no one has built such a thing. Perhaps you are the person to do it? If so, don't be put off by the fact that you're not a research scientist. I don't believe research should be a specialist profession, any more than should plumbing or carpentry. Most of us are capable of making careful enquiries into things we would like to know about. And there are some pretty good sociological reasons for believing that research is better carried out by the people who are going to have to live with the results than by a special breed of white-coated fanatics. As a friend of mine once put it, 'It's too late to turn scientists into humanists, so we'll just have to turn people into scientists'. Why not?

Chapter 8

❧◦❧

Wind power

I DON'T know exactly how many amateur, back-garden windmills have been put up in the past five years, but it must be several hundred. Most of them, it's fair to say, either blew down straight away or failed to do what their makers thought they would. Never mind. A lot of new information has been generated (if not much electricity), and at least most of the enthusiasts have now learned that wind power needs sound craftsmanship if it is to be used effectively. If you are going to build a windmill for electricity generation (which from now on I'd better call by its correct term, an aerogenerator), you will have to become a good metal worker, a reasonable mechanical engineer, and a competent electrician – or at least have quick access to people who are. You must also be capable of climbing a high pole or tower, with your tools, probably in a storm, to put right whatever it is that has gone wrong. On the other hand, most of the really bad mistakes common in small aerogenerators have now been made – and providing you study the field assiduously, there's no reason for you to repeat them. Further, if you do succeed, your success should last for many years to come – and save you a good deal of money in the process.

At Eithin we erected a Savonius rotor windmill – one with a vertical axis and made from two oil drums, each cut in half and mounted as shown on page 130. This kind of windmill is theoretically attractive because it's cheap to make, and it'll turn whichever way the wind blows. Its history is a salutary one for anyone thinking of getting into wind power.

We planned to use it to pump water from our spring into the attic storage tank. That meant it had to be near the house and spring, and that in turn meant installing it on the lee side of a hill, about 500 feet below the summit. Mistake number one. The gusts and eddies never turned the thing, and it only worked properly when we had a stiff north-easterly blowing. That was about once

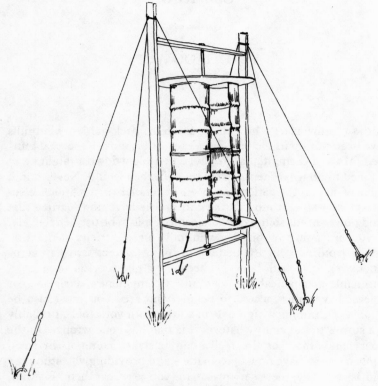

SAVONIUS ROTOR

a month. We were also persuaded to buy a rather expensive and advanced pump which we buried immediately below the rotor's vertical axis. We never got that pump to work properly. For one thing, it was too powerful for the size of the windmill; for another, we got into all kinds of trouble with air locks in the long pipe-run from the mill to the spring. The water at Eithin is still pumped electrically. Like almost everyone else's windmill, that one still stands there, useless, and eventually it'll end up as a mass of tangled scrap. Tragedies like that can be found in the backyard of almost any windmill enthusiast.

Quite soon now someone is going to come up with a fool-proof design for a good family-sized windmill. At least if you decide to have a go now, there are plenty of good leads to follow, and a lot of useful and recent information to absorb. Five years ago there wasn't even that. At that time any information about wind power came from traditional knowledge of huge sail windmills used for grinding flour, from rural companies who used to make those fan-type windmills for water pumping on farms, and from a spate of renewed interest in wind power which occurred in the 1940s and early 1950s. At that time, nuclear power was not given serious consideration, and the electricity people decided they had better come up with some alternative to coal and gas. They did do a lot of work on large wind-powered devices, and some impressive machines were erected, ranging in size from small ones producing 8 kW or so up to a real giant in Vermont in the United States which got up to 1,500 kW before it was blown to pieces. The promise of cheap nuclear power snuffed out all that valuable work in the late 1950s, and as a result we've lost a couple of decades in the race to find energy substitutes.

Wind power will certainly be back with us in a big way by the next century. Wind and water power catered for all men's energy needs for about 99·99 per cent of human history. Our brief contemporary flirtation with fossil fuels will certainly look very much like a one-night stand in the history books of the future.

What form wind power will return in is not yet clear. I'm pretty sure that those 1,000 kW monsters are far too big for happiness. On the other hand, much as many people would like it, I don't really relish the day when every home has its own windmill perched on the roof top. TV masts are bad enough, and anyway I suspect that that scale is really too small to be truly beautiful – at least as far as windmills are concerned. Perhaps something around 25–50 kW will prove the best, supplying power for a road or street or hamlet. Meanwhile there are plenty of people about who would like to build their own.

The theory

The first thing you need is some idea of how much power you can get from the wind. The theoretical maximum is given by the formula $P = 0.59 \times 0.00064 \times A \times V^3$, where A is the area swept by the windmill (in square metres), V is the speed of the wind (in metres per second) and P is the power available in kilowatts. In practice, no windmill will produce more than 60 per cent of this, due to friction and other inevitable losses, and for a normal design the formula boils down to $P = 0.00071 \times r^2 \times V^3$, where r is the radius of the mill blades in metres. To save you the trouble of the calculation, I've done it for you:

Maximum Practical Power Available (in watts)

diameter of mill (in metres and feet)

Wind speed	1 3′ 9″	2 6′ 6″	3 9′ 10″	4 13′ 1″	5 16′ 5″	6 19′ 8″
2·5 m/sec						
(5·6 mph)	3	11	25	44	69	100
5 m/sec						
(11 mph)	22	90	200	355	550	800
10 m/sec						
(22 mph)	180	710	1,600	2,840	4,440	6,400
15 m/sec						
(34 mph)	600	2,400	5,400	9,600	15,000	21,600

Two things are very intriguing. First, as in a solar roof, it pays to increase the size. In fact, it pays even more than in a solar roof in that, if you double the length of the roof, you get only twice as much solar power. But if you double the length of your windmill propellers you get 4 times as much power. If you triple them, you get 9 times as much. But against this is the fact that as your windmill gets bigger, it gets very much more difficult to make – while a large solar roof is as easy as a small one.

Secondly, you get an even bigger gain if you have high wind speeds. Double the wind speed and you have 8 times as much power. Triple it and you have 27 times as much. But there's a snag. These figures apply only when the windmill or aerogenerator is operating at its most efficient speed. Every wind device has just one speed at which it will pick up the theoretical maximum of some 60 per cent of the available wind energy. This is called the rated speed, and it varies mainly with the type of propeller or sail used.

If you use 2 or 3 propellers in an aerogenerator, the rated speed will be when the tips of the propellers are travelling between 5 and

7 times as fast as the wind speed. For most designs that occurs at about 11 metres per second (25 mph). If you use a sail to turn the machine, the optimum or rated speed is much lower – when the tip of the sail travels twice as fast as the wind, perhaps at 6 to 8 metres per second (13 to 17 mph). And finally, the multi-blade fan-type of rotor, the kind used on farm machines, rotates with a tip speed to wind ratio of near 1. Its rated speed is at most 5 metres per second (11 mph), often a good deal less.

This puts windmill designers in a bit of a spot. Unless they're in a very windy place, the average wind speed is not likely to be much more than 5 metres per second (11 mph) – probably it'll be lower. To get much energy out of that will need a very large machine – but it will be one which will turn most days of the week. This is why the traditional grinding mills had sails and were so big – they were designed to give power from the low winds which blew most of the time. Of course they had no means of storing up extra power on windy days for use in calm periods. This also explains the design of farm pumping windmills, which were required to work in almost any weather and were designed to operate at very low wind speeds.

Yet the energy available from the strong winds which blow less often is a great deal more. For instance, at a typical site winds of 13 to 18 mph may blow for only 200 hours a month, while lighter winds blow for nearly 500 hours. Yet the energy in the 13 to 18 mph winds is twice as much, even though they blow for less than half the time. But to make good use of the stronger winds you have to have some means of storing the energy of windy days for calmer periods.

For a small machine – say anything below 6 metres in diameter – I think the way out of this impasse is becoming clearer. For a start, I would not recommend you design a wind machine for pumping water or grinding corn. If you need to do those things, you might as well go to the trouble of building an aerogenerator which will give you electric power to do whatever you want (within reason). That way you can pump and grind when you have to, and run lights and radios and maybe a fridge when you don't. Further, with a generator, you can store the energy in batteries and hence make use of those stronger winds, which will mean your machine can be smaller. That rules out multi-bladed fans, and favours propellers over sails.

If you're now looking covetously at the table which says you can get 21 kW from a 34 mph wind with a 6-metre diameter machine, be careful. You can – but to make any sensible use of it you're going to have to have so many storage batteries that you'll either bankrupt yourself or rupture yourself in moving them to the site. A 34 mph wind blowing for 24 hours will give you over 500 kWh. To store that amount of energy, using say lead/acid car batteries, will involve you with more than 10 tons of batteries – around 900 average car batteries in all. Forget it.

Furthermore, trying to catch that much energy will mean you need an alternator capable of producing more than 20 kW – and that's a big, heavy and complicated piece of equipment. As we'll see, by far the best bet for your alternator will be one from a car or truck – and most of them give about 500 watts. Of course, you can hook more than one up to your aerogenerator, but 4 would be a maximum. Two would give you 1 kW and 4, say, 2 kW.

Assuming you don't live on top of a mountain, and hence your 34 mph winds are few and far between, you can get between 1 and 2 kW with a 22 mph wind and a 3-metre diameter rotor, of the propeller type, or between ½ and 1 kW with a 5- or 6-metre diameter propeller in an 11 mph wind. The latter would best be a sail rotor, which is anyway easier to make and easier to replace if it breaks up. So my advice boils down to this: if you've a windy site try a 3-metre diameter propeller; if you haven't, go for a sail machine with a diameter of 6 metres or so.

The site and the tower

First things first. The best place for a windmill is right on top of a smooth, rounded hill. If you can't manage that, you should have a site exposed to the two main prevailing wind directions. And if that's not possible, the site must at least be exposed to the prevailing wind. If it's not, skip this chapter because it isn't worth building a windmill.

Secondly, your propeller should be 15 feet higher than any obstacle within 400 feet on the windward side, and 100 feet on other sides. There must be nothing substantially higher than the propeller within 800 feet upwind and 200 feet on the other sides.

The only exception, I suppose, is your house, because you'll gain in the amount of electric power the nearer the mill is to it.

In other words, you're likely to lose more power in running a long cable to the house than you'll suffer from eddy effects if the house is near. Try to keep the mill within 100 feet of the house.

If you've a very small windmill, say 2- or even 3-metre diameter, you can probably make the tower either from a telegraph pole to even 2-inch diameter steel pipe (though pipe has been known or buckle). Towers like these use a central column to hold the mill up vertically, but depend for their lateral stability on a really efficient system of guy wires. Most people think immediately of using 4 such wires – but 5 or 6 are better. One of them can then be taken down for repair, or can fail completely, without endangering the structure.

Each wire must be firmly fixed to the mast, as high as possible without danger of getting entangled with the propeller. The best means of anchoring the wires is to drive a thick piece of angle iron 3 or 4 feet into the ground, angled towards the mast like a tent peg. But first dig a hole where the angle iron is to go the size of a 2-foot cube, drive the iron in and fill the cube with concrete. You now have a fix which even the mightiest wind will not budge.

Each wire must be fastened to its angle iron via a turnbuckle which you use to tighten the wire. Ideally you want a lot of people when erecting a mast – one to each wire, certainly, and preferably a couple more taking the main weight with an extra rope. Pull it upright, and adjust each wire in turn on to its turnbuckle with the clamp that holds the wire together after it has passed through the turnbuckle. When that's done, the thing will be stable but not vertical. Use a level to make sure the mast is absolutely vertical, and adjust the turnbuckles on each wire. Don't overstrain, though, or you'll easily snap the wire. The wires should be taut, but not so taut that they make a high-pitched musical note when plucked.

A wooden mast of this kind is very strong indeed; nothing more elaborate would ever have to be devised were it not for the problem of what to do at the top. Because somehow you have to fit a platform on which to mount the whole windmill assembly with its hub which allows it to rotate to face the wind. This is tricky, because it must withstand high forces. The platform must be of 1-inch marine ply, or, better, a steel plate. It will be fixed through its centre to the top of the mast, but stability will only come with steel straps or rods, at least 2 feet long, running from the edges of the platform down to the mast a foot or so below. Use 5 straps or rods – and

take care how you fasten them. Those fastenings will be the
weakest point of the structure. When building windmills, always

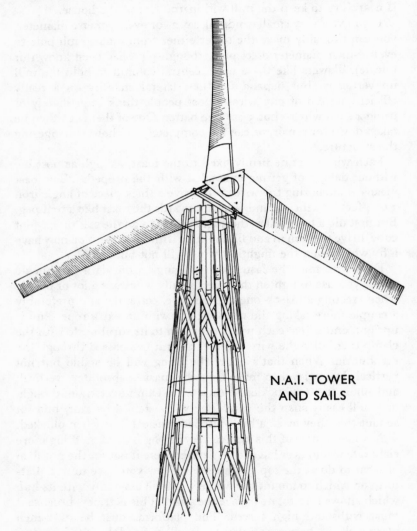

N.A.I. TOWER
AND SAILS

overestimate the strength of the wind and the forces involved. It
pays to be safe.

This platform problem is so acute that there is a good case to be made for building a tower and not using a mast. The top platform then adds strength to the tower, and another half-way up as well will help even more. The best design I know is for a 26-foot high tower built by the New Alchemy Institute-East on Cape Cod and fully described in the *Journal of the New Alchemists*, No. 2. The basic structure is made from 8 lengths of 2 × 4 timber each 26 feet long (all timber must be treated with wood preservative). The 2 platforms are fixed to the tower by nailing down into short lengths of 2 × 4 bolted to the main uprights (with eye bolts, on the centre platform, to provide a fixing for the guy wires). The NAI wires run inside the tower but anchoring them outside would in my view provide a better hold. The tower is tapered to a shape given by making the top platform an octagon 28 inches across and the centre one a circle of 48 inches diameter. The main uprights are fixed at the bottom with large bolts to 8 bits of telegraph pole 6 feet long driven deep into the ground. The top half of the tower is braced diagonally with 16 40-inch lengths of 1 × 3, and the bottom half with 16 58-inch lengths.

Such a tower (this one was designed for a 18-foot diameter sail machine) will give pretty good service. Bits of wood attached up the lee side will make a safe ladder, and some more pieces mounted all round about 3 feet from the top will give an easy toe-hold for working on the machine. If you want even more strength (and who doesn't?) the price of a third platform will be minuscule and help out of all proportion to its cost. By the time you've finished, such a tower is going to cost $200 or more, but a metal, commercially-available model to do the same job will add up to 3 or 4 times as much when you've finished paying for transport and import duty and all the other extras people can manage to think up. Build your own.

Sails and propellers

There are two nice things about windmill sails. First, they're easy to make, which means they're also easy to replace. Second, they'll never be as strong as the rest of your machine. That's an advantage because in a gale the sail is likely to get ripped up first, and once that's happened, of course, the wind machine will stop turning and no more harm can come to it. A rigid propeller, by contrast, can go on and on turning in a gale until the whole machine disintegrates.

The sailwing idea has been recently developed by a team of

scientists at Princeton University who were struck by the efficiency of a glider wing, with its blunt, rounded leading edge. The New Alchemy Institute has adapted the idea to make an 18-foot diameter water-pumping mill which works pretty well, even in a very low wind speed. The Princeton idea led to a 25-foot diameter machine, designed to produce 7 kW in a 9 metre per second wind.

The leading edge of the NAI sail is a $1\frac{1}{4}$-inch diameter steel television mast, while the trailing edge is made from a taut wire or nylon cord. As a result, the shape of the sail changes with windspeed, to take up the most efficient aerodynamic shape. The sail itself, made from cotton or, better, dacron (as in boat sails), slips over the steel and nylon cord frame like a sock. The drawing on page 141 shows the essentials. The steel masts are fixed with U-bolts to a 1-inch thick triangle of plywood, which serves as the hub, each side of the triangle measuring 30 inches. The rest is apparent from the diagram. Note the door springs fitted to give an automatic governing device for high winds. These have two positions, one for use in storm conditions. The NAI design has, however, come through gale force winds in the normal spring position. I would recommend an additional governing device (see next section), so I think you could dispense with the storm position for the springs – not a very practical idea, in any case, for they involve climbing the tower in a high wind to make the adjustment.

This unit has been tried and tested, and if you get into problems write to Marcus Sherman, c/o New Alchemy Institute-East, Box 432, Woods Hole, Mass. 02543 for advice. The NAI machine was for water pumping, so the hub was connected to a crank shaft used to power the pump. Our machine will be an aerogenerator, so we will use a different system (see below). But it's worth pointing out now the main disadvantage of sails for electricity generation. The rotor will revolve relatively slowly, and will be far too slow to turn a car alternator at the right speed. Even with propellers, you need to gear up by about 10 to 1. For a sail machine of this type, you will need to gear up 20 or even 25 to 1. But, even allowing for the frictions that introduces, you'll still make more efficient use of slight winds than would a propeller machine.

If you are to go in for the more complicated propeller design, the first problem is finding a pattern for the most efficient aerodynamic shape. It will be a complicated, three dimensional figure, and slight deviations from the specification may make quite drastic

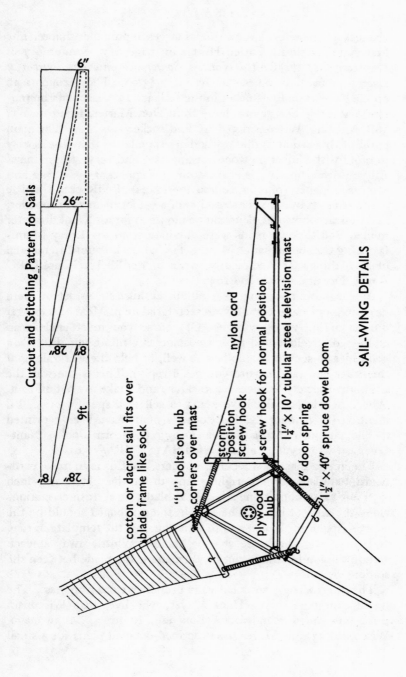

Cutout and Stitching Pattern for Sails

6"

26"

28"

8"

9ft

28"

8"

cotton or dacron sail fits over
blade frame like sock

"U" bolts on hub
corners over mast

storm
position
screw hook

nylon cord

screw hook for normal position

$1\frac{1}{4}$" × 10' tubular steel television mast

16" door spring

$1\frac{1}{2}$" × 40" spruce dowel boom

plywood
hub

SAIL-WING DETAILS

changes in efficiency. I know three sources of propeller shapes. The first is an article by Ulrich Hutter on page 217 of volume 7 of *Proceedings of the United Nations Conference on New Sources of Energy* (1964; UN Sales No. 63.1.41, $3.50). The second is an article by Winnie RedRocker in the January 1973 issue of *Alternative Sources of Energy* (available from Don Marier, Route 1, Box 36B, Monong, Wisconsin 54859). RedRocker says in it: 'The main point of this article is that a wooden propeller of this type is easy to build with almost no woodworking skill and very little money.' All you need, he says, is a drawknife (or spokeshave), a rasp and some sandpaper (plus of course the plans). RedRocker's article describes step by step construction of a 7-foot diameter propeller, and indicates how the plans can be modified for a 10-foot diameter model. RedRocker's plans were obtained from the LeJay Manufacturing Co., Belle Plaine, Minnesota 50011, who publish a manual of such things. If in difficulty, write to RedRocker himself, PO Box 3, Farisita, Colorado 81037.

A word about writing to windmill enthusiasts. Most of them have no money and certainly no secretarial help. Most of them get dozens of letters every week. Of course you must enclose an addressed envelope and return postage as a minimum. But it's a good idea to send a few dollars as well, to help the work along at the other end (and ensure you get a reply). This is the way the alternative society finances its research, and I take my hat off to it. Where people actually have plans to sell at a specific price, I'll mention it. Incidentally, RedRocker's plans have been reprinted in the *Survival Scrapbook on Energy* (Unicorn Books, Nant-Gwilw, Llanfynydd, Carm., Dyfed SA32 7TT, £1.50).

The key to making wooden propellers like this is to make cardboard templates of the right shape to fit the blade at 7-inch intervals or stations along the 7-foot blade, or at 10-inch stations along the 10-foot blade. The hole in the cardboard should be the exact shape of the blade, and to fit it you snip the template in two, and fit it over the blade at each station. Whittle away at each station till you have an exact fit, then shape the blade between the stations by eye.

The alternative is to make your propeller from fibreglass. The world expert on this is Hans Meyer, who lives in a Wisconsin commune called Windworks (Box 329, Route 3, Mukwonago, Wisconsin 53149). Meyer has described detailed plans for a small aerogenerator in the November 1972 issue of the American journal *Popular Science*. The key to his technique is the use of expanded paper, of honeycomb pattern, which can be drawn out and twisted to give exactly the right aerodynamic shape. It is held in this position and then fibreglassed to give a very rigid and light propeller. I won't describe how to do it, because Meyer is the expert, not me. Apart from getting his article in *Popular Science*, you can also buy for $11, plus postage if outside the US, enough expanded paper for one of his three-bladed rotors. Since the 1972 article Meyer has made an improved and larger model of his machine, and you can buy from him for $15 complete plans plus the expanded paper (called hexcel) for the rotor.

When you've made your sails or propeller you have to fix it to something which will rotate in a bearing which can be anchored to the mast. The best thing is the complete rear axle and differential of a scrap car, which can now be obtained very cheaply from a junk yard (see next section). But assuming for the moment you've done that, you must now balance the rotor. This is important: if you don't balance the thing, the vibrations and the uneven weight will certainly be enough to shake the whole contraption loose. Your rotor, electrical equipment and probably your tower will crash to the ground. So balance you must.

Any good engineer will tell you you must balance dynamically – that is, when the thing is revolving fast. You can't – it needs complicated equipment. So you have to balance statically, which means first setting the thing up with the rotor in a vertical plane and spinning the rotor hard by hand a few times. Watch the point at which it settles to rest. If it's always the same point, you are unbalanced, and you'll have to weight the lighter arms. With a propeller you do this by cutting out an oval shape of metal and screwing it to the lighter blade with the screw offset from the centre. Find the right point by trial and error to screw in, which will give you rough balancing. Then twist the metal oval round on its screw to give you fine balancing. Then tighten the screw. To balance a sail, use your common sense; some pieces of lead flashing cut into thin strips and twisted round the metal strap at the tip of the wing might be good – but make sure they're firmly fastened or they'll come off in a high wind.

Transmission and governors

The problem of how to transmit power from a rotating sail or propeller to a device for producing electricity can be solved in two ways. You can build a shaft which will turn pulley wheels linked by a belt to an alternator. That will take you into buying and fitting bearings and pillow blocks from small mail order firms, or finding the right junk pieces in the right place. Jim Sencenbaugh has built a pretty successful 500-watt aerogenerator in this way and for $15 he'll send you a complete set of plans. They'll take you through not only all the mechanical problems, but round the electrical circuit (see below) as well. Even if you don't intend copying someone else's plans exactly, it's not a bad idea to get them because they contain many hints which you might otherwise spend much time puzzling over (address: 673 Chimalus Drive, Palo Alto, California 94306).

The second way of doing it, which I reckon is much easier, is to buy a complete rear axle and differential from a junk car dump. If you don't know much about what happens inside a car, now is the time to find out; the information will not only help you make the windmill, but it'll be very handy later on if you're still running a car. The beauty of this scheme is that it is cheap – and that you can use a wheel hub to solve your main bearing problem. Leave one hub on, and bolt a plywood plate on which the propeller is mounted to it. You then have to mount the entire axle and differential on a 1-inch piece of marine plywood, or a steel plate which is even better. This is the platform which will carry all the gubbins at the top of the machine – notably the axle, the alternators and some electronics.

Your second bearing problem is how to mount this platform on top of the tower. It must rotate freely so that the propeller or sail can always face the wind. The expensive way of solving this is to buy, as the New Alchemy Institute did for their sail mill, a steel turntable. For the record, theirs was a model no. M4-1214 series 1,000 Econotrak bearing (9-inch inside diameter) from Rotek Inc., 220 West Main Street, Ravenna, Ohio 44266, and it cost them about $129. It's undoubtedly a splendid device but you can do the same thing with another wheel hub. Ideally, I would buy a scrap tractor hub and axle. Disconnect it from the differential and bolt the differential housing to a platform near the top of the tower. The top platform can be cut out to take and support the axle housing near the hub. Now mount the propeller platform onto the wheel mounts on the tractor hub.

It's a good idea to leave the handbrake cable trailing from both these hubs – the propeller mounting hub and the platform hub. That will then give you a manual method of (a) stopping the propeller from turning in a gale; and (b) stopping the turntable at a position where the propeller is at right angles to the prevailing wind in a gale. A double precaution.

The axle and differential can be mounted most easily on the platform with the differential sticking up – in other words, the vehicle drive shaft, were it still attached, would be pointing vertically towards the heavens. It then remains to attach a pulley wheel, spinning horizontally, to the car drive shaft mounting, and to link that pulley with a belt drive to the alternator(s). When you've done all that, you've got another balancing problem. It's very important that the platform, and all that you've installed on it, is weighted in such a way that the centre of gravity falls immediately over the mounting on the tower. If it doesn't, the weight, plus the vibrations from the rotation, is certainly going to tear the top platform out of its tower mounting, and you'll lose the lot. If you are using more than one alternator, the balancing can probably be done by positioning them to achieve the desired effect. Otherwise you'll have to devise some other method of weighting the platform.

Mounting the differential this way may lead to two problems. The lubrication may not work well and pulley belts may slip off. There is a case, therefore, for mounting the thing as it was in a vehicle – with the differential horizontal and the pulley wheels vertical – but it's usually more difficult.

The drawing on page 144 shows the main elements of the platform and its mounting. You must now build a fairly substantial vane, and attach it to the rear axle at the opposite end to the propeller or sail. This is what will turn the mill to face the wind. And you're now straight up against the problem of governors.

If you just leave your mill to go faster and faster in stronger and stronger winds, make no mistake but that you will lose the lot. Maybe not in the first gale – but certainly within a few months. You must therefore install some device either for slowing the propeller down in strong winds, or for turning it somewhat out of the wind.

You can, of course, simply do it manually – but the time will surely come when you don't want to get up in the middle of a stormy night to shut the thing off. You'll lie cosily in bed, convincing yourself it'll be all right, when you'll hear the crash that will cost you a few hundred dollars and several months' work. Don't risk it. There are many things you can do to make the thing perfectly safe.

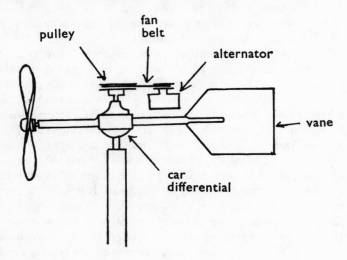

DIFFERENTIAL MOUNTING

The easiest is to mount a subsidiary vane, at right angles to the main one, about 50–70 per cent smaller. In a good breeze the mill will still turn to point to the wind. But as the wind strengthens, the relative importance of the second vane will increase, and it will slowly begin to turn the top platform so that it points somewhat out of the wind. The stronger the wind, the further round the platform will rotate to avoid it. It's a good, cheap and simple system.

But I'm not sure how effective it is. My advice would be to try it. It may work on its own. It will probably work well enough if combined with the spring feathering device I described for use with the sailwing. Be cautious. Watch your mill carefully through its first gale or two. If it looks like you're still in trouble, you'll have to add something else.

One solution is to mount the main vane on a hinge, so that it can be folded back parallel to the subsidiary vane in gales. That will certainly solve the problem, but it will of course still mean that you have to close the thing down manually in very severe winds. According to that real veteran of windmill manufacture, Marcellus

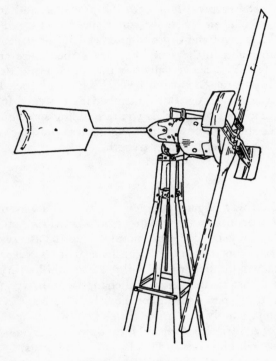

WINCO 1222H

Jacobs, most manufacturers of windmills in the 1930s did this in the wrong way. They spring-loaded the vane so that in normal winds it was kept in the operating state. Then they provided a pulley and cord used to fold the vane back for storm conditions. What happened was that eventually the pulley or cord broke, and the operator was left helpless to watch his mill disintegrate. What you have to do is spring-load the vane so that it normally shuts off the machine. If you want it to work you have to pull the cord and align the vane against the spring. If anything breaks then the vane snaps back and shuts the mill down. Fail safe.

Most commercial mills have more sophisticated governors. Some of them feather the angle of the propellers so that they don't catch the wind if they revolve too fast. Others, like the Wincharger (Winco 1222H), incorporate a centrifugal air brake. Two circular pieces of metal revolve along with the propeller, and are spring-loaded to offer no air resistance at low speeds. As speed increases, however, they pivot and begin to intercept the air stream. As they come further and further out, they brake the device and stop it going too fast. You can actually buy this air governor for a cost of $13.31: it's part no. 8830 from Dyna Technology Inc., Box 3263, Sioux City, Iowa 51102. But remember it's designed for a 6-foot diameter, 200-watt machine. If you're building something bigger, the air brake may not be strong enough unless you adapt it in some way to give a greater braking strength.

The electrics

The simplest way of generating electricity with a windmill would be to hook it up to an alternator which provides you with a.c. current, as in your domestic supply. But it's the worst way. Domestic a.c. comes to you at a constant 50 or 60 cycles a second. What your windmill alternator will produce will be very a.c. – so a.c., in fact, that its frequency will change with every gust of the wind (the frequency depends on how fast the rotor is turning). With such a supply you could run only two things – heating elements of an electric stove, and incandescent electric light bulbs. Even those will blow hot and cold as the wind gusts.

If you're building a windmill, as distinct from buying one (see last section), it means you don't have much cash. In which case you don't want to go out and buy a new alternator or generator. That would cost you a lot of money. Instead you can get one for almost nothing from a junk vehicle lot. There are two types of device used on vehicles – earlier models had a generator which produced 12 volts d.c. direct, and later models (and most trucks) produced a.c. but incorporated a rectifier to change the a.c. back into 12 volts d.c. It is the latter, the alternator, that you want – it's simpler, more effective and produces current at a lower rotational speed than the old-fashioned generator. You'll find alternators on all trucks, and on the larger and newer cars. When you've found the alternator you want, it's a good idea to purchase a service manual for the vehicle from which it came. The manual will tell you the performance of the alternator, and give you some idea of how to treat it, test it, and service it. When you disconnect the alternator from the vehicle make sure you take the voltage regulator that goes with it. You need this to ensure your batteries get charged at the proper rate.

At this point you need to know some basic electricity – power in watts equals volts times amps. For instance, if you get hold of the alternator from a Volkswagen bus with a 1,700 cc engine, you'll find it's rated at 14 volts and 55 amps. Multiplying those together tells you you can get up to 770 watts from the device. That's only the nominal rating. You can take more power from it than that, providing you do it intermittently. That's quite a lot of power, and you certainly won't need more than two such alternators.

You'll also find the optimum power of the alternator comes at 2,200 revolutions a minute. If your aerogenerator ever gets up to that speed, you'd better run for your life because the surrounding countryside will shortly be spattered with bits of windmill. In fact, the sailwing type will not produce more than, say, 150 rpm and the propeller rotor no more than 300 rpm – unless conditions are exceptional. As I've said, you must therefore gear up – by, say, 10 to 1 for a propeller and 20 to 1 for a sailwing. Don't forget there is already a gear up between your rear axle and the drive shaft. If you don't know what it is, then test it by rotating one and counting the number of revolutions of the other. It'll be something between 2·5 and 5 to 1. The rest of the gearing up is done with different sized pulley wheels fixed to the drive shaft mounting and the alternator (when calculating the effect, it's the ratio of the diameter of the wheels to each other which gives the gear ratio). Use a fan belt to connect the pulley wheels. Don't worry too much about the exact ratios – you can't know what will give the perfect result, and anything roughly right will give you the power you need.

If you're using two alternators, you can connect them both via one belt drive to one pulley wheel on the axle. But I'd recommend you use two belts and two pulleys. For one thing, if one belt snaps or some other fault develops, you've still one left and the batteries will go on being charged. Further, you may find that the heavier winter winds will work two alternators all right, but that in the summer you're better off with one. It's then easy enough to remove one of the belts.

The alternator has three connections. One must be earthed to the differential. The second, to which will have been originally connected a very thick cable, is the stator terminal which supplies the juice. This you connect to the positive pole of the battery, using very thick cable capable of carrying whatever current the alternator is rated at (the VW alternator, for instance, should carry 55 amps). Now to get the current from the top of the tower to the bottom, where the batteries will be, is a bit of a problem. It is done on manufactured wind generators by a complicated series of slip rings which transfer the current to some part of the tower. The reason is that the platform on which the alternator is mounted is constantly revolving to follow the wind. If you connect a cable from the alternator on this platform to the battery on the ground it will eventually get twisted round the tower. Now I reckon that the design of slip rings for a 55 amp current is beyond my, and probably your, capabilities. You must therefore use plenty of cable – enough to allow it to get twisted round the tower two or three times – and provide a plug and socket for it before it enters the battery. You can then periodically disconnect the plug, untangle the cable, and start again. No good using an ordinary 13-amp plug and socket, though. You'll need to find a special one capable of carrying the 55 amps.

A solemn warning. You must never disconnect the plug when the alternator is turning (that is, when the propeller is going round). If you do, you will damage the alternator, as you also will if you ever connect the battery terminals to it the wrong way round. If alternator and batteries are ever separated from each other, the propeller must be anchored or the alternator disconnected from its drive belt.

There is an obvious danger that your power cable will twist round the tower and eventually pull itself off one of its connections. To prevent that you must attach a length of strong wire, slightly shorter than the cable, from the platform to some point on the tower so that it will physically restrain the platform from making that last revolution which will snap the power cable. A bit of common sense will see you through all right.

The third connection on the alternator is to the field coils, and this provides you with your last problem on top of the tower. It is connected by ordinary electric cable to the positive side of the battery, and draws only a small current. But it's a crucial one, because it provides the magnetic effect which causes the alternator to produce current when it is rotated. The trouble comes in calm periods when the wind is too feeble to turn the blades. If you leave the field coils connected to the batteries, the latter will soon drain away, and you'll lose a lot of valuable stored juice. Some system has to be devised for breaking this connection when the wind isn't blowing, and for making it when it starts to blow. For that you need a relay.

The first way of operating it is to mount a small additional vane on the side of the platform. Spring-load it so that it will trip a mechanical relay, and thus connect battery to field coil, when the wind gets to the desired speed. Jim Sencenbaugh operated his machine this way, adjusting the spring to work the relay when the wind got to 8 mph, and he says it works very well.

Possibly a better way is to use an electrically operated relay. For this you need one of those bicycle dynamos which rub up against the rim of the bicycle tyre. Set this dynamo to rub against one of the drive belts to the alternator, and use it to operate the relay which will connect the battery to the field terminal. When the wind starts to blow, the alternator will begin to revolve, and the belt will start to turn the bicycle dynamo. The current produced will close the relay and the alternator will start to charge the batteries.

An advantage of both these systems is that they overcome another starting problem. Propellers and sails do not get under way very easily in light breezes. If the field connection is made, they also have to turn against the load of the alternator, and so will not start to move until the wind is fairly strong. But if in a calm the field connection is broken, there is no load to work against. The rotor will start to turn in calmer conditions and, once turning, will close the field connection and you'll get power at lower wind speeds than would otherwise be possible.

All your electrical units on the tower – alternator, voltage regulators, relays, must be well earthed to the differential. They must also be protected from the rain by some kind of cover. At ground level earthing is provided by a long stake driven deep into the ground. As your windmill is a perfect target for lightning, you must arrange at some point for there to be a $\frac{1}{4}$-inch gap between the positive lead from alternator to battery and a lead coming from the earthing stake. You can either make such a gap, or buy one designed for use on a television aerial.

Batteries

How much energy do you need to store? And how much can you expect to collect from the wind? Two difficult questions – and as the second depends on the answer to the first, I'll deal with it first.

To work out accurately how much you can collect, you need to have at least a ten-year wind profile of the exact position of your propeller. That would tell you what winds of what strength blew for how many hours each year. As you certainly won't be able to get such a wind profile, you'll have to make intelligent guesses, and the easiest way is to refer to a table published by Low Impact Technology in England. I don't know how accurate you can expect it to be, but my impression is that it's probably a bit pessimistic. You may do better than it suggests.

Average monthly output in kilowatt-hours

nominal rating of alternator (watts)	average wind speed (mph)					
	6	8	10	12	14	16
50	1·5	3	5	7	9	10
100	3	5	8	11	13	15
250	6	12	18	24	29	32
500	12	24	35	46	55	62
1,000	22	45	65	86	104	120
2,000	40	80	120	100	200	235
4,000	75	150	230	310	390	460
6,000	115	230	350	470	590	710

This table has no meaning at all, of course, if your propeller or sail is not powerful enough to work your alternator. So it's best to check back at this point with the other table on page 132. Suppose you plan to consume 80 kWh a month (quite a lot), and your average wind speed is 10 mph. You will then need about 1,500 watts of alternator output, which would be given by two VW alternators. But you can't expect those alternators to produce their full power in an average wind. You should expect to get full power in a wind somewhere between 22 and 24 mph (say 10 metres per second). Thus a 3-metre mill will give you more than 1,500 watts in a 22 mph wind (from the table on page 132) – but you'd be better off with a 4-metre one. That would be all right for a propeller which works more efficiently at high speeds. Go a size or two bigger if you have sails.

Actually, I doubt that if you're using wind power – and have thus become conscious of not wasting the juice – you'll need as much as 80 kWh a month. One way to work it out is something like this:

light : three × 40 watt fluorescents for 6 hours	=	720 watt-hours
radio : 10 watts for 5 hours	=	50
TV : 75 watts (transistorized model) for 3 hours	=	225
iron : 600 watts for ½ hour	=	300
washing machine (hot water added) 275 watts for 1 hour	=	275

1,570 watt-hours
a day
or 47·1 kWh a month

If you want a refrigerator you must add another few kWh a month. Almost certainly you won't be able to run a deep-freeze, which takes 20–30 kWh a week. But you're unlikely to come out much above 60 kWh a month, even allowing for occasional use of electric drills and coffee grinders. It goes without saying you must do no electrical heating on windmill power – and you should throw out your electric kettle as well as your electric toaster.

The next step is to work out how much battery storage you need. You should allow – unless you're in a very windy place – for enough power to keep you going for at least 5 days without wind. At 2 kWh a day, that means you need to store 10 kWh. Battery storage is usually rated in ampere-hours, but don't let that put you off: just divide the watt-hours you need by the voltage, and you have the ampere-hour figure. Thus 10 kWh is 10,000 watt-hours, which divided by a voltage of 12 (for car batteries) gives you 833 ampere-hours.

Now for the bad news. A small car battery stores around 45 ampere-hours and costs upwards of $20. To be safe you would need 20 of them. Total cost: more than $400, and that's doing it by far the cheapest way.

151

There are two kinds of battery suitable for this job. The first is the familiar lead/acid battery, of which the kind you buy for cars is by far the worst. It's designed primarily to provide the enormously heavy currents needed by the starter motor in the car, and you won't need that sort of capacity. It's also designed to take a lot of beating as it travels round bumpy roads. Your batteries will be stationary, and don't need to be that robust. But you do want them to have a long life, and as anyone who's ever run a car knows, his battery sometimes lasts only a couple of years, exceptionally 4 or 5 years. Never longer. But with a wind generator you'll be using your batteries more often, and discharging and charging them more often, than in a car. You'll be lucky to get 5 years out of new ones, and of course much less out of second-hand ones.

You can do a bit better if you go for the lead/acid batteries designed for radio receivers and as stand-bys in telephone exchanges. They may well be assembled as 32-volt units, though, and you have to make sure there is provision for charging them at 12 volts, or transform your voltage before it reaches the batteries. Now be careful, because a 32-volt battery may well have a storage capacity of more than 200 ampere-hours. But that doesn't mean you need 4 or 5 of them to make up the 833 ampere-hours needed at 12 volts. A 32-volt battery storing 200 ampere-hours rates at 6·4 kWh of storage (32 × 200 watt-hours). You would need at most 2 such batteries, but that's a much more expensive way, in terms of initial outlay, than car batteries, for such a battery will cost around $700. But you might do better in the end, because it will last longer than a car battery would.

The de luxe solution is to go for an alkaline battery, and there are only two feasible choices: a nickel/iron or a nickel/cadmium battery. These are very expensive indeed – but they should last up to 15 years or so if you take good care of them.

How to decide between all these choices is difficult. It really boils down to what you can get hold of cheaply. You may find batteries at government surplus sales, and if they are really cheap I'd buy them regardless of whether they're lead/acid or nickel. On the other hand, if you're near a used junk car depot, and you're friendly with whoever runs it, you may be able to pick up lots of reasonably good batteries for very little. In which case it's the short-life lead/acid battery every time.

Wind power in the home

Your last wind power decision must be whether to use the 12 volts d.c. direct from the batteries in your house, or whether to convert it to a.c., either 110 or 240 volts, depending on where you live. It's a difficult decision, and you must understand the implications of both systems thoroughly.

If you use 12 volts d.c. you are constantly up against the problem of amps. For instance, if you had all the devices mentioned in the last chapter going at the same time – washing machine, TV, radio, lights and iron – you would be drawing 1,080 watts. At 12 volts that means you will be handling 90 amps in the main cable which runs from the batteries to the house. If you used ordinary cable, as used in house wiring, it would simply melt.

So you have to work out how thick your main cable should be. It is standard practice in good wiring not to let the resistance of the cable reduce the voltage available to an appliance by more than 2·5 per cent of its intended value. That means, working at 12 volts, that the voltage drop along the cable from batteries to house should not be more than 0·3 volts. The radius of the copper cable you should use is then given by the formula:

$$r^2 = 1{\cdot}55 \times 10^{-6} \times L \times I/3{\cdot}14 \times 0{\cdot}3 \text{ cm}^2$$

where r is the radius of the cable in cm, L is the length of the cable in cm, and I is the current in amperes. It works out that a 50-metre length of cable carrying 90 amps should have a diameter of 17 mm. And that's an awful lot of copper – and nearly twice as much aluminium, if you're using aluminium conductor. Of course, if you halved the load, you would reduce the diameter of the cable needed by one-quarter.

But what is more striking is the saving you'd make if you ran the power to your house at high voltage. The same sum at 240 volts would work out at a cable diameter of only about 4 mm. That would save you a lot of money.

Unfortunately, the problems of using 12 volts d.c. do not end with the cable from battery to house. You will need to re-wire the house for 12 volts d.c. That's all right if you don't already have a.c. domestic wiring, but if you have it's a bit of a waste to have two circuits. For d.c. wiring you can use normal a.c. ring main cable (rated at 30 amps for 220 volts a.c.) for small appliances like lights

and radio. But for TV, washing machine, iron and freezers you'll
need heavy duty cable again.

You can get some 12-volt d.c. equipment – both 8 and 13 watt
12-volt fluorescent fittings as used in trailers are good. You'll need
a transformer for a 9-volt transistor radio in order to run it off 12
volts (they're surprisingly cheap). You can buy a 12-volt refrigerator and a water pump (as used in small boats). What you do
about the iron I frankly don't know. And though normal domestic
switches may be all right for light fittings, you'll need heavy tumbler
switches for power devices. Finally, you must consult a qualified
electrician about all this – particularly for advice on cable sizes and
where to place fuses. The figures I have given are to illustrate the
problem, not to plan a practical circuit.

I reckon the moral of this story is pretty clear. If you don't
already have any electricity in your house, and if you just want to
run lighting and perhaps a radio (possibly a transistorized TV),
then 12-volt d.c. will be good enough, providing your windmill is
very close to the house. If it isn't, if you want to run occasional
power devices like drills, irons and washing machines, and if you
are already wired up to a.c. from the grid, then use a different
system. Transform your 12 volts up to 120 or 240 volts a.c.
(depending on your domestic supply) at the batteries.

This is really a much simpler solution, for it involves you in one
problem, and one problem only. You need a solid state inverter to
convert 12 volts d.c. into high voltage a.c. They are expensive, and
viciously so if you go above about 500 watts. An inverter for 500
watts may cost you $150, but one for 1,500 watts will cost you
many times as much. So the answer is to use 2 (or if you plan to be
really profligate with your power, 3) smaller ones. Install them with
the batteries at the foot of the tower (well protected from the
elements) and from then on your problems are identical to those of
normal a.c. wiring. It may sound as though you're going to spend
a lot on the inverters, and you are. But probably not as much as the
very high power cable you would otherwise need to carry the huge
currents required for 12 volt d.c. and the extra wiring for the house
current.

And the really big advantage is that you can connect your
system up so that you can use either grid supply or wind supply, in
the same sockets, at will. Compromise again. And what's more,
it'll mean you could cut down on the number of storage batteries

you need. Plan for, say, 3 days without wind instead of 5, and go over to the grid if you get caught out by a calm spell.

The best way to do this is as follows. Turn off the main line, and cut through the lighting circuit a few feet away from the distribution panel. Connect the cable from the panel box to a 5-amp socket, and put a 5-amp plug on the cut end of the lighting circuit. If you want to use mains lighting, just push the plug into the socket. Now bring the supply from the inverter into the house and terminate it in a double point wall socket. Push the lighting plug into one of them, and your house lighting is now wind powered. Make up another plug and cable to fit the other of the two sockets. Lead this cable to 2 or 3 power points at special places (workshop, kitchen, TV point) and use them for power appliances when using the wind. When forced back to the domestic supply, go back and use the power sockets which are already fitted.

Alternatively you could of course treat the ring mains from the grid supply as I've suggested for the lighting circuit. The danger is, however, that if you use the same power sockets in your rooms for both wind and grid power, you may forget which is in operation and overload the wind system. In which case you'll certainly drain the batteries and may damage the inverters if you draw more power from them than they are capable of. Once again, check it all out with a qualified electrician. There's no point in going to all that trouble to get wind power if you die from electrocution the first day of operation.

That is the basic story about getting the electricity into your home. I'm now going to go into some more detail for the person who's actually in the throes of doing it, because there is a lot more to it than I've so far suggested. There's a good case for re-thinking the whole electrical system, and regarding it as quite different to the grid supply, which of course it is.

First, if you want to use low voltage d.c. you don't have to use copper as the conductor from mill to house. Aluminium is cheaper, even though you need to use twice as much because it has a lower conductivity. But why use wire at all? With very low voltage you needn't worry about insulation or danger, because no one is going to hurt himself with 12 or even 24 volts. You could carry your juice into the house with copper pipe, suitably connected at each end. Or even long lengths of aluminium guttering which is much cheaper. Providing it's thick enough not to get warm when carrying the current, and so dissipate a lot of your precious power before it gets into the house, it'll work perfectly well.

Then the business of inverters is quite complicated. There are many different kinds on the market. The expensive ones are those which convert the d.c. into the same kind of a.c. as the grid supplies. That a.c. is called sinusoidal, and its frequency is either 50 or 60 cycles a second. But inverters which convert to a square wave, rather than a sine wave, and produce frequencies of up to several thousand cycles per second are very much cheaper. That kind of a.c. will power any of your normal devices except those which run off a motor – drills, clocks (buy a clockwork one instead), refrigerators and deep freezes, plus kitchen gadgets. And though, as I've suggested, you could buy 3 sinusoidal inverters if your pocket can afford it, you will have to hire a very competent electronics engineer to wire them up so that they run in phase if you want to run your motorized equipment off them.

Time for another re-think. First, your biggest problem might be solved most easily if you use your wind power to run first all your devices which don't have motors – lights, heating devices such as irons, and anything else without a motor. Use a square wave inverter, of the appropriate rating, to power that lot, which will be most of your load. Then start asking yourself how essential your motorized devices are. Throw a few out. If you find you don't need any then your problems are solved. If there are still some you feel you must run, then work out how much juice the biggest needs, determine never to use more than one at a time, and buy a much smaller sinusoidal inverter to power the biggest. Run that supply to a special socket, used only for things which must have conventional grid-type a.c. That way you could save yourself a lot of money.

Buying an aerogenerator

You can buy ready-made aerogenerators easily enough, ranging in size from the small 200-watt Wincharger to a Swiss 10,000-watt model. The smallest will just provide you with a few lights and cost over $500. The largest will cope with lights, power equipment, refrigerator, deep freeze and most of your electrical heating. It'll set you back more than $10,000 by the time you've paid for all the ancillary equipment. The kind of machine I've been mostly describing in this chapter, say 1,200–2,200 watts, will cost over

$7,000, excluding tower, import duty, and transport from Switzerland. So if you make your own you've a lot of money to play with – but yours will never work as well or as reliably as a custom-made machine.

The commercially available machines boil down to this: from the States, the Wincharger (from Dyna Technology Inc., PO Box 3263, Sioux City, Iowa 51102) or the larger Aerowatt (actually a French machine), the biggest rating at 4.1 kW (Automatic Power, Inc., division of Pennwalt Corporation, 213 Hutcheson Street, Houston, Texas 77003). In the US, Henry Clews is the agent for both the Australian Quirks windmills and the Swiss Elektro models (Henry Clews, Solar Wind Co., PO Box 7, East Holden, Maine 04429; Clews has a booklet, *Electric Power from the Wind*, which is well worth getting for $2). Many other water pumping machines are commercially available, and some people suggest buying one and adapting it for electric generation. Don't. They're not designed for that and you're better off making your own. A list of the manufacturers of aerogenerators, with their addresses, is included in the Book List on page 287.

Chapter 9

❧

Water and plumbing

EINSTEIN once said that if he could live his life again, he would
have been a plumber. I can understand why well enough. Of all
the building jobs, plumbing is the easiest, saves most money and
is the most fun. But it is surrounded by more mystique than an
oriental religious cult. If you are going to plumb, your biggest
problem is to convince yourself that there's no special magic involved which only plumbers know about. Once you've done that,
the problem is three-quarters solved.

Not so long ago all plumbing was done with lead, and plumbing
jobs were all those which involved lead – pipes, wastes, tank
installations and also such extras as chimney flashing and lead
beating round sills. You don't find much lead in the building trade
now, and I shall restrict this chapter to the business of getting
water from a source, running it through your house to do whatever you want it to do, and then providing a means for getting the
wastes out again. No lead is involved – you'll use only copper and
plastics, and perhaps salt-glazed ceramic pipe for the main drains.

Getting the water in

Chances are that your house is connected to a public water supply.
If it is, go on using it, for the moment anyway. I say for the moment
because the United Kingdom, like many countries in the world, is
now chronically short of water. I have little faith that the authorities
are going to be able to cope with a growing population with a
growing thirst for water. If they do, it will only be by wrecking
yet more of the country with water catchment areas and enormous

reservoirs – which would be totally unnecessary if we changed our water habits just a little. We shall certainly be looking hard for different ways of getting our water before the century is out.

But if you are connected to the public supply, the expense of making the connection has already been paid for and you might as well use it – sparingly, if you have any thought for tomorrow. The rest of this section is for people who don't have public water, and for those wise enough to start thinking of alternatives for today.

People who live outside the big towns and cities can often find their own water supply. It is surprising that even in the most civilized of countries there remain millions of wells and boreholes still perfectly serviceable. Hundreds of thousands of them are still in use. If you own one of them, your only problem is getting water up out of the ground and into the storage tank. Unfortunately, those beautiful 6 feet high, long-handled brass pumps that used to grace many a farmhouse cellar or pantry are now nearly extinct – although while house hunting recently I found two still in perfect working order. But if you can't get one of those, you can get a small hand pump that will do a fairly efficient job – the kind of pump used for a thousand and one things on most farms.

Or you can use an electric pump, if you are prepared to spend the money it takes to buy one (or less for a second-hand one). But there is one thing the would-be plumber must learn early on about pumps. No pump will suck water up more than about 27 feet (basically because even a complete vacuum can support a column of water only 32 feet high). If the water surface in your borehole or well is deeper than that, you have no choice but to lower the pump so that it is never more than, say, 25 feet above the water in the driest period. All this has nothing to do with how high a pump will lift the water after it has sucked it into the pump chamber. That is determined only by the power of the pump, and if you want to you can easily use a small pump to raise your water 100 feet or more (the higher you raise it, the slower the pump will work, of course).

Amateurs almost always have trouble in making pumps work because they fail to understand how important the priming action is. Before you start a pump, you must fill the pump chamber and the suction pipe with water. If you allow any air bubbles to remain, the pump will simply stretch the air bubble out along the pipe, and no water will ever appear. In practice this means you prime the pump slowly and carefully with water before starting to pump, and jiggle it and the suction pipe about to make any air left in rise up and escape. If your suction pipe snakes along the ground, rises up here and there and drops down here and there, the pump will never work because you will never eliminate the last traces of air. The suction line must fall all the way from pump to water, with no places where air bubbles can get stuck.

And on the far end of the suction line, you must fit a foot valve – a very cheap device which will allow water to enter the pipe and not flow down and out of the pipe. If you don't use a foot valve, every time the pump stops the priming water will escape back into the source, and you'll have to prime every time you want to use the pump. With a foot valve you should only need to prime once. Thereafter you can forget all about priming, except after prolonged periods of inactivity.

Pumping used to be a daily ten-minute, after-breakfast chore. There's no reason why it still shouldn't be. If you fill your tank daily, either with a hand pump or an electric one, nothing much will ever go seriously wrong. As you probably can't pump and watch the level in the tank rise at the same time, you must arrange the overflow from the tank to spill out somewhere within sight of your pump. You then just pump until the overflow starts to run. But with an electric pump there is a device which enables you to do this automatically, called a float switch. It costs very little and is easy to fit into the tank. Basically it consists of a float which moves with the water level. When the float gets to the bottom of the tank it hits a stop and throws a switch which turns on the pump. As the water level rises the float moves up until it hits another stop, near the top of the tank, which throws the switch off. If you use an electric pump it's a good idea to invest in a float switch. With luck, you can then forget about your water supply for a good many years.

If you are taking your water from either a stream or a spring, you use much the same system. You must build a sump somewhere, either in brick or concrete or by digging a hole and inserting a plastic tank so that the water will run through it (the cheapest and easiest solution). Providing the water supply is flowing faster than your top pumping speed, the sump needs to be only large enough to house the end of the suction line with its foot valve. If your supply is really only a trickle, then you'd better start looking for another source of water now, because it's a sure thing it's going to dry up completely in a dry summer. At Eithin we had both a stream and a spring (and they both dried up in very dry weather). Early on in the building operation we devised a water system which has yet to be bettered anywhere in the world. At a point well above the house we wedged a bucket into the stream bed and ran about 100 feet of garden hose from the bucket direct to the kitchen tap. With a lot of sucking we got a siphon going, and from then on had water on tap without the help of pumps, float switches, sumps or any other modern invention. It worked perfectly, and we could easily have run the siphoning hose to a ball valve in the attic tank, and worked the plumbing system for the whole house in that way. The only trouble with the system was that not only did the stream eventually dry up in the summer, but sheep had access to it further up, and eventually we began to connect occasional bouts of disturbed stomach with the purity of the water supply (rightly or not, we shall never know).

Living and working at Eithin was in many ways like trying to run the whole world on a very small scale. At the micro-level, we experienced there many of the economic, food, water, building and other crises which are now occurring, or will soon occur, in the much bigger world outside. So what happened to our water systems may well be of some general interest.

January and February of 1974 were the two wettest months of my life. For days on end, literally, the rain never stopped. But then at the end of February there began a drought which lasted until well into July. It was the driest period known in eastern Montgomeryshire for more than 50 years, and water supplies which had never before been known to fail did so. Acres of spring crops had to be ploughed back in because they never germinated. And by the middle of May both our stream and our spring had disappeared.

We solved the problem for a few weeks by siphoning water about 400 yards up the hill from a cattle trough supplied by public water from a site a couple of miles further away. As we had previously elected not to join the public water system (at a cost of some £700), it was hardly surprising to be told after 4 weeks by the otherwise friendly farmer that we would have to think again. At the time it never occurred to us that a Welsh drought could last more than a month. But the time came when even our cattle trough was disconnected; the nearest, and probably heavily polluted water, was then half a mile away and, worse, some 300 feet below us.

We started to pump our well, unused probably for half a century. The water level soon sank beneath the magic 30-foot contour, and there was no sign of the well filling up again. We dug in damp places, and found a puddle big enough to dip a bucket in and provide a couple of gallons a day for the cow. But it didn't help us. We called in a water diviner and one of us even found he could divine as well. But whether the divination revealed deeply hidden water or buried treasure we shall never know, because it soon occurred to us that catching rainwater from the roof would be less trouble than trying (and probably failing), to dig another well.

We did have a big roof – nearly 1,600 square foot in all, plus two 400-gallon galvanized water tanks. We positioned one under each down spout from the two gutters, and then waited for the rain. From a roof that size, even a reasonable shower made quite a sizeable pool in the bottom of the tanks, and so we started by pumping the water from the outside tanks to the attic storage tank. Perhaps I should add our plumbing was complete by this time: two conventional lavatories, four hand-wash basins, a kitchen sink, a bath and a separate shower, not to mention a bidet. Working that system off rainwater, and with all 13 of us well aware of the water crisis, we found we got through 100 gallons of water a day as an absolute minimum. The few showers we were getting that summer were nothing like sufficient to cope with that demand. We disconnected the plumbing.

From then on we shared the outside earth toilet, washed in a plastic bowl in the farmyard and carried the kitchen water in by bucket to the cook. All told we probably cut our consumption down to 15 or 20 gallons a day for the whole community, plus a rather more than average consumption of pints of beer in the evening at the local pub. The community survived that way until the end of September, when the spring started to flow again. There were times, of course, when there was an occasional downpour and the two 400-gallon tanks started to overflow. Those were the bath days, when everyone tried frantically to use as much water as possible to prevent wasting any.

The moral of this story is simple enough. You can work out theoretically that the average rainfall falling on the average roof in a country like the United Kingdom cannot supply enough water to cope with demand inside the house. So much for the theoreticians. At Eithin we survived, without any real hardship, for 4 months of the worst drought for 50 years.

So survival is not at issue. The gap between what you can collect from a roof, and what would still be a reasonable level of comfort, is more difficult to assess. In the developed countries of Europe and the United States, the average domestic consumption of water is not far off 35 gallons a head a day – three times what we used at Eithin for 13 people. Of that one-third is used simply for flushing the toilet, and another third for washing the person. The rest goes to laundry, dish-washing, cooking, drinking, and odds and ends.

How much you can collect depends, of course, on the rainfall and the area of the roof – but a rainfall of 60 inches a year on a roof of 50 square yards would give you roughly 14,000 gallons a year, or an average of nearly 39 gallons a day. In practice, you would have to count on somewhat less, to allow for losses and evaporation. Further, a rainfall of 60 inches is about the highest known in the United Kingdom, and most other places in Europe and the States receive considerably less.

But there are plenty of ways to cut water consumption down without much inconvenience. The one-third we waste in flushing toilets *is* a waste – there is no reason under the sun why precious clean water should be used for that job. So one-third of your water can be saved at a stroke by arranging for the waste from hand-wash basins and baths and showers to be collected in a tank, which overflows in the normal way to the main drainage. The water from this tank is pumped up to the toilet to fill the tank. No need for expensive electric pumps here. Just install a simple foot pedal pump, and users can pump and then flush for themselves, sitting down to do it if they want!

Another big water saving can be made by taking showers instead of baths when what you really need is to be cleaned and the psychological luxury of the long hot soak is not what you're after. A shower takes less than one-sixth the water of a bath. Or you can save water by bathing with a friend. Further, if you fit atomizer sprays onto your taps used mainly for hand washing, you'll cut the water used there down to a tiny fraction of what it used to be. If you do all these things, the average domestic consumption of 35 gallons a day will come down to less than 10 gallons. In most places, that will in effect mean you could depend on rainwater from your roof for most, if not all, of the year.

But as most houses are connected to the public system, is all this really necessary? What I would like to see is a dual water system in every house – just as solar energy requires alternative heat sources. If households would only collect and use their rainwater when they had it, and revert to public water when they didn't, we would solve the water crisis for all time. No need for more big reservoirs or pumping schemes. There'd be enough water to go round for centuries to come in most places. And all you need is a big tank to collect the water and a pump to deliver it to your plumbing system.

Which brings us to the big reason why hardly anyone any longer uses rainwater. Purity. How clean must your water be? What precautions can you take? I have to be careful here, because a mistake can undoubtedly mean serious illness, even death. So do take water purity seriously – but on the other hand use your common sense. It's obvious enough that today we have over-reacted to the filth of previous centuries, and insist on water standards that are far above what is necessary. In most places in the world, and certainly anywhere more than 20 miles from an industrial city, you could drink untreated rainwater for the rest of your life and never feel an ill-effect. In my time I've drunk all manner of really filthy water and never had more than a mild stomach-ache to show for it. Now you can arrange to filter your water with sand in settling basins, treat it with chlorine to kill the bugs, and then pass it through a filter fitted on the kitchen tap. But I wouldn't bother. At Eithin we always drank untreated stream, spring or rainwater. Had we been more sensible, we would have fitted a filter on the kitchen tap, and used that for drinking and cooking. Unless your water supply is really foul, the other taps don't matter too much – even if you clean your teeth from them.

A filter will look after everything for you – except heavy metals. Of which by far the most serious is lead (make sure there's not too much on your roof if you intend drinking rainwater). All this boils down to one simple precaution: if you live near an industrial centre, consult your public health authority before drinking rainwater off the roof. If you get a clear warning from him, use water from the main for cooking and drinking, and rainwater for everything else.

Plumbing

When plumbing your house, you start from the point where the water comes in, and then work through the system to the point where the wastes leave it. The best way to tell you what to do – and how to do it – is to go through the whole system from start to finish.

The start is the cold water storage tank, as high as you can get it, almost certainly in the attic. I'd use a 50-gallon tank – smaller is too small and bigger begins to involve you in unnecessary weight problems. You need to build a good solid platform for your tank from 2 × 4s, designed to spread the load over as many rafters or roof trusses as possible. Try to situate the tank at a point where the main weight falls over a load bearing internal wall. And do buy a fibreglass tank – they're excellent and far cheaper and longer-lasting than anything else. You then need to cut holes in the tank, and to do that you buy a tank-cutter which will fit your electric drill from a hardware shop. You now come up straight away against the problem of pipe sizes.

In my opinion plumbers make a bit of a meal about this. If you are plumbing anything larger than a substantial domestic house you probably should get some technical advice. But if your plumbing is fairly conventional you can do nearly all the work using $\frac{3}{4}$-inch (now called 22 mm) and $\frac{1}{2}$-inch (15 mm) pipe. Do all the long runs and the main supply and return from hot water cylinders in $\frac{3}{4}$-inch. When you are within, say, a few yards of the appliance you can go down to $\frac{1}{2}$-inch, but avoid taking too many T connections off a $\frac{1}{2}$-inch pipe. Instead use that very useful T connection which converts $\frac{3}{4}$-inch supply lines into $\frac{1}{2}$-inch outlets.

The main exception to all this is where you have gravity feed from a heated back boiler, or cooking stove, to an indirect hot water cylinder. For that you now normally need 1-inch pipe, or possibly $1\frac{1}{4}$-inch – instructions on the appliance will make it clear. Larger pipes are needed here so that the low pressure differences generated by the heat are sufficient to push the hot water round the circuit.

Back to the tank. You need to cut three holes – two about 3 inches below the top rim to take the main supply and overflow, and one about 3 inches from the bottom to take the water to the house. Into these holes you fit connectors. With a fibreglass tank you don't need washers, but do use plenty of good quality plumber's jointing compound, smeared round both the threads and the surfaces which will fit against the tank walls. Wherever you have screw fittings in plumbing, use plenty of compound, or teflon tape which is less messy, to make sure there'll be no leaks.

The second exception to pipe sizes is, of course, the overflow. Overflows must always be at least one size bigger than the pipe that is supplying whatever you are providing the overflow to. This is so that if something does go wrong, the water will drain away through the overflow faster than it can fill the tank. Overflows must never run upwards but must fall away to wherever they discharge. The best route is usually between the roof members and out through a small hole in the fascia to a place where water overflowing will be spotted at once.

The plumbing lines fasten to the connectors mounted in the tank. At this point, you need to know how to fasten various types of pipe lines to the connector.

Pipes first. The standard pipe these days is copper, and very good it is too. It is also much easier to work than you probably suspect. Its only drawback is expense. In some localities you must use copper or iron pipe for hot-water runs. In others, special plastic pipes are permitted by building codes for both hot and cold. Both plastic and copper are easy to work with. Soldering makes copper simple. Cements or "solvent welding" make plastic even simpler. Iron pipes require special cutting and threading tools and techniques, considerably more difficult than copper or plastic. These fittings are really very cheap – you can buy them to make 45° or right angle bends, to make T connections, to screw onto the bottom fitting of a tap or a tank connector, or to reduce from one pipe size to another. This is what you do.

Cut copper pipe with a rotary cutter – never with a hacksaw. The standard cutter is provided with a reamer that you twist into the end of the pipe, to remove the burr. Failure to remove the burr effectively reduces the inside diameter of the pipe. Clean the end of the pipe and the inside of the sleeve or fitting with steel wool until they shine brightly. Smear the pipe with flux (available at hardware or plumbing outlets, along with solder in rolls) and insert it in the fitting. Twist it back and forth slightly, to distribute the flux around the entire joint.

Heat the fitting and the pipe with a blow torch until the copper becomes hot enough to melt the solder. Do not let the flame from the torch melt the solder. If the copper itself is hot enough, the solder will flow completely through and around the joint, making a solid, completely watertight joint. In practice, you don't of course solder one joint at a time. You set up a run of pipe with the necessary bends, clean all the joints and flux them, and then move all along it, from one joint to the next, soldering as you go. If you solder close to woodwork, hold a piece of asbestos sheet between the pipe and the wood to prevent fire.

Another way of making copper joints is with compression fittings. These are more expensive and in my experience more

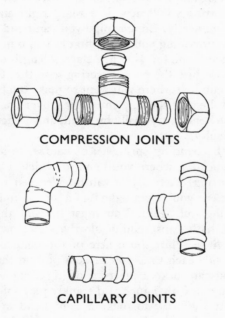

COMPRESSION JOINTS

CAPILLARY JOINTS

difficult to use. Again they provide a fitting into which you plunge the ends of the pipes, and you must then tighten two nuts on each side of the connector to grip the pipes. As the nuts tighten they compress a small copper ring inside the fitting round the pipe and – you hope – make a watertight joint. They usually do, but you must tighten the nuts very well, and you must have your pipe correctly angled to the fitting.

167

Plastic pipe and fittings come in all the varieties and sizes available in copper, and handling them is quite similar. You must ream out the burr, making sure not to leave shavings in the pipe. Then you fit things together. A small brush (usually the water-color size is big enough) carries the solvent to the joint. Capillary action spreads it in and around the joint. The plastic dissolves – then hardens again, making a tight seal. Some plastic pipes are also joined with an adhesive similar to rubber cement.

Now you can do nearly all your plumbing by using straight lengths of pipe and buying ready-made bend connectors to take you round corners and angles. But it's an expensive way of doing it. Plastic you can drape more or less wherever you want it, and the only bend fitting you'll need is a sharp right angle elbow to turn tight corners neatly. Copper pipe you can bend more or less how you want – providing you invest first in two pipe springs, one for $\frac{1}{2}$-inch pipe and one for $\frac{3}{4}$-inch. Attach a length of wire to the spring and drop it into the pipe, lowering it so that the middle of the spring ends up just where you want to make the bend. All you do now is bend the pipe the way you want it over one knee. You'll find $\frac{1}{2}$-inch pipe bends very easily by hand, and $\frac{3}{4}$-inch pipe bends with some difficulty.

The job of the bending spring is, of course, to stop the pipe crinkling and buckling where you bend it (which it certainly will do without a spring). Actually, it can buckle even with a spring, and if that happens you've got a devil of a job on your hands ever to get the spring out again. You must prevent the pipe from buckling – and that means bending slowly, very slowly, and care-fully, little by little. Shift the centre of the bend on your knee slightly to side each time you make a pull on the pipe. With $\frac{1}{2}$-inch pipe you can make a pretty good right angle bend – but where you need one with $\frac{3}{4}$-inch, I'd frankly play safe and buy an elbow fitting. It's difficult to make a tight bend in $\frac{3}{4}$-inch pipe without a pipe bending machine. It's also impossible to bend any-thing bigger than $\frac{3}{4}$ of an inch in copper without a bending machine, so any 1-inch work will have to be done either with ready-made fittings or by hiring a machine (if you can find one).

You'll meet two other snags in pipe bending. The first will be that you'll probably find the spring won't fit in the pipe. There's nothing radically wrong, except that when you cut the pipe with a pipe cutter, you may have squashed the pipe end to a smaller diameter than it is meant to have. Use the reamer to make the end of the pipe the proper diameter. When I started plumbing I didn't know this trick, and it took me the best part of a day to work out what was going on and how to correct it. If you do know, it only takes 20 seconds to ream the pipe out.

The second problem will be when you've carefully made your first perfect bend. Flushed with pride, you seize the wire on the end of the pipe spring to pull it out with a flourish. It won't budge – nor will it however much you pull, twist or screw the spring. What you have to do is to bend your pipe through slightly more of an angle than you finally require. Then, again very carefully, bend the pipe back to the angle you need. The spring will now pull out easily enough, and if it doesn't, it will if you withdraw it by pulling and screwing it round simultaneously.

That's really all there is to know about the business of working with copper. The rest is simply a matter of knowing how to connect everything up and what fittings go where.

Back at the tank, you have 3 tank bosses connected, with male threads protruding from the outside of the tank. To these, of course, you must attach a fitting with a female thread on one end, and a soldered joint on the other into which the copper pipe goes. A word about the supply to the tank. If it's from a pump then you simply connect the pump to the tank with ¾-inch pipe, and then fit the float switch. If you are using a supply main, then ½-inch pipe will be quite sufficient because of the high pressure – but you attach the line, not to a tank boss, but to a ball valve. There are two types of ball valve – high pressure and low pressure. Make sure you buy the right one – high pressure for a mains connection, and low pressure for everything else such as feeding one tank from another (see below).

The cold feed coming from the tank to the fixture is now run to the taps. Branch into ½-inch pipe at whatever point in the circuit seems convenient. Ideally you should run a separate ¾-inch cold feed from the tank direct to the inlet on the hot water heater (it's the connection at the bottom of the tank, on the side away from the 2 connectors used for the indirect hot supply). But if you want to cheat a little you can simply make a T connection from the main feed pipe supplying the taps – although it's not good plumbing practice. The rest of the cold system is straightforward enough. Use ½-inch taps for everything except the bath, where you usually use ¾-inch. Each tap must have its tap connector, which screws on to the bottom. Use plenty of jointing compound on the thread and make sure you tighten really well. Tap connectors are the most likely places for leaks to occur. And make sure that when you buy the connectors, they come with a washer in the threaded end. Without that they certainly will leak. When you attach a tap to a bath or basin, you usually use a plastic washer supplied with it to prevent the tap biting its way through the enamel or porcelain. If you can't get plastic washers, then you can use plaster or putty as a bed. But I find the best and easiest stuff to use is that sealing strip you buy in long lengths for stopping leaks round the edges of a bath where it just fails to make a good connection with the wall. The same applies to fitting wastes in basins and baths.

The hot water system works the same way, except that of course the water passes through the water heater to be warmed on its way to the taps. Your indirect heater has four connections. The one right on the top is for the pipe that supplies the taps and for the expansion pipe. The one at the bottom, on its own, is for the cold water feed. And the other two, mounted one above the other on the other side, are for the indirect hot water supply – the top one for the feed and the bottom one for the return. You need tank connectors for all four fittings, and plenty of compound (yet again) on the threads which are another likely source of leaks. Inspect the cylinder to see what sizes, and whether male or female threads, are needed for the tank connectors.

The one thing you must remember about the water heater is the expansion pipe. Fix the supply pipe for the taps to the top connection, turning the pipe through 90° so that it runs horizontally as it leaves the heater. Then, after a few inches, fit a T junction, with one output horizontal and the other pointing vertically up. The horizontal connection you then run to the hot taps. The vertical connection is joined to a pipe which runs up to the attic, rises above the cold water storage tank, and then bends over it. Its function is to discharge boiling water and steam harmlessly into the tank should anything over-heat. Your vent pipe must always be left open and there must never be a shut-off or any other valve between the open end and the heater itself. I know, because a stupid plumber once fitted a shut-off in one of my vent pipes. One day I accidentally turned it shut, and the hot water heater simply caved in and split, like an eighteenth-century experiment demonstrating the force of a vacuum (which is what it was). Believe me, 30 gallons of hot water suddenly discharged through the bathroom floor and into the kitchen is no joke.

Don't forget shut-off valves in other places, though. If you have a public supply, you need one before the supply gets to the ballcock in the cold water storage tank. You need another in the feed from the tank to the taps. And you need a combined drain and stop fitted just before the cold water enters the hot water heater. If you work it out, you'll see that a drainfaucet at that point is in fact the only way of ever emptying the hot water heater, because it is so connected that hot water can never be drawn off if the cold water supply is turned off. You can in fact drain a cylinder without a draincock in that position by disconnecting the top connection and siphoning out the water with a garden hose – but it's a messy business.

It is usual also to fit a shut-off in front of any other fitting which houses a ball valve. So use one between the cold water tank and subsidiary top-up tanks used for central heating or back boiler systems. You should also install a shut-off immediately in front of each toilet tank – but if your main cold water shut-off is easily accessible, it's not really necessary.

One thing remains. You must plumb in the hot water heating system – about which I've already said a good deal in the chapters on heat and solar energy. For a solar roof, follow the directions in that chapter. If you're heating water only with an immersion heater (a deplorably wasteful practice), then you need only a straight-forward copper tank with a fitting for an immersion heater. But if you have some other heat source to warm the water, then you need an indirect cylinder and a separate plumbing circuit for it.

This is known as the primary circuit. It must start from a separate cold water storage tank, though this need only be very small, 5 or perhaps 10 gallons. The supply to this should be branched from the main before it reaches the principal cold water tank; if you are pumping water, you have no choice but to take a further supply from the principal cold water tank to the smaller tank. From there the water is run to join the primary return somewhere before it re-enters the boiler; a separate expansion pipe must be installed over the smaller tank. The rest of the circuit consists simply of joining the flow from the boiler to the top connection of the two on the

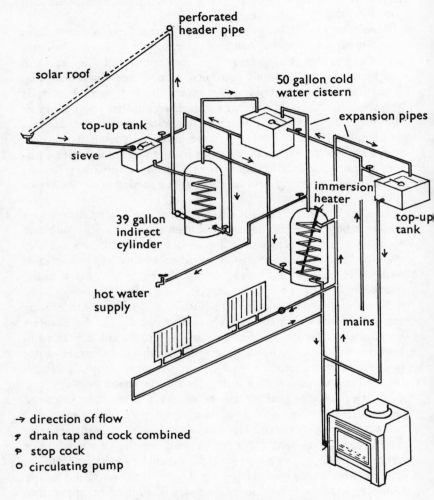

perforated
header pipe

solar roof

50 gallon cold
water cistern

expansion pipes

top-up tank

sieve

immersion
heater

top-up
tank

39 gallon
indirect
cylinder

hot water
supply

mains

→ direction of flow
⌇ drain tap and cock combined
⌀ stop cock
○ circulating pump

PLUMBING FOR COMBINED SOLAR ROOF,
WATER AND SPACE HEATER

Note: In US systems, immersion heaters are not normally used. The stop-cock is the shut-off valve and the top-up tank, the storage tank.

indirect cylinder. The return flow links the bottom connection on the cylinder with the return connection on the boiler – don't forget a drainfaucet at the point where the return enters the boiler. If you're fitting radiators, branch them off in parallel – so that hot water will still flow, even if all radiators are turned off – from the flow pipe before it reaches the cylinder. If you don't get enough flow in your primary circuit, try to make sure all air bubbles are gone, and bleed the radiators of air with the key provided. If it's still no go, you'll have to install a circulating pump.

If your plumbing is now complete, and all the wastes connected, now is the time for the test. For this you need all the family and as many friends as you can find. Station them at strategic points round the circuit armed with mops, cloths and plastic bowls. Turn on the main shut-off but keep all the others closed. By opening one valve after the other, let the water progressively into the system, checking at each stage for major leaks. There's bound to be at least one, and you'll usually be able to cure it simply by tightening a nut. If not, drain the system and remake the joint.

When everything is turned on, you'll find the cold water flows perfectly but the hot hisses and spurts and dribbles. You've got an air lock and you need to know what to do about it. Some will just go away with time. But if you've any sense, you'll have fitted to the bath what is called a mixer valve with a shower attachment. This has two taps for the hot and cold, and one spout. A lever above the spout directs the mixed water either into the bath through the spout or up to a shower head. This is the cheapest way of providing you with a bath and a good shower. It's also a ready-made device for clearing air locks. Turn on the hot water tap in the bath and one other hot tap at the lowest point in the circuit. Then place the palm of your hand firmly under the bath spout, push up hard, and turn on the bath cold water tap. Because you've closed the spout with your hand, you'll force the cold water back through the hot water system and eventually out through the other open tap. On its way, the cold water will chase out all air bubbles. You'll know when it's done the trick because the circuit will convulse with an immensely satisfactory series of jerks and hiccups.

If you don't have a bath mixer tap, you can do the same job less easily by connecting a cold tap to a hot tap with a piece of hose, and opening both taps. Hang on to the hose, though, or the water pressure will tear it off.

173

One final plumbing tip. Every good plumber carries with him the inner-tube of a motor tire, a pair of scissors and a compass. With that you can make your own washer to fit any device. And it's surprising how often you need a washer you haven't got. You can also repair the flush valve in a toilet with that kit for nothing. After a few years the large washer that sets up the siphon in the tank often falls to pieces. If you drain the tank and remove the siphon attachment, you'll see easily enough what has happened. All you need to do is cut a piece of inner tube slightly smaller than the diameter of the siphon chamber inside, and attach it as was the original washer. It's a quick fix that will work perfectly for many years and will cost you nothing. But this depends very much on the type of valve and on other factors – so don't count on its working in every case.

Drains

However ambitious you want to be in devising new ways of disposing of waste, and to use what is normally thrown out as garden compost and as a source of cooking gas, you won't get very far unless you know how to operate the conventional system. So I make no apology for describing how to connect your house to main drainage or a septic tank. The trouble with so many alternative technologists is that they never learned how to cope with ordinary technology. Hence their marvellous new ideas rarely work in practice.

The heart of your drainage system is known as the stack. It's a 4-inch diameter pipe, bought in 3 or 4 metre lengths, which runs vertically from the main drain to not less than 3 feet above the nearest opening to an inhabited room. Into this stack you attach your waste pipes – baths, basins and toilets – and the section of pipe which lies above these connections is left open, capped with only a grill to keep out leaves and debris. This half is called the vent pipe, and one of its jobs is to let the stink away at a level where no one's going to notice it. The other, lower section of the pipe is attached to the main drain – you buy a special connector with the pipe – and is called the soil pipe. Fitting it all up is about the easiest building job you'll ever have to do.

The stack pipe can run either inside the house and up through the roof, or outside attached to the outside wall. If it's inside, you need a flange through which you stick the vent pipe. The flange has a collar around the pipe and prevents any moisture coming in off the roof. As I've said before, if you are re-roofing make sure to get the flange fixed in the right place in advance. To fix a flange on an

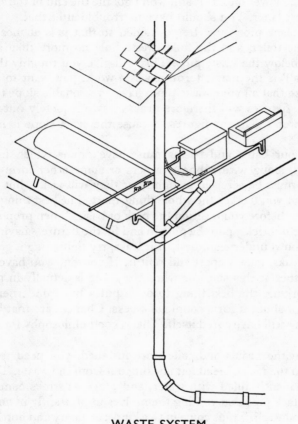

WASTE SYSTEM

existing roof means taking off, and then replacing, an awful lot of roofing.

Each length of stack pipe comes with a 'push-fit' connection at the bottom. The connecting section, with two waste inlet holes and a toilet inlet, you buy separately and is only a foot or so long.

Believe me, the push-fit method of connecting two of these pipes together does need a lot of push – unless you know how to do it. First try smearing the inside sleeve well with wax or detergent. You'll have to twist as well as push and once it starts going in, it'll slip home easily enough until you feel the upper length hit a rim inside the lower one. If it still won't go, file the end of the sleeve to a smooth taper. You should have no trouble after that.

The stack pipe must be positioned so that it is at most 3 feet from the toilet, and the toilet waste hole no more than about 6 inches below the waste pipe. This will give you roughly the right fall. 'Fall' is the magic term in waste work; you want to arrange things so that all your waste pipes have a reasonable slope to them, and the fixtures will therefore drain away adequately but not too fast. I won't give any figures, because the exact slope is not very critical.

All your baths and basins must have drains which fasten in position, along with rubber washers or some other form of seal. Drains must be screwed in tightly or they will leak – but not too tightly or you'll crack the whole thing apart. The best thing is to fit the drain before you position the bath or basin. Then prop it up on a couple of bricks, pop the plug in and fill the fixture – having put a plastic bowl underneath first. If it leaks, try tightening it gently. If it still leaks, take it apart and refit it. If you find you have a slow leak, either at this stage or when the thing is actually in position and working, the best thing to do is put a bowl underneath and forget all about it for a couple of weeks. Chances are that by then the thing will have cured itself. This is good philosophy for all slow leaks.

When the basins and toilets are installed, you need to attach a trap to the male thread left sticking out from the waste. The trap is permanently filled with water, and prevents stinks coming out of the stack pipe and venting themselves unpleasantly in your face while you wash. Traps come in two kinds: ordinary and bottle-type. Use the bottle-type if you have an exceptionally steep fall to your waste line, or if the waste pipe connects to another waste pipe before entering the stack – in which case there is a danger that when one basin empties, the water flowing away will suck out the water from the trap on the other basin, and your bathroom will stink to high heaven. The bottle trap is designed to prevent that.

At Eithin we had only one problem with all this. And that was fitting the drain onto a shower tray. Showers, and some old-fashioned sinks, come with a roughly fashioned hole in the bottom into which you have to fit the drain. The fitting inside the basin is easy enough but the underside is so rough that when you tighten the nut, using a big rubber washer or putty or sealing strip, you never get anything like a good seal. We sweated with this for hours, and eventually went off to consult a builder's merchant. His advice turned out to be good. Make two large leather washers, he said, and sandwich between them a lead washer cut out from a piece of lead flashing. Put plenty of compound between them, and on the underside of the shower tray, and tighten it all up. We did, and it worked first time.

You may also have a problem with the height of the bath. If the lavatory is on the floor, and the holes in the stack positioned to give the correct fall to the waste pipe connecting them, you'll probably find that if you stand the bath on its own feet and screw on the trap, the trap exit is almost level with the drain it has to be connected with in the stack. In other words, your bath is going to take a couple of days to drain away – and there's nothing worse than a bathful of someone else's scummy water when you want to get in it. You have to raise the bath. At Eithin we propped it up 6 inches by nailing 3 pieces of 2 × 4 together and placing them under the legs. The bath will look ridiculously high when you do it, but it will drain well. And you'll soon find the height seems perfectly natural.

If you want a sunken bath, or for some other reason your levels don't work out, you'll have to drill a new hole in the stack pipe to receive the waste. But it must be more than 9 inches below the nearest toilet fitting on the stack, or all manner of very unpleasant happenings may take place. You buy a special fitting to go in the hole, and fix it there with special plumber's glue for PVC fittings. By and large, it's easier to prop up the bath, if you can. Don't forget when you do that to prop the back slightly higher than the drain end so that the last drop of water does find its way into the plug hole.

Finally, a salutary story about the connection between the bottom of the stack and the main drain. The drains will have been laid along with the floor slab, and for months you'll have had the end of a ceramic drain sticking up somewhere in the kitchen floor (or in the garden if your stack is outside). The stack simply fits into this, and you buy a special end connector to fit on the pipe to ensure that, when you finally make a nicely rounded joint between the two with cement, it all holds together well. When we finished the plumbing at Eithin, we were of course so keen to start using it (we'd had no plumbing facilities apart from the kitchen tap for eight months) that we didn't bother waiting to seat the joint. Nor, foolishly, did I think to clear the main drain between the kitchen and the manhole outside – it had after all been laid new only a few months previously. For a day or two all went splendidly – and then one morning we came down to find the kitchen floor afloat, and liquid bubbling up from the loose joint where the cement should have been.

We pushed the drain rods up from the manhole to see what the obstruction was, and found the rods reached about one foot short of the clear end in the kitchen floor. That meant lifting out the stack pipe and plunging the hand down a foot into the main drain. It came up with bits of old timber, concrete, hardcore, a piece of sacking, half an old cement bag, a ping-pong ball and a child's toy car. So what you should do is clear your main drain, fit your stack pipe, test it thoroughly and when you're sure it's working, cement that final joint. Luckily for us, we hadn't started to use the toilets seriously before we discovered the flood.

Chapter 10

❧❀❧

Waste and compost

THE nuclear arms race and the sewage disposal system of the so-called developed countries must surely be the two greatest follies of the contemporary world. First we lace our countries with huge networks of underground pipes to carry our waste away. Then we spend millions building factories to hasten the decay and control of that waste – a process which nature can manage quite satisfactorily without help from man. And then we chuck the result into a nearby river or sea, where it over-fertilizes the environment and produces a great deal of havoc. Rational men would be hard put to devise a more expensive way of throwing out a valuable resource.

Small wonder we're going bankrupt. And small wonder that our farm soils get poorer and poorer every year. They need – and doubtless will continue to get as long as farmers can afford it – more and more artificial fertilizer every year. Whereas what they should be getting is the human waste that is polluting our beaches. A sensible system, like the one the Chinese have practised for millennia, of returning human shit to the field might not solve the world food problem overnight – but it would go a long way towards it.

If you live in a block of high-rise flats, there may be some excuse for using a public sewerage system until the authorities come up with something better. But everyone else ought to be hard at it devising alternatives. You'd be better off with an old-fashioned outside privy, a chemical toilet in the house, a septic tank system, or one of the composting lavatories that have the additional benefit of needing no water for flushing. If you want to go one better than that, turn to the next chapter to find out how to use your waste to make methane for cooking.

But before you start, it pays to know where you stand legally. If you buy a cottage which has an outside privy or a chemical toilet (or of course a septic tank or cess pit) it's perfectly legal to carry on using it. But if you start to change the plumbing around, the Building Inspector will end up by making you install a septic tank, or connect to public sewage drains if they're nearby. So if you want to stick with a primitive device you have either to leave your building much as it is, or carry out a series of clandestine alterations.

Actually, a septic tank is not a bad solution, apart from its cost. We put one in at Eithin, largely because of Building Regulations. We would have preferred to install a composting Clivus (see page 191), but found they could not deal with the liquid wastes from baths and sinks. Of course, there was a perfectly good liquid drainage system, ending up down the hill in a soak-away – a large pit filled with small stones and topped off with earth. But because we were doing so much work on the house we had to put all our waste water through a new and 'improved' system. The irony, of course, is that the waste water from a septic tank eventually finds its way into a soak-away of exactly the type already in use. But at least we ran the drains from the tank down under the vegetable garden – and both we and the vegetables did well enough on the result. A septic tank needs emptying only every few years, but if you do it yourself – or persuade the emptier to part with his pickings – there's no reason why your solid waste shouldn't end up in the garden, where it belongs, as well.

Septic tanks

A septic tank needs to be as far away from the house as is convenient – say at least 50 feet – and downhill from it if there's a slope to the land. From the manhole immediately outside your house, you run a 4-inch pitch-fibre pipe to another manhole immediately in front of the tank. From there the wastes flow into the tank which acts as a digester, a settling basin and a storage pit. In other words, the solids sink to the bottom, the bugs work on the chemicals to break them down and the liquids which flow out should be completely sterile. They run into land drains, usually arranged in a herring-bone pattern, and are then meant to drain away into the ground. But it doesn't always work quite like that in practice – at least not until your tank has settled down, which may take a few years.

My experience of tank building is not very happy. For a start, you have to decide whether to build your tank or buy a fibreglass one. The latter look like enormous yellow onions and the smallest hold 600 gallons. No septic tank should be smaller than that, or it won't work at all; in fact, it should be big enough to hold the effluents from two days' waste from the house. If you work it out, and find you need more than 600 gallons, the answer is not to build a bigger tank – which is expensive and time-consuming – but to cut down water consumption in the house. We estimated that by using 2 skins of semi-engineering bricks we could build our own tank for half the cost of buying a yellow plastic bubble. In the end I don't think we did, and the trauma of trying to build it was certainly not worth whatever saving we did make.

We must have had at least 10 inches of rain the month we built our tank. The steep path down to the tank turned into an avalanche of mud through which we tried to barrow bricks, mortar and concrete. Water poured into the hole from every conceivable direction so we worked all the time standing ankle deep. Some days it rained so hard that the mortar between brick courses was simply washed away and the bricks had to be relaid the next day. Conditions were so foul that we each took short spells at brick laying, and that meant that the bricks ended up all over the place. The moral of the story is to build your tank in a dry month. We'd have done it twice as well and four times as quickly in the summer. In fact, if I were doing it again, I'd buy a plastic onion; only if the prospect of saving $100 to $200 is a matter of life and death would it be worth building your own.

If you do decide to do so, you can choose between using semi-engineering bricks and building a concrete tank. If you've a lot of manpower, and have had some experience of concrete and formwork, the latter will be quicker. Of course, in both cases you start with a 6-inch concrete floor, and you must cover the insides and floor of both types with waterproof sealer so that the tank doesn't leak. Both need a lid and we cast concrete slabs, 5 feet long, 9 inches wide and 3 inches deep to go over the top of ours. That worked fairly well, but don't forget to put a couple of pieces of reinforcing in each slab or they'll simply break in two when you lift them up. Slabs like that can be transported fairly easily by one man balancing them across a barrow, with the slab positioned fairly near the handles. One of these slabs should be poured with a piece of pipe stuck in the middle to allow gases to vent away, and to receive the end of the pump when the tank must be emptied.

The drawing shows the basic design for a septic tank. We built a single compartment model but by all accounts a double one works better. If you use that, the first compartment should be twice as big as the second. Note that both the input and the output pipes terminate well below the water level. This is so that the tank fills and empties without disturbing the thick crust which will form on the surface. This is important for good operation. The entry

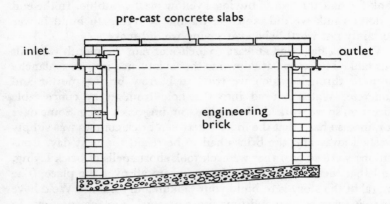

SEPTIC TANK

and exit T pipes are made specially for septic tanks – make sure you buy the proper ones. But one awful warning. We used them full length, so that the down pipes stopped about 9 inches above the tank floor. After a couple of weeks we found our manhole full of waste and the whole system relentlessly backing up towards the house. The solids had jammed in the space between the floor and the pipe. I spent an indescribable February morning with my arm immersed to the elbow in freezing shit trying to saw the end of the pipe off under water. I have to report that it's considerably easier and more pleasant to saw the pipe off before you begin to use the tank.

When you've finished the tank, and put the slabs in place, cover them with some old plastic and put 6 inches of earth and some grass seed on top. By the summer the grass will have grown up and you'll never know a tank is there, apart from the vent pipe sticking up.

Installing a septic tank involves quite a lot of excavation. You can certainly dig the main drain to the tank, and the trenches for the herring-bone land drains, by hand. You can also dig the hole for the 600-gallon tank, although it may take you much longer than you reckon. Once again it's a question of cost. A mechanical excavator will scoop out the big hole in an hour or two – and of course while you have one on the site you may as well have it excavate all the trenches as well. If so, the operator will have a full day's work on his hands – but one which will save you a couple of weeks' steady digging. If you're on stony ground use an excavator every time.

For land drains, you can use short lengths of ceramic pipe butted loosely against each other to leave a crack large enough to allow some of the flow to drain away. But it's cheaper to buy special plastic land drain – 3-inch pipe for the back bone which comes fitted with T junctions to take the 2-inch pipes which run off in herring-bone fashion. When you install the pipes, 'blind' the bottom of the trenches with a couple of inches of gravel first to make a better drain. If you don't have gravel, use broken slate or some small stones and rocks. The plastic pipe, incidentally, is slitted at about 1-foot intervals to let the effluent drain away.

Once your tank is working, inspect the ends of these drains very carefully (you should leave them exposed for this reason). If all the liquid is draining away in the ground before it gets to the end, well and good. Cover the ends up and forget them. But if liquid is still coming out of the ends, you must terminate each one in a soak-away. Dig a biggish pit, much deeper than the drains, fill it with rocks to above the level of the drains and then back-fill with earth. That should do the trick. The drain trenches, incidentally, should be about 2 feet deep.

The only trouble with the herring-bone system is that it's rather a hit and miss affair as to how much liquid goes down each pipe. You can go one better by building what is grandly known as a distribution box below the tank itself. This consists of a small square brick box, once again sealed to make it waterproof. The effluent is led in on one side. And 3 drains lead away from near the bottom of the other sides. The effluent then begins to fill up the

Section

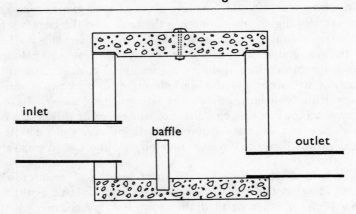

Plan

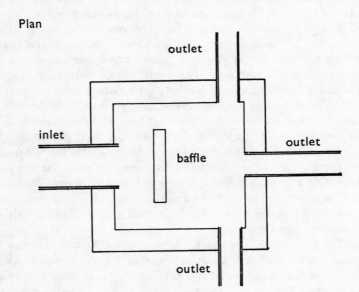

DISTRIBUTION BOX

box and when it reaches the levels of the drains it flows out through them equally.

Whatever you do, don't forget the manhole just in front of the tank. If you try to economize and miss it out, it's a safe bet that one day your main drain from the house to the tank will block up. If it does, you'll then have to dig down, saw the main drain in half and try to insert drain rods up the end. If you've got your manhole there, you'll never be frightened of blockage because it's the easiest thing in the world to push drain rods up from a ready-made manhole.

The privy

Wherever you live, providing you have at least a pocket-sized garden or yard, you should also have a privy. A privy is the most ancient and simple method of disposing of human waste. It uses no water, costs no more than the price of a piece of board to install, and keeps your wastes where you want them – under your control. But there is no point in having a privy as well as a septic tank or main drainage unless you are prepared to make use of human compost.

Except for the past 50 years or so in western society, human waste has always been put back on the land where it belongs. Even in our society, we shall not be able to afford to throw out such a valuable resource for much longer. The alternative, of synthesizing nitrogenous fertilizers using other natural resources, is already proving a great expense for most farmers. The only solution is once again to make use of human compost.

That idea has long been out of fashion – mainly for reasons of hygiene. And of course it is true that some of the most diabolical epidemics of history were caused by disease organisms being passed from person to person via their excrement. To overcome that problem, we have tried to hide the excrement away where it won't show and where no one can ever again come into contact with it. Instead we should have learnt how to render it simultaneously both harmless and useful.

Nine times out of ten you'll catch nothing from handling excrement because if you are healthy what you excrete will not contain anything very harmful. You can spread cholera or typhoid or food poisoning in that way only if someone is already suffering from the disease. Of course what you excrete is full of bugs – always. It's possible that a few of those bugs, with which you have learnt to live in harmony, may cause a very mild upset if they find their way into another human body which is not so used to them. But that should not be counted as disease – but as the same kind of internal adaptation which you have to go through every time you travel to a different climate and eat different kinds of food. So, particularly if you don't live in the tropics, there's little to worry about in an otherwise healthy society.

Nevertheless, we shall always have to treat excrement with respect. And that means good composting to render your wastes biologically sterile before you start using them in the garden (see next section). Anyone who uses untreated manure of any kind on his garden is asking for trouble anyway, because he'll probably 'burn' most of his plants into the ground.

The privy at Eithin was a two-seater housed in a stone hut on the hill behind the house with a magnificent view. Even after we installed all our plumbing most of us continued to use it. On a farm it's nonsense to have to walk to a house, change your boots and take off your coat every time nature calls. So use your privy. If you build one, you need first of all some kind of shelter to put it in, and then simply a board into which you cut bottom-sized holes. A two-seater is a good idea – providing you use one hole at a time. You need a sack of hay or straw or some similar compostible material. Throw a handful on every time you use the privy. Hay is a marvellous absorber of odour, and a privy used like that should never stink. There was a time in England when pubs used to hang balls of hay from the ceiling to absorb tobacco smoke and other odours – a practice which any sensible publican would revive forthwith.

If you have hens, you'll need to put an old slate over each hole to stop them laying their eggs down there. Ours always did, and that was the messiest and most revolting part of an otherwise very satisfactory arrangement (yes, we did eat the eggs!). When one hole was full it was left unused until the other was filled up. Then the man of the week took a rake, and pulled out the garbage through a hole in the back of the privy, threw it on a nearby compost heap, and covered it with another layer of straw or old hay. One detail we found helpful was to encourage people to learn to shit and pee at different times – it's quite possible, for both men and women. A special bucket was provided for the pee, which could then be thrown almost anywhere. Pee is normally completely sterile and will not do any great harm in small amounts. But don't throw it directly on to valuable plants or it may well burn them. This separation of two normally associated functions makes the handling of decaying matter much more pleasant.

There are plenty of variations you can work on this system. For instance, in south-east Asia a similar two-seater system is in operation, with each hole being topped up with a mixture of sand and ashes after use. When one hole is full it is sealed off and allowed to rot down until the other hole is full (they use buckets in each hole). Because of the high temperatures in that part of the world, the first bucket is fully composted by the time the second is full. Its contents are then put straight on the farm or garden. That might work for you too, depending on where you live. But if you think the composting hasn't completely finished, play safe and compost it again before using it.

Don't, on any account, use a chemical toilet out-of-doors unless you have some particular reason for wanting to waste money. Those chemicals are expensive, and all they do for you is render your waste sterile. You must still compost the result (the chemical won't harm the workings of your compost heap, the manufacturers claim) and the smell of the chemical is if anything more objectionable than the one it's meant to disguise.

Chemical lavatories are useful only indoors – where you obviously can't muck about with sacks of hay and rakes. In fact, they're a very good solution to the whole problem, providing you train your family to pee somewhere else wherever possible (otherwise you'll be emptying the bucket nearly every day). When we first arrived at Eithin we had chemical toilets in the trailers, and used laboriously to dig a hole in the ground for each bucketful and pour it away. Doubtless it was good for the ground, but we later found that you could add the stuff to the garden compost heap without endangering the heap. The whole art of using both privies and chemical toilets depends in the end on your being a good enough composter to use the stuff on your garden.

Composting

Anybody can compost anything using any technique. All you have to do is throw all your organic waste into a heap, and leave it. It will, in time, turn into that black, crumbly soil so beloved of old-fashioned gardeners. But unless you want to wait five years or so, you must use a bit of common sense in composting; if you really need to you can compost from 14 days up. If your own personal wastes are going on as well, then you must really compost well; unless your heap gets to very high temperatures, the organisms which might prove dangerous one day will never be killed.

Don't compost anything that can be eaten. If *you* can't eat it, then give it to the pig, or the cow, or the chickens, or the rabbits. They are much better compost heaps than anything you'll ever make. And they'll grow fat in the process, which is presumably why you're keeping them. But if you don't have such animals then you should compost all your organic wastes, even if you have only a few square yards of garden. No point in buying expensive fertilizer, and overloading the garbage collection system, when you need do neither.

A good compost heap is started with around 6 inches of rubbish – lawn clippings, potato peelings, discarded lettuce leaves, ordinary leaves, weeds, straw or whatever. To that you add a couple of inches of good honest manure. Poultry droppings are the best of all, but anything, including human shit, will do. If you don't have any manure, then squat down on top of the heap a couple of times and provide the necessary – because your heap will go the better for it. Then add an inch or so of compost from the last heap – or, if this is your first one, the same amount of the richest soil you can find. Finally, sprinkle a layer of ashes or ground limestone or some other mineral powder which will correct the mineral balance of the heap, and prevent it getting too acid. Then get the heap good and wet – not sopping, but just right. Go on building up layers like that until you reach a height of 5 feet or so.

What should then happen is that the heap gets very hot. It will take a few days, depending on the weather, and on how wet your heap is. If you don't get the required results, you'll have to add some compost starter which you can buy commercially under various names, to provide you with the right bugs (it's very cheap, but not as cheap as muck, which should do the same thing). Make very sure the inside of the heap has got good and hot. And then, after say 3 to 6 weeks, when the temperature has died down, you must turn the heap. The best way is to move all the material on to another heap to one side. Try to get the outside of the old heap into the middle of the new one. Wet it again. Watch the temperature rise again. Turn and compost twice more, and in a total of 3 to 6 months, depending on whether it's winter or summer, you'll have the most beautiful compost in the world.

If you want to do the same thing in less than a month, you'll need both compost activator and a mechanical shredder. You put all your compost through the shredder first, which turns it into tiny morsels which the bugs will get their teeth into much more quickly. You don't have to worry too much about the layering because a shredded heap works pretty well whatever way you build it up. And you turn it every 3 or 4 days until it's done.

If the contents of your privy are eventually to go on to your garden, I would recommend that you make this routine a bit more complicated. Make a couple of heaps behind the privy and just compost that material on its own there. It'll rot down perfectly well. When the first heap is pretty much done, cart it to the garden compost heap and incorporate it there layer by layer in the way I've just described. That means all human material will be composted twice. And that means it'll be pretty old by the time it reaches the garden. The chances that all the bugs will have been killed by the high temperature will therefore be twice as high. It plays to be a bit safe.

Most of the rest of the art of composting is a matter of architecture. You should build your heap to about 5 feet high but the other dimensions will depend on how much stuff you have to compost. In any case, you need to make some kind of box to put it in, and the art is in making the box compost-tight but not air-tight. You need all the air you can get to make it go quickly. My favourite is chicken wire around three sides, with an arrangement on the fourth which allows you to drop boards in a slot and keep the compost in as you build it up. That means 4 stout posts, one at each corner. If you're blessed with an abundance of old planks, you can use them all the way round, making sure you leave air gaps between each. It's also a good idea to build your heap up with 2 or 3 stakes planted firmly in the middle. When the heap has gone as high as it can go, pull the stakes out to leave ventilation shafts reaching right down to the bottom of the heap.

Start your heap off on some old bits of timber, arranged criss-cross so that air can get underneath, with brushwood over the top to support the compost. And if you really want to make the best of your compost, pour a concrete platform for each heap, sloping down to a drain which drips into a tank or tub of some kind. What you collect in that tub – called by the enthusiasts compost tea – will be nothing short of the elixir of life. It'll make anything grow. And you'll overcome the worst problem of composting, which is leaching. Many of the chemicals you want from the heap are water-soluble and, if the heap gets too wet, will simply be washed away. You can prevent that to some extent by covering the heap with some old plastic in very wet weather (and in very dry weather, to stop it drying off). But collecting the washings via a drain is certainly the de luxe way of doing it.

In any case, the area round your compost heap is going to get very rich. You might as well make good use of it by growing grape vines or some other exotic perennial plant round the edge. If you choose something that grows tall, you'll hide the heap as well.

When we lived in London my wife used to make compost in a couple of old trash cans. She simply shoved all the waste in, and forgot about it. They were never watered, there was no air flow, no manure and no activator. But we always got a couple of good trash cans full of compost every year. So why worry? Unless you're in a hurry, or you want to include human manure and make sure of killing bugs and weed seeds, it doesn't really matter much how you compost.

The ultimate solution

If you stop and think about the problem of waste for a bit, it's pretty easy to see what the final answer should be. You need a device that brings both the compost heap and the outside privy into the house. That way you could make your compost and evacuate your bowel at the same time, in comfort, use no wasteful water, and produce fertilizer for the garden. In other countries some devices have got near the idea. In South Africa and Japan, for instance, they often use a kind of septic tank which houses the toilet seat right on top of the tank. The chute from the toilet leads down into the tank, under water, and you don't really need to use water to flush. But a septic tank is not a compost heap.

The most sensible waste disposal device so far invented comes from Sweden. Basically it's a huge plastic tank which you install in the cellar or underground. There are two fittings to the top of the tank, into one of which goes a specially designed toilet seat. The other houses a chute for kitchen garbage. And there's a vent pipe which leads up to the roof to take the smells away. It sounds simple, but the inside is scientifically designed to produce currents of air

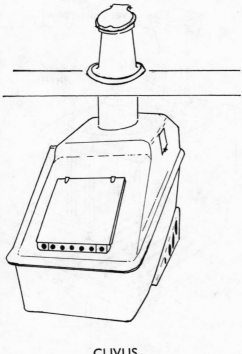

CLIVUS

in exactly the right places. They are arranged so that there is always a down draught through the toilet seat and garbage chute, and no smells can get out. The air also flows round the composting material to speed decay, and helps remove excess moisture as vapour through the vent pipe. A family of four using this device – called a Clivus – makes only a few buckets of good rich compost a year. Emptying is easy, and done annually. Every house should have one.

As yet there are plenty of reasons why they don't. Last time I enquired, the total cost of such a device, imported from Sweden with all the trimmings, was about $1,500. Cheaper by far to build a

septic tank – especially as you may have to anyway, to take care of
liquid waste (technically, foul water). Why a large piece of plastic
should cost that much I have no idea – though of course the price

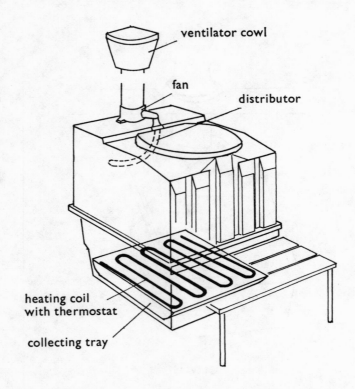

ventilator cowl

fan

distributor

heating coil
with thermostat

collecting tray

THE MULLBÄNK COMPOSTING LAVATORY

would come tumbling down if the demand were bigger. Again,
the Clivus is just too big – about 10 feet long, 8 feet high and 4 feet
wide. Considering how little material it has actually to store, it
should be possible to make something similar but smaller. More
research needed. And lastly the Clivus is not yet fully capable of
taking all the liquid wastes from baths and sinks, as well as
excrement and kitchen rubbish. You still need a separate waste
water drainage system. You can, of course, use the 'farm-style'

soak-away system for bath and sink wastes, which is good enough –
though it does involve a fair amount of digging and will not be
approved by a building inspector.

Nevertheless, the Clivus is winning a battle for us. It's been
approved by a number of official Swedish bodies, and it's passed
all manner of scientific tests with flying colours. Incidentally, it's
also one of the few alternative devices which is labour-saving.
There's less work involved in taking out two bucketfuls of compost
every year or so than there is in keeping a flush toilet clean and in
good running order. In the US, write to Clivus Multrum Inc.,
14A Eliot Street, Cambridge, Mass. 02138 for information.

The only alternative that is currently available is best described
as an electric toilet. This is basically the Clivus scaled down to a
size not much bigger than an ordinary toilet. Again no water and
no drains, and a good few bucketfuls of rich compost every year to
boot. But there is a snag. Although small, it does its job only with
the benefit of a small electrical heating element and a fan to push
the warm air around. You need an electrical outlet, and a hole in
the roof for the vent pipe. The device itself rates around 150-200
watts, but even so one of the manufacturers claims that their
toilet uses around 4 kWh of juice a day. And that's a lot of electricity. Currently I'm running a Swedish-made electric toilet – the
Mullbänk – and very good it is too. As the Ecolet, it sold in the US
in mid-1976 for about $630. A similar composting toilet, the
Bioloo, also manufactured in Sweden, was available from Ecos,
Inc., 69 Hickory Drive, Waltham, Mass. 02154, for $750. Also
similar, and requiring even less frequent waste removal, is the
Biu-Let (manufactured in Sweden as the Mull-Toa), distributed
in the US by Bio-Utility Systems, Inc., Box 135, Narberth, Pa.
19072, at $595. If the electricity consumption could be cut down,
these composting toilets would certainly be the final answer to the
problem of sewage.

Chapter 11

Methane

ANYONE who's really gloomy about the future of energy ends up by worrying about food. If our farms were suddenly denied access to diesel fuel, the flow of food they produce would dry up in a few months. To get back to horses would take quite a few years, and even then we'd find our food production greatly reduced – for horses eat up a lot of acres.

But there's no need to worry. There's a perfectly good alternative solution which would make all our farms more or less self-sufficient in energy. If they composted all their wastes – manure and straw and vegetable tops – anaerobically, without air, they'd produce enough methane to run their tractors, power their machinery and light their buildings. If a country like the United States composted all the organic waste that it could easily get its hands on in that way, it would produce enough methane to provide about 2 per cent of its total power needs. That may not sound a lot – but with good insulation, sound fuel economy and a more sensible set of priorities, it would go a long way towards avoiding disaster. We may yet come to it.

This business of methane production is nothing new. During the last war many farms operated methane plants, and many farmers, particularly in Germany and France, could be seen driving about with plastic bags full of methane on top of their cars which they used instead of petrol. Some of those plants are still working. And in India there has been a spate of research over the past 20 years to produce what they call gobar gas – literally cow gas – from cow dung. As a result an estimated 2,500 Indian farms now make their own methane from very simple plant. Even in the developed world quite a few sewage works compost anaerobically. They use the methane produced to run electrical generators, and usually provide more than enough electricity for their own wants. On that scale, there's nothing unusual or very difficult about it.

But whether you can do the same and produce anything worth the effort is another matter. The household methane digester has yet to be perfected, and it's easy to see why. The average human being produces enough waste each day to produce just 1 cubic foot (0·028 cubic metres) of bio-gas – the stuff which actually comes out of a methane digester and which contains some 65 per cent methane (CH_4), 35 per cent carbon dioxide, and a few traces of this and that. If you burn that bio-gas it gives off energy – about 600 BTU for every cubic foot of gas, or 6·3 kWh for every cubic metre. Now 600 BTU – or its metric equivalent 0·176 kWh – could be used either to boil a little less than 3 pints of water or to provide the heat equivalent to running a single-bar electric fire for just 10½ minutes. You aren't going to get very far with that. For cooking alone, the average family needs about 32 cubic feet or nearly a cubic metre of bio-gas.

But the picture changes dramatically if you add in vegetable waste, grass clippings and, better still, waste from any domestic animals you may keep. For example, 1 lb of undried vegetable scraps should produce nearly 2 cubic feet of bio-gas. Chicken shit produces at least half a cubic foot per day per hen (your hens will be free range, so you must count on only half that, from night-time droppings only). And a house cow produces a queenly 30 or 40 cubic feet a day – again you can count at most on half that, unless you're prepared to follow the cow round the field with a bucket and spade.

So a family of four, keeping 30 hens and anaerobically disposing of 3 pounds of vegetable matter a day, could expect to produce enough bio-gas to do at least half its cooking. It begins to make sense. Of course, there are some snags and, as always, you'll produce less gas than the theoretical figures suggest. No one closely tied in with the western economic system could possibly regard a methane venture as economic. It involves a lot of digging and plumbing and messing around with smelly piles of rotting shit. There's also a danger you may blow yourself up in the process, because if methane is mixed in a 1 to 4 to 1 to 14 ratio with air, the mixture becomes highly explosive (but no more so than natural gas, which is composed almost entirely of methane). On the other hand, if we let western economics dictate our energy policy, we'll end up with no energy at all.

What the bugs do

All composting depends on bugs – but those you use in anaerobic composting are different from the ones you try to encourage in the garden compost heap.

When you first load a methane digester up, you're bound to get some air in the system. None of the bugs you want will function if there's air in the digester. So first, ordinary aerobic bacteria will start eating away, and will continue to do so until they've exhausted all the air they can find. No methane yet.

Then, when the last traces of air have vanished, the anaerobic bacteria will begin to get to work. At this stage you get mainly liquefaction – the solids are broken down and liquified and complex chemicals turned into much simpler ones. The main products are organic acids, and mostly acetic acid – the main constituent of vinegar. At a later stage this acetic acid will provide at least 70 per cent of all the methane you collect. Fortunately, the acid bacteria reproduce very fast and don't care a great deal about the temperature they work at. You'll have no problem getting this first anaerobic stage of digestion to work. But still no methane.

That comes in the third stage, when the acids have been produced and the solids mainly liquified. Then the methane-producing bacteria – providing you've got some in the mix – will take over. Their job is simply to convert the acids into methane. The problem is mainly that methane-producing bugs are fussy little devils – they like to have the right temperature and the right acidity or they sulk and nothing much happens.

The right temperature is about 36°C or 95°F. There is another set of methane-producing bugs which will work best at even higher temperatures, but they're not generally used because high temperatures are difficult to maintain and the sludge these other bugs produce at the end isn't very good as fertilizer. Maintaining your digester at 36°C is quite difficult enough.

Lots of ways have been suggested. You could build your compost heap (the aerobic one, if you're still keeping one going) round the digester and hope the warmth it produces will do the trick. You can arrange for your hot bath and sink waste to run out through a coil round the digester or into a sump underneath it. You can add warm water to every mix of slurried manure and vegetable matter you feed into the digester. Or you can just insulate the thing very well and hope you'll get the right temperature by luck.

If you do any of these things I don't reckon you'll get much methane. The bugs responsible not only like to have the right temperature but, fussy things that they are, respond very badly to even small changes in temperature for short periods. So you need some constant source of heat for the digester, and the best way is to run a coil of pipe carrying warm water through the digester itself. The water must obviously be warmer than 36°C, but it shouldn't be more than 60°C or muck inside the digester will cake around the pipes. Obviously you need at least a thermostat in the digester to control the temperature and, in a de luxe model, another one on the water heater set at the higher temperature of 60°C. You need roughly 1 square foot of pipe area for every 100 cubic feet of digester capacity.

How to heat the water? You could do it simply with an electrical immersion heater, though that's expensive unless you've surplus free energy from a windmill or aerogenerator. You can take a lead out of your normal hot water supply. You can build a separate small solar heater and use that for heating the digester – though, unless your supply of sun is incredibly reliable, I don't recommend it as a couple of cloudy days could make havoc inside the digester.

The best way is to use some of the methane coming out of the digester to heat the water (use bottled gas for the period during which the digester is warming up and no methane being produced). That may sound like putting the cart before the horse, but of course you'll only use some of the methane that way – maybe 20 per cent, possibly as much as 30 per cent in a cold winter. But if you don't heat, you may get no methane at all. The importance of correct heating is shown by these figures. If your temperature drops by 5°C, the rate of methane production will roughly halve itself. If the temperature goes down another 5°C you'll get only one-third the optimum rate. And if it drops below about 15°C you won't get any methane at all. Worse, it's not only the rate of production that's altered. The total yield from the digester from a given batch of muck will go down in much the same way. So don't build a digester unless you're prepared to go to the trouble of maintaining the right temperature inside it.

You can economize, of course, on the energy needed by insulating the tank well. First, it's a good idea to dig it into the ground, as the ground itself insulates very well. Then wrap some insulation round the digester, making sure no water can seep in from the surrounding earth. Finally, you must take care not to use an insulator with open pores, such as fibreglass. If you do, and there's a leak, methane may get in the pores and form an explosive mixture with the air already trapped there. Styrofoam is the recommended insulator.

The next problem is acidity. During the liquefaction phase, the mix in the digester will get very acid, which the methane-producing bacteria don't like at all. They'll gradually begin to correct that, but don't expect much methane to come off until the pH reaches at least 7 (pH 7 is neutral – higher values are alkaline, lower ones acid). Then the methane bugs will come into their own, and at a pH of 7·5 to 8·5 will really start producing. You can check the acidity of your mix by running off a little liquid and testing it with a calibrated litmus paper.

If your digester runs too acid for too long, you'll have to take action. It may be because you're adding fresh material too fast – in which case slow down. Your temperature control may have gone haywire, in which case check it out. Or you may have got a build-up of scum on the surface (as in a septic tank). You can remove that by agitating the contents in some way, and things should return to normal. When you build your digester (see page 206) you must make provision for agitating the muck in the tank. Ideally you should stir it about for a few minutes every day, either by hand or mechanically. That will improve production. But continuous agitation – you'll be pleased to learn – is bad for it.

When the digester is running smoothly it should produce an environment which stabilizes itself. If you add too much acid material, the bugs will quickly restore the pH to what they want. Similarly if you add too much alkaline material, they'll correct it for you. When your digester is going well, you can then sit back and collect the methane.

Methane digesters have a chicken and egg problem. That is, you must seed each new batch of material with the right methane-producing bugs. Those bugs are contained in copious amounts in the end product – the sludge you use for fertilizer – of the previous digestion. Just add a few cupfuls of that to the new batch and off you go. But what if this is your first digestion? If you know a pond which bubbles from the bottom, go and get some of the mud from low down because that pond is producing anaerobic methane in the same way as a digester (occasionally the methane from it will catch fire, producing what are known as will-o'-the-wisps).

Otherwise you must make a starter brew, and it may take a few weeks. Put a few inches of either the active liquid from a sewage farm or the run-off from an intensive stock farm in the bottom of a glass jar. Add an equal amount of fresh manure, and leave the top off (otherwise you'll get a very smelly explosion). Go on adding fresh manure once a week and, with luck, you'll end up with a brew containing the right bugs. Chuck it in the digester when you first load up.

You may then have to wait up to a month for the first two stages of bacterial action to finish. The methane-producing stage will last between one and two months if you manage to maintain the temperature accurately – longer if you don't. But it'll be fairly obvious from the amount of methane you collect when the process is exhausting itself. You may want to wait the best part of a third month to get all you can out of it. Then you release any remaining methane and dig out the slurry that is left. That will make you the best garden compost you ever had – but it's normally a good idea to let it compost aerobically before you add it to the garden. You must certainly do that as a safeguard against infection if the original material contained human manure.

Getting the right mix

When you load a digester there are two things you must watch out for. The first is the size and dilution of the material you put in. The second is the amount of carbon in relation to nitrogen that it contains.

It's no good adding logs of wood or bales of hay to a digester. The bugs simply won't be able to get their teeth into them quick enough. The best rule I know is that anything you put in should be small enough for you to be able to eat (never mind whether you want to or not – I'm talking about size). And the second rule is that you must usually dilute it with water to make a suspension of at least 6 per cent solids, and not more than about 9 per cent. If you add too much water, the solids will settle out and you'll be running what is in effect a septic tank. A septic tank does indeed produce methane, but by no means at the optimum rate. So you can't, for instance, just run all the house waste from the soil pipe into the digester. Most of the water must go somewhere else.

To get the right percentage of solids in the mix is again easy enough. You want a slurry the consistency of moderately thick cream. Usually, you'll add stuff to the digester by mixing the slurry in a small compartment which drains through a plughole into the digester. You mix until the creaminess is right, then pull out the plug, and if you've got it right the stuff will flow down the drain into the digester. If it won't flow, you've made it too thick.

The carbon to nitrogen ratio is just as important, but much more tricky to get right. Methane-producing bugs need the right food, and that means they need food in which the carbon to nitrogen ratio is fixed at between 30 and 35 to 1. There's no easy way to work out the ratio of the stuff you're putting in, except to weigh it and look up the C:N ratios in a good table. I've put just about all the quantitative information that is available on methane production into the table overleaf, but readers should take it with a good deal of caution. The information comes from many different countries and has been accumulated over many years. The only real test of performance is to see what actually comes out of your digester. Such figures as these offer at best a rough guide.

The first two columns of figures can be used to work out the C:N ratio of any mix you need. But you must remember the difference between dry and wet weight. All the % N figures are given for dry weight, and hence the solid content of any batch must be worked out before trying to find out how much nitrogen it contains.

Suppose the digester were being fed with a mix comprising 3 lb human sewage, 5 lb poultry manure, 4 lb vegetable waste and 5 lb oat straw. The first thing to do is work out the solid content or dry weight. As a general rule of thumb you count 20 per cent of the total weight of most animal manure as solids. One-fifth of the wet weight, in other words, is the dry weight. Poultry are a bit different, and you should count one-third. Humans are different again, and you count 28 per cent for shit, and only 6 per cent for pee. For green matter, the amount of water varies enormously, but you can

Methane Production Data

Material	%N*	C:N Ratio	Digestion Time (days) 25°C	Digestion Time (days) 35°C	Daily Amount (lb)	Solid Content (lb)	Gas Production ft³/lb*	Gas Production ft³/day
cow dung	1·7	18–25	50	25	52	10	3·1–4·7	30–50
horse ,,	2·3	25			36	7		
pig ,,	3·8	20	40+	30+	7·5	1·5	6–8	9–12
sheep ,,	3·8	22			3·0	0·5		
human ,,	5·5–6·3	6–10	20–45	11–15	0·5	0·14	6–9	0·8–1·3
poultry ,,	6·5	15–25	30	10	0·3	0·1	6–13	0·6–1·3
urine	15–18	0·8						
blood	10–14	3–4						
meat scraps		5·1						
grass/hay	4·0	12						
cabbage	3·6	12						
tomato	3·3	13						
alfalfa	2·8	17						
seaweed	1·9	19						
red clover	1·8	27						
mustard	1·5	26						
potato tops	1·5	25						
average								
greenstuff	2·7	20		40–50		25%	2 (wet) / 7 (dry)	
wheat straw	0·5	150						
oat straw	1·1	48						
sawdust	0·1	200–500					unsuitable	

* dry weight

reckon an average of one-quarter for the dry weight. Straw, of course, is already dry.

From the dry weight you can work out how much nitrogen the original material contained if you know the % N figure (column one of the table). If you also know the C:N ratio (column two) you can then work out how much carbon it contains. If you have 1 lb of nitrogen, and the C:N ratio is 25, you then have 25 lb carbon. The whole calculation goes like this:

	wet weight (lb)	dry weight (lb)	%N	weight N (lb)	weight C (lb)
human manure	3	0·84	6·0	0·050	0·40
poultry manure	5	1·67	6·5	0·108	2·16
vegetable waste	4	1·00	2·7	0·027	0·54
oat straw	5	5·00	1·1	0·055	2·64
				0·240 lb	5·74 lb

hence C:N ratio = 5·74 : 0·24 = 24

This would be somewhat low for an ideal mix. If a further 5 lb of oat straw were added, the C:N ratio would rise to 28·4, which would be as near perfect as makes no difference.

This does not mean, of course, that an elaborate calculation has to be made every time you add some muck to the digester. In practice you probably end up adding roughly the same mix every time – varying it perhaps between winter and summer, when there will be more greenstuff available. You'll end up being able to adjust the C:N ratio by intuition.

How much?

As with a wind generator, you need to know both how much energy you can expect from your digester and how much you're going to need. The answer to the first question will only really be known when you've run the digester for a few months. There are figures available on what other people have achieved – but the results depend enormously on such things as how well you control the temperature and acidity, what kinds of bug you manage to capture, what sort of mix you feed in, in what quantities and what amounts, and even on what kinds of food you and your animals eat.

But to get an idea, take the example we used in the last section. From the figures in the table on page 201, we would expect:

	wet weight (lb)	dry weight (lb)	production/ lb	total
human manure	3	0·84	6 ft³	5·04 ft³
poultry manure	5	1·67	6 ft³	10·00 ft³
vegetable waste	4	1·00	7 ft³	7·00 ft³
oat straw	10	10·00	7 ft³	70·00 ft³
		13·51 lb		92·04 ft³

I have of course used the lowest quoted production figures. And to be thoroughly pessimistic, you should count on using, say, one-third of your production for heating the digester. That leaves you with only 60 cubic feet. What can you do with that much gas?

The gas itself will probably be only about 60 per cent methane, and so its calorific value cannot be taken as anything above 600 BTU per cubic foot. In other words, 60 cubic feet is worth 36,000 BTU, or 10·6 kWh. That should produce energy for a family of four to cook for a couple of days. Or you could use it for lighting, running a small refrigerator (gas, not electric), powering an engine or turning an alternator. Probably the greatest world authority on methane generation is the Indian Ram Bux Singh, Director of the Gobar-Gas Research Station, Ajitmal, Etawah (U.P.) India. (If you write to him, Singh will send you two very useful booklets his research centre has prepared on methane.) Singh quotes the figures on page 204 for gas consumption.

So 60 cubic feet of gas will run a single mantle lamp for 20 hours at least, power a small refrigerator for 24 hours, or boil up 6 gallons of water (theoretically, 60 cubic feet of gas is sufficient to boil 22 gallons, but in practice the result depends on how efficient the burner is and how much heat you waste in warming up the surrounding air and not the water). Or you could run a 10 h.p. car for about 20 minutes which, at 30 mph, would take you just 10 miles. That, incidentally, tells you a lot about the economics of motor vehicles. Sixty cubic feet of bio-gas is the equivalent of one-quarter of a gallon of petrol. See next chapter for methane as a possible alternative to petrol.

appliance	specification	gas consumption (ft^3/hr)
gas cooker	2″ diameter burner	11·5
	4″ diameter burner	16·5
	6″ diameter burner	22·5
gas lighting	1 mantle lamp	2·5 to 3
	2 mantle lamp	5
	3 mantle lamp	6
refrigerator	18″ × 18″ × 12″	2·5
incubator	18″ × 18″ × 18″	1·5 to 2
boiling water		10 per gallon
running engines	converted diesel or petrol	16–18/h.p./hr

If this doesn't seem too encouraging, Robert and Brenda Vale have done a much more elaborate calculation. They assume that a household of 3 people keeps 1 pig and 2 goats. They collect all the human waste, all the pig waste, and half the goat waste because the goats are put out to graze during the day. In addition, all the green waste from a ¾-acre garden is put in the digester, assuming it is worked intensively and provides two crops a year. With the addition of 1 lb of straw a day, used as bedding for the animals, they reckon to collect about 60 cubic feet a day (which would reduce to 40 cubic feet if the gas was used to heat the digester). That would be just enough to provide for all cooking needs for an average family. The gas authorities use a figure of 80 therms a year as the average family cooking requirement. This is equivalent to 8 million BTU a year, which works out at about 37 cubic feet of bio-gas a day.

By far the easiest way to use the gas from a methane digester is with burners designed to run off natural gas (which is almost pure methane). To do this, however, involves removing the carbon dioxide from the bio-gas produced. It's also a good idea to remove hydrogen sulphide and water vapour, both of which will be present and both of which are corrosive. So the gas is bubbled through lime water (which removes both carbon dioxide and any ammonia present) and then passed through beds of calcium chloride, to remove water vapour, and iron filings, to remove hydrogen sulphide. If the calcium chloride is heated after use, the water vapour will be driven off and it can be used again. If the iron filings are exposed to air, they can be used again as well. Any sensibly designed methane plant will include two of these scrubbing arrangements, with a system of taps to make the gas flow through one or the other. The chemicals in the one not in use can then be regenerated or replaced while the other is being used.

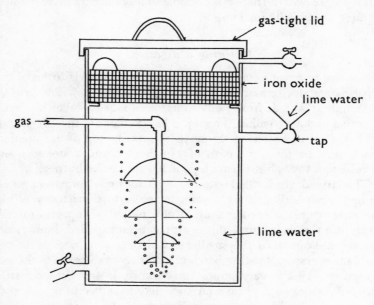

SCRUBBING UNIT

The result will burn well in a normal natural gas burner, providing it is raised to the same pressure as natural gas supplies – which is about 8 inches of water gauge or 0·3 lb per square inch above atmospheric pressure (just over 2 kiloNewtons per square metre, for the metrically minded). Don't be put off by complicated-looking figures. The pressure needed is very small and easily made by adding a weight to the top of the gas holder (see next section). To find out what weight to add, attach the gas supply pipe to a glass tube filled with water and bent in a U-shape. Go on adding weights till the water on one side of the tube is about 8 inches higher than on the other. Then you've got roughly the right pressure. You may find the gas burners work at lower pressures. Don't be deceived, though, because if they do they'll be working very inefficiently.

There is an alternative to the problem of burners, which is to make your own. I don't recommend it. Playing around with methane is quite dangerous enough, without inviting explosions. But if you're ever in India it is possible to buy burners there manufactured specifically for bio-gas.

Building a digester

My advice to anyone starting on a methane venture is to make an experimental device first to get the hang of the process. The easiest and simplest is made from 2 oil drums, one about 30-gallon size and the other about 55-gallon. The top is knocked out of the larger and the bottom removed from the smaller. Into the top of the smaller drum must be fitted a length of 1-inch pipe and a stopcock or valve. From the valve, plastic pipe is led to the gas burner.

The large drum is filled with some starter brew and whatever is being digested, diluted with water to the right consistency. With the valve open, the smaller drum is now placed on top, and forced down into the slurry until all the air has been expelled. Now close the valve. Wait until the smaller drum begins to rise. With all methane digesters, the first batch of gas is always vented to the air for safety. This is very important because, if any air were still trapped inside, an explosive mixture may have been formed, and disaster may strike if you try to light it. So you open the valve, force the smaller drum back down into the slurry and close the valve again. Next time round you should have your first methane.

A sump digester like this will give you a chance to try out the effect of heating, of changing the mix and watching acidity levels. It won't ever give you much gas – but there should be enough for you to experiment with burners and even to cook a simple meal. You'll also get used to handling slurry and other waste material, and you'll have a chance to find out how much work it all involves. Reloading a sump digester is a bit of a pain because you must wait till you've used most of the gas in the container, remove it, take out some 5 gallons of used slurry, replenish with the same amount, stir it all round, and put back the smaller drum (first venting the air, of course).

The next step is to decide whether your final working model is going to be a batch digester, or a continuous one. A batch digester you just load up and leave, using the gas until it is all spent. You must then empty it, re-load and wait another three weeks or so until your second batch is ready to start producing methane. If

OIL DRUM DIGESTERS

you're using methane daily, one batch digester won't be enough, because there'll be long periods without gas. You'll have to build at least 2, preferably 3, and run them at staggered intervals so that you've always got gas on tap. The advantage of batch digesters is that they're simpler, and need no inlet or outlet devices.

Continuous digesters are a bit more complicated but should give you a more constant supply of gas. But every digester has occasionally to be emptied and serviced. One problem is that eventually continuous digesters get stopped by thick scum forming on the surface. You can prolong the moment when it has to be taken apart and the scum removed by good agitation. But the day will certainly come when the gas holder has to be removed and the scum taken out by hand (or fork). If a constant daily supply of gas is essential, you'll have to build 2 continuous digesters. There's

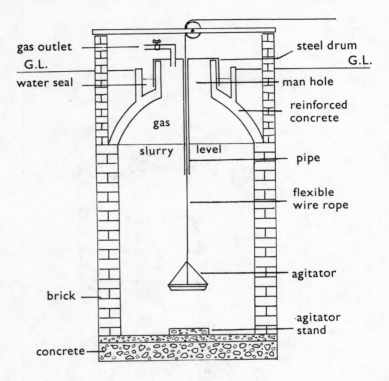

INDIAN BATCH DIGESTER

also the complication that the inlet and outlet pipes may eventually get blocked with slurry. Trying to unblock them with drain rods could vent air into the digester, with disastrous results. And that means you really need a slurry pump at hand to force the material through when things get tricky.

Either way, the critical parameter for your digester is size. Work out how much gas you need, and then see from the table on page 201 whether you've enough dung and vegetable waste to produce it. Remember that you may not get as much gas as the table suggests. I'd allow a 25 per cent margin, as well as reckoning 30 per cent for heating, in working out how much you'll need.

You must then make an estimate of how long your digestion is likely to take. If you use only dung, digestion will be much quicker than if you add vegetable waste and straw – but it will also be much less productive. Unless you're an intensive stock farm, the odds are you'll be using quite a high proportion of vegetable matter. I would then allow 60 days for digestion if you have devised a good means of maintaining a high temperature, and nearer 80 to 90 days if you haven't. Of course, the quicker your digestion, the smaller the digester can be.

Suppose you need gas for cooking (say 35 cubic feet a day) plus a bit more for lighting when it's available. The mix outlined on page 203 should give you that comfortably, with some to spare. You then have to work out how much space you are going to need if that amount of waste is added for 60 days.

The table on page 203 shows that the total dry weight of the mix is 13·5 lb. This you must dilute so that the solids form about 9 per cent of the total mix – in other words, you have a solids to liquid ratio of 9 : 91 – which simply means you add 10 times as much water by weight. As 1 gallon of water weighs 10 lb, 135 lb of water is 13·5 gallons. And as there are 6·24 gallons to the cubic foot, the water you add will have a volume of about 2·15 cubic feet. In comparison to this, the volume of the dry solids will be very small indeed. Reckon on adding a total volume of 2·5 cubic feet a day, and you won't be far off.

Of course, in practice you don't add as much as 13·5 gallons of water to your wet mix, which already contains approximately 8·5 pounds of water, or nearly one gallon. You should find about 12 gallons will give you the right degree of creaminess. Don't bother to measure it. Just aim to get the right creamy consistency (and replace as much water as you can with urine for that will speed up the digestion and increase the yield of gas).

But you can now work out the size your digester has to be. You'll be adding 2·5 cubic feet of material a day, and it must stay in the digester for about 60 days. You need a digester of about 150 cubic feet capacity. If you build a circular one, it will then be, say, 10 feet deep and just over 4 feet in diameter. Or, perhaps easier to build, 6 feet deep and just over 5½ feet in diameter. In all continuous digesters it's a good idea to make the surface as big as possible, and keep the depth to a minimum. This way the scum that forms will have a much bigger area to cover, and hence will take much longer to stop the process. Indeed, John Fry, a pig farmer from South Africa who has done a lot of pioneering work on methane, even suggests that a long horizontal digester may be the best design. Something like that can be made either from a disused boiler or from ferro-concrete.

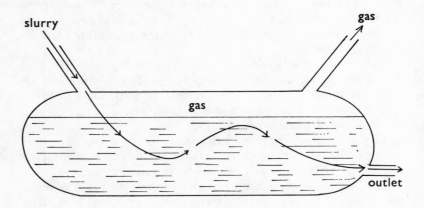

HORIZONTAL DIGESTER

I mentioned in chapter 10 that the minimum size of septic tank that can be used is 600 gallons – which is about 96 cubic feet. So if you could make do with slightly less gas, and added less mixture every day, you could buy a fibreglass onion-type septic tank and convert it to methane. For sure, that is the easiest way, though by no means the cheapest. Incidentally, if you found by really good process control you could get your digestion time down to 40 days, you'd find that a septic tank digester would be exactly the right volume for the mix we are talking about.

The drawings to this chapter show you some of the possible designs for a methane digester. I'd put a lot of faith in the 100 cubic feet per day design by Ram Bux Singh because he has had more experience of methane production than any other living person. The Book List includes articles by Singh which give you a detailed, step-by-step account of how to build that digester.

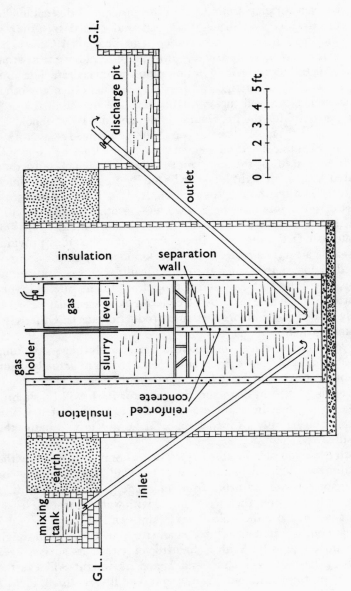

INDIAN 100 CU. FT. A DAY CONTINUOUS DIGESTER

If you want to play around with other designs, I'd recommend you get *Methane* by Steven Sampson and edited by Andrew MacKillop (published by the Wadebridge Ecological Centre, 73 Molesworth Street, Wadebridge, Cornwall, UK). I have to say that the book is full of misleading information and inaccurate data. But it does contain more designs for methane digesters than any other publication. Note well that most of them are untested; this is a feeding ground for the imagination only, and not a handbook.

But whatever type of digester you build, you'll need a gas storage tank in which to collect the methane. This can either be built over the digester itself, or the gas from the digester – which must then be fitted with an air-tight lid – can be led by pipe, usually of 1-inch diameter, to a gas holder somewhere. This will be a small-scale model of the giants used by gas works – in other words, a cylindrical metal container which fits down inside the slurry, if you operate it over the digester. The slurry round the sides provides the seal against incoming air. Some kind of a guide system is needed to ensure that when the collector fills with gas, and begins to rise, it will rise vertically and not topple off to one side. It is very important that whatever type of collector you use must be completely voided of air before methane production starts. Otherwise, you know what.

If you use gas daily, your collector need only have a volume about half that of your daily requirement. If you're actually using 60 cubic feet a day, make a collector of about 30 cubic feet. If your collector is $5\frac{1}{2}$ feet in diameter, the collector itself will be slightly smaller, say 5 feet in diameter. To house 30 cubic feet it would then have to be only 18 inches high. Make it 2 feet to be on the safe side.

With luck, you may be able to pick up a container of roughly the right dimensions from a scrap yard. If not you'll have to make – or have made for you – a drum from 12 gauge (2·5 mm thick) mild steel plate. Rivet first, then weld and fill with water to test for leaks. Weld again to close the leaks. Test again – and so on.

A gas collector that size (5 feet diameter, 2 feet high) will weigh approximately 230 lb. With a diameter of 5 feet, its surface area will be 2,820 square inches, and hence its weight will exert a pressure on the gas it contains of about 0·08 lb per square inch. I said earlier that natural gas is supplied at a pressure of about 0·3 lb per square inch, and that is the pressure you'll need if your natural

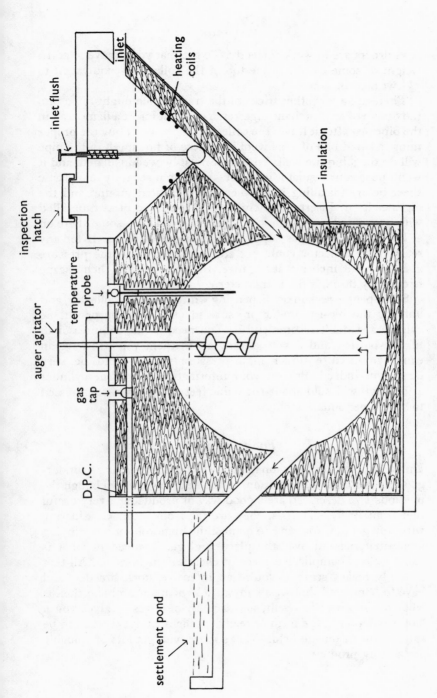

SEPTIC TANK DIGESTER

gas burners are to work correctly. To get that you'd have to add a weight of some 620 lb to the top of the collector – equivalent to 5½ cwt bags of sand.

There are a few other tricks of the trade which ought to go into the design of any methane digester. You must insert a flame trap in the pipe just after it leaves the collector. If you can't buy the proper thing, a small ball of steel wool or a piece of fine mesh in the pipe will do the job quite well. Your tank must be well insulated, and it won't be if your insulator gets wet – so wrap it securely in a plastic sheet before installing it between the excavated ground and the digester itself. Insert a manometer – a U-shaped glass tube filled with not more than 6 inches of water on each side – somewhere on a T from the main gas supply pipe and out-of-doors. If for any reason (the collector could get stuck in its guides) the pressure goes above 8 inches water gauge, the bio-gas will then escape harmlessly through the manometer.

Some people reckon on dispensing with a large gas collector, and bottling the bio-gas under pressure in used propane or butane cylinders. I don't recommend it. You need an air compressor to fill the bottles, and if you get any air in them you will have an explosive mixture under high pressure which could be very dangerous indeed. But for your information a propane cylinder 4 feet high will hold about 160 cubic feet of gas when compressed to 200 lb per square inch.

The next steps

Unlike wind power, I reckon methane technology is going to undergo some radical transformations in the next few years. Though the methods I've described are a good way of producing a very useful fuel from waste materials, they are far from ideal. Considering what you get out, you have to manhandle huge volumes of stinking waste materials all over the place, and get involved in what is really quite a complicated piece of chemical engineering. All that certainly makes sense if you're an intensive stock breeder, and have to handle all that waste anyway. Your main problem then is what to do with the result, and a methane digester gives you a handy solution in the form of really excellent sludge which can be sprayed direct on the field. What's more, you get lots of valuable gas as a by-product.

But for you and me the economics are less sure. One intriguing improvement that might be made is to run the methane digester in conjunction with algal beds. The liquid slurry run-off from the digester would be piped to shallow flat beds in which green algae would be allowed to grow. The production rate, with a bit of sun, and perhaps a plastic cover to raise the temperature a bit in the daytime, would be prodigious. And there's a lot you can do with algae. These single-celled green plants make very good animal fodder because they contain a high proportion of protein. This might be a way of supporting more animals than your land area would allow. You'd simply give the animals the algal water to drink and their need for other foods would be cut down quite considerably.

Or you can make a modern-day perpetual motion machine by collecting the algae without too much water (which is difficult) and feeding it back into the methane digester. A few algae make a lot of methane, and your output might be substantially increased in that way. Of course, it's not really perpetual motion, because you're simply trapping solar energy in the algae (instead of in grass or vegetable waste) and converting it to methane. But someone has worked out that the algal system ends up by trapping 2 per cent of the solar radiation that falls on it. If it's true, that's quite an efficient process compared with the much more laborious one of growing grass or vegetable waste, not for the table, but for the cooker. One snag, maybe, is that I have seen it suggested that algae are converted to methane by those bugs which work best at the much higher temperature of 50–60°C (120–140°F). If this is true, it is most inconsiderate of nature because it means the algae would have to be fed into a different methane digester from the one which was handling your other wastes. More research needed.

The other big problem with methane is that it's a gas, and it can't be easily liquefied (see chapter 12). So storage is difficult, and particularly so if you want to use the fuel to power a moving engine, such as a car or tractor. Those plastic gas balloons lolling about on the top of vehicles can hardly be considered either a safe or a permanent solution to the transport problem. There's no way round that one – unless you can convert the methane to a liquid fuel in some other way. In 1974 ICI won a technological prize for developing a process which would convert methane to methanol on a massive scale. They now do it by the million tons. Methanol is wood alcohol, the main constituent of meths. It's a clear liquid and an excellent fuel. It could well be used as a substitute for petrol or diesel fuel.

The snag, of course, is that the ICI process is not for the likes of us, and depends on being able to transport methane to a huge centralized factory for conversion to liquid methanol. And the process itself involves impossible chemicals, pressures, temperatures and catalysts which would be quite impractical on the small scale. Anyone who can invent a small-scale process, which is easy to operate, for doing the same job on the farm or the home, should be given the next Nobel Prize for Chemistry. It would change the whole process quite radically.

Finally, there's no reason why we should get stuck into a methane groove. If organic waste can be converted into methane or methanol, it could also be converted to other fuels. I have on my desk a recent technical report from the United States, the abstract of which runs as follows:

'The Bureau of Mines is experimentally converting cellulose, the chief constituent of organic solid waste, to a low-sulfur oil. All types of cellulosic wastes, including urban refuse, agricultural wastes, sewage sludge, wood, lignin and bovine manure, have been converted to oil by reaction with carbon monoxide and water at temperatures of $350°$ to $400°C$ and pressures near 4,000 psig, and in the presence of various catalysts and solvents.'

Would that that process could be scaled down. Converting methane to liquid methanol is one thing, but if we could transform our solid wastes on the farm and in the home to oil for heating, cooking, lighting and running vehicles, then the days of alchemy will finally have arrived. Turning base metals into gold is small fry compared to turning one's excrement into oil.

Chapter 12

⊷⊶ ∘ ⊷⊶

Transport

THE best way of getting from one place to another is not to go. We've now got so used to easy travel that journeys have lost their significance. Whether we like it or not, they're going to get it back. It's a safe bet that never again will we be able to move so freely about the Earth's surface as we were in the 1960s. And, in some ways, a good thing too. Most of the places people really liked to go to have been ruined beyond repair simply because they went there so often.

But if you must go, don't do it alone in a powerful six-seater sedan. There are plenty of other methods, many of which cost less, pollute less and in the end are more enjoyable. The most important of these is:

Walking

An average pair of legs will take you over 20 miles on a good day. In the Army, mine once took me 100 miles in 3 days, but it wasn't an experience I could recommend. Actually, the reason we don't walk these days is not that we're lazy, but that we're in too much of a hurry. When time is money, and you can earn £2 or £3 an hour, walking turns out to be the most expensive form of transport ever, costing you nearly £1 a mile. Small wonder no one wears boots any longer.

Only you can get yourself out of that bind. Hurry and rush are two of the worst features of civilization; without them everything would get done much better, with more enjoyment, and probably not much more slowly. The walker is certainly going to move about more slowly. That price is only worthwhile if you value the exercise, the things you can see en route, and the chance to slow things down a little. But don't try to make the best of a bad job by walking fast. If you're going to do it, do it at a suitable pace, which is not more than 3 miles an hour.

In town or city, walking in fact may not lose you much time in any case. Buses and subways usually involve a walk at both ends, a wait for the transport, a delay in buying the ticket. If the journey is 2 miles or less, you could walk it quite easily in something over 30 minutes. I'd be surprised if you can do it by public transport in less than 20. Isn't 10 minutes worth the pleasure of walking, if you're the sort of person that can cultivate it?

Walks of that distance don't require any special gear, except perhaps shoes which are more waterproof than those you'd use to drive to the office or factory. But one reason many people jibe at walking is that their journey is to go and fetch things, not simply to move themselves about. Walking with a couple of parcels under one arm and some lengths of copper pipe under the other can be a real pain. You need a sensible carrier. A pram is one such, as housewives know very well. Another is a wheeled trolley, as used by those who frequent the big supermarkets. Don't be put off by the image. A wheeled trolley or shopping bag is a first-class way of moving goods around.

The point is to avoid ending up looking like a gibbon, with your arms so stretched by constant carrying that they reach nearly to the pavement. You want the stuff out of your hands, which means either on to wheels or your back. A milk-maid's yoke would be a good though cumbersome solution for crowded streets. A rucksack, which puts the weight on your back where it belongs, is probably the ideal. But if you can balance stuff on your head, African style, by all means give it a try.

And if you're building, and delivery is a problem, don't forget the humble barrow cart – the kind with a couple of wheels and two handles. Many odd-job builders still use them, and they're perfect for small loads. I wouldn't try moving 5 tons of anything in that way, but the odd bag of cement, a little sand and a great many tools are easily pushed in a barrow.

If you're going to walk more than about 5 miles a day, you'll need special gear for your feet. And that means leather boots. Don't fall for the cheaper, artificial leather kind which, though apparently warm and comfortable, will end up unused in the cellar. I have a pair of those and they're exquisite for the first 2 miles. After that, because they don't allow any moisture to escape, you feel more and more as though you've been paddling with your socks on. Your feet won't get cold because the moisture can't evaporate, but in summer they'll get much too hot. They're very bad for your feet, your socks, and your morale.

The cheap way of buying leather is to get ex-Army boots but you'll have to endure a couple of weeks of real agony before they're worn in. Leather moulds itself to the foot, and the person who had the boots before you will have had very different shaped feet. You'll get blisters to start with, the only cure for which is not to prick them but to cover them with Band-aids until they go away. That'll give you a chance to go on walking without too much discomfort. A good tip is to get two pairs of boots, and work them in simultaneously. One pair will give you blisters in one place, and when they get unbearable switch to the other pair, which will blister somewhere else. By the time you go back to the first pair, your skin will have hardened up. After two or three switches the problem will be over.

Leather boots need wool socks, long enough not to ride down and disappear inside the boot. The problem then is that you'll spend the rest of your life darning holes. I've found a solution to this which seems to work well. Wear two pairs of socks, wool next to the skin, and nylon, or some artificial fibre which won't wear, on the top. The rubbing against the boot then doesn't wear holes in anything and you have the comfort of wool next to the skin. Unless there's something very peculiar about my feet, that'll work for you as well.

Never wear rubber boots unless you're going fishing or to muck out the cows.

The bicycle

Anyone over 30 can remember a time – which now seems like an aeon ago – when everyone had a bicycle, and used it. In some more sensible countries, such as Holland, they still do. Elsewhere the bike is fast on the way back.

But if you live in the Rockies, or the Welsh mountains, or on a 4-in-1 hill, you'd best forget the bike. I know there are plenty of cycle enthusiasts who'll tell you that the modern light-weight frame, with 10 gears thrown in, will take you up anything. It'll cost you over $150 new, though. And you have my assurance that in steep country it'll only get you about with a great deal of pain, and the expenditure of more energy than you'd use in walking. I know, for Eithin was on a 4-in-1 hill, and we had two of those aggressively modern and hugely expensive machines. I went down and up once, and once only. Needless to say, going down was fine – except for the girl who broke her shoulder when she went over the top of the handlebars. Others at Eithin used those bikes more than I did, but even so they lay unused in an old barn for 99 per cent of the time I was there.

Actually, any new bike is now ridiculously expensive, I suppose because demand has fallen to such low levels. Maybe they'll get cheaper again. Meanwhile, go for a second-hand machine. I personally can't abide drop handlebars, and unless you're an enthusiast I doubt that you will. So go for a nice gentlemanly up-right handlebar, and check that the frame is sound. If you don't want additional expense, turn the thing upside down, revolve the wheels and watch for irregularities. If the wheels are uneven, you'll have to get replacements, so allow for that in the price. The rest of the machine doesn't matter too much. Chains, pedals, brakes and gears can all be replaced if defective. And when you've got a good one, do put a nice large comfortable saddle on. The tiny, unsprung leather jobs which the enthusiasts use must, I reckon, be directly traceable to the medieval torture chamber.

If you live in Kansas, or somewhere equally flat, a bike without gears will do you fine. But most of us have to cope with some hills from time to time, and at least 3 gears will make an enormous difference. Five might be even better, but anything more than that is ridiculous unless you're going to enter for the Tour de France.

You don't need a light-weight racing frame, but on the other hand some bikes can be really heavy, and that makes a big difference up-hill. A few years ago it was the rage to buy collapsible bikes that folded in two to go in the boot of a car. Not a bad idea, but to make them strong enough those bikes had to be very heavy indeed. It would be better to run a small van, into which you can throw your bike whole, without having to break it down to its constituent parts.

A bike without baskets is no good at all. Get one for the front, and either another for the back, or a pair of paniers which will hold more. Keep an old rucksack in them, and you'll be surprised how much stuff you can carry without great difficulty.

The only real problem with the bike is the rain. Rain takes on its nastiest aspect on a bike, particularly around the knees where the water ends up after it's dropped off your coat. A proper bike cape is the only thing which will actually keep you dry (more or less) in wet weather. But biking in the rain is not one of life's greatest experiences. Walking can be, and I tend to keep my bike for drier weather. Incidentally, if you've got a good pair of gloves, you won't get as cold on a bike as you might expect.

In a city such as London the bike is the ideal transport. It's the fastest way there is of getting about. Don't be unnerved by the thought of using a bike in crowded city streets. All you have to do is alter your route, using one-way, back streets that few cars venture down. You'll leave the traffic snarled up at coloured lights far behind, for it doesn't matter on a bike how much you twist and turn. And as for mpg, someone at Eithin – Philip Brachi – once worked it out. Taking into account the amount of energy used to propel you so many miles on a bike, it turns out you get the equivalent of several thousand miles to the gallon. And you can't do better than that.

Finally, if you really want to know about all the pleasures you can get from biking, read Dan Behrman's superb book *The man who loved bicycles*. It's not the work of a cycle fetishist, but a very personal account of how much fascination can be had from the bike.

Public and private transport

Even the most stoic sometimes need something quicker or drier than Shanks' pony or the bike. I refuse to endorse the current vogue against the motor car which, in spite of its many faults, remains a superb invention. The problem is what we've done with it. It should have made country living a real delight, and a realistic option for a great many people. The fact that nearly all of us have clung obstinately to town or city living, and taken the car with us where it certainly doesn't belong, is our problem not the car's.

If you live in an urban area, don't own a car. Today the economics of doing so are pretty marginal; tomorrow, when there will be special city taxes for urban car owners, they'll be impossible. So sell your car and use the money you save on public transport, taxis and hiring a car or van when you really need it.

The basic cost of keeping a small car on the road – completely stationary – is now approaching $25 a week, including depreciation, road tax, insurance, maintenance and repairs. A large car will cost much more. If, on top of that, you actually use the car, and travel say 10,000 miles a year using high test gas, you'll have a fuel bill of some $400 this year (and almost certainly $500 next year). Total: more than $35 a week, or over $1,750 a year.

Instead you could use that money to hire a car for a long weekend once a month (and travel 300 miles each time in it), and spend more than $10 a week on taxis, trains and buses. After all that, you'd still be spending less on transport, and with none of the hassle car-owning entails. If you walk and bike a bit as well, you'll be dollars ahead.

What's more, that sort of calculation is very much a *status quo* sum. It assumes that everyone else goes on using their own car, and the public transport systems are no more used than they are today. If we sorted our priorities out a bit better, public transport could get cheaper – if, for example, trains were used more often and bus services used to carry goods and mail as well as people (as the sensible Europeans do).

As things stand, the cost of going by car (reckoned only on gasoline consumption) is about the same for one person as it is by train. With a low-consumption car, and with 3 or 4 passengers, the car is considerably cheaper – at the moment. Actually, a car with 4 or 5 people in it – for which after all it has been designed – is quite an economic proposition. So if families could get together and share motor vehicles, we'd all be better off. Less fuel consumed, cars fuller, less pollution, less insurance, less road tax – you name it, and you win. Thus there's good reason for getting to know your neighbour better. If you know him or her well enough to share a bath (as I've said), you'll save something. You'd probably have to know him or her even better to share a car, but you'll save a lot more.

The same applies if you live in the country, except that the alternative of public transport and car rental is probably not practical. But I think country dwellers should own a car – shared if possible – because the car can bring something to the country never before possible. It can end isolation, and hence help to repopulate our now almost empty countryside.

But if you are a car-owner, particularly in the country, it won't do to carry on as the ads tell you. Routine garage maintenance is now impossibly expensive and for a country family impossibly inconvenient (I discount the absurd idea that any one family should ever own two cars). You've got to do it yourself. And most of what I could say about that counts for nothing because I'm a lousy car mechanic.

The big battle, as in plumbing or building, is one of mystique. Mostly we convince ourselves we can't fix our own vehicles – and if you've done just half the things mentioned thus far in this book you should by now be over the 'I can't do it' hang-up. The other problem, I have to admit, is the way cars are built these days. They're made for other people – and only specialists in that particular make – to service. It's just no good taking a VW to a Ford garage for it won't have the right tools for even some of the simple jobs. I can't think of a fate bad enough for the car manufacturers who thought up this insidious method of making the most money out of their expensive parts and their poorly put-together bits of machinery. May their souls rot.

Unfortunately, there's really no way round it. If you own a vehicle which needs a special hub-puller to dismantle the hub, the chances are very slim that you'll be able to do without that tool. And you'll soon discover that though the garage will charge an exorbitant amount to do the job for you, the manufacturer will charge you even more to supply the tool; and he may not supply it at all if you're not registered as one of his specialists. When you hit that problem, you can only grin and bear it.

But there is much else you can do. Cleaning and maintaining the plugs and distributor, setting the spark gap, tuning the engine and keeping it in good shape are all best done in your yard, not the garage. If you're really pig-ignorant about all this, get some good car mechanics' books as a start – simple ones. And, second, you must have a service manual for your particular model. With that in hand, most of what were before complete mysteries will unravel themselves. A good manual in your vehicle is just as important as some car tools and a good spare wheel.

There are two kinds of manual. The first you obtain, at quite a high cost and probably in 2 or 3 volumes, from the manufacturer.

The second kind is more popular, written by motoring journalists, a good deal shorter and cheaper and also specific to your model. I've worked on vehicles with both kinds, and I have to say that the manufacturer's are far, far superior. For a start, they're written for mechanics who just have to get your vehicle back on the road. The popular sort are written for people who like to tinker about a bit but, if they can't manage it, can always take the vehicle to a garage to put right a boshed job. Get the manufacturer's manual.

As in building, the rest is experience – and best of all shared experience with someone who knows more than you. It really doesn't take much to learn enough to deal with all the routine stuff. When you've mastered that, then by all means get into re-bores and valve grinding and the rest.

I'm on firmer ground when it comes to buying cars. There's one school of thought that you should buy new cars only, and keep them 2 years before replacing them. If you don't want to get your hands dirty, that's probably the best policy – though I do know plenty of new car owners who've got their hands so dirty in the first 6 months they've never bought a new vehicle again. But buying a new car every 2 years is as good a way as any to bankrupt our planet of resources and your pocket of ready cash. I've owned 7 vehicles in my time and none of them was less than 6 years old. I doubt any one knew less about how they worked than I did, and in 15 years I can remember only two breakdowns when I had to send for help. Two of those vehicles I sold for more than I paid for them, and the other 5 cost me a grand total of £925, of which I got £120 back on one and am still using the last. Another was left me by my father. The average cost over 15 years has been less than £50 a year, with a vehicle in hand so to speak. At that rate you can afford to spend a bit on parts.

But a 5-year-old car, no matter what the salesman says, is going to have a lot wrong with it. Car mysteries seem a bit simpler if you think of your vehicle as containing 7 different systems: body, engine, clutch and gears, steering, brakes, suspension and electrical system. Most people think of the engine first, but in fact that is not the most expensive part. A reconditioned engine, or even a second-hand one, can be had relatively cheaply – and, if you've a block and tackle, can be replaced fairly easily; even a garage will do it for less than you might imagine. A defective gear-box, particularly an automatic one, can be much more expensive. Even a new braking system, with new liners, master cylinder and piping all round, will cost just as much as an engine. Defective electrical systems are easily and cheaply put right. Steering is not something to play around with if you don't know the ins and outs – and that can be a really expensive item. And, strangely, the body work can be the most expensive of all. If it's rotting away from the sills up, it's going to take you a long time to remake it all with fibreglass. A complete re-spray, if you must have one, for a van or something similar will almost certainly cost more than a new engine.

So where does all this leave you? Try and assess the brakes, the steering, the engine and the body. If more than two of those are obviously in need of serious attention, don't buy it. If only one is really bad, buy it but do something about the defects as soon as you get delivery.

A vehicle of this kind is going to cost you only some $400–$600 And that means you can make another saving on insurance. It's just not worth insuring for all risks, and it's debatable whether you should even bother with fire and theft. Legally, all you have to have is cover for Third Party liability, and that won't cost you much at all, particularly with a good no-claims bonus. If, in spite of the fact that you are going to drive more slowly and less often than most other people, you do manage to write your vehicle off, you just have to find another $400–$600 and buy another. As complete insurance cover is going to cost you more than $150 a year, it's obviously only worthwhile if you make a write-off of your vehicle every 3 or 4 years. If you do do that, you shouldn't be on the roads in any case.

The only other tip to cheap motoring is not to buy new parts. When your current vehicle finally expires, it's excellent sense to buy a replacement of the same model, and keep the old one. You can then cannibalize it for new bits and pieces, for the chances are that most of the parts on your old vehicle are still perfectly serviceable. If they're not, then a visit to the nearest car scrapyard is called for. By this time you should be quite familiar with whoever runs that, and you'll know whether or not he's a rip-off merchant. You should be able to get old parts, particularly if you prise them off the wrecked vehicle yourself, for less than a quarter of the cost of a new part.

Alternative fuels

The only other thing you can do to cut the cost of motoring is to burn something other than gasoline. The alternative technology movement has a long standing dream that one day all motor vehicles will be propelled by methane generated from human sewage and farm waste. It's a beautiful dream, but for reasons I've already hinted at, I doubt if it'll ever make it into reality.

The conventional internal combustion engine doesn't have to be run off gasoline – which actually is a rather poor fuel, of which a great deal is wasted in imperfect combustion and which emits staggering levels of exhaust pollution. Chemically, the three gases known as methane, propane and butane are all very similar and are potentially much better fuels. They burn more completely, give as good an mpg and in Britain at least, are a great deal cheaper because they're not taxed in the same way. In the US there's less economic incentive to convert to alternative fuels, so the material on the next several pages will not be as useful.

There has thus arisen a new trade in converting gasoline vehicles to run off what is called LPG – liquefied petroleum gas, the blanket name for butane and propane, which are the ones used in bottled gas. Haulage contractors and fork-lift truck operators have been running their vehicles off LPG for decades, and they operate quite a thriving little industry behind the scenes, which has for some strange reason been kept more or less completely hidden from the likes of you and me. But that is all to the good. It means that the bits and pieces you need to convert your car to run off LPG are manufactured and easily available.

Before I launch into the details, I must give vent to some reservations. If a substantial number of people convert to LPG, no one is going to be economically much better off in the end. The taxes needed to make nuclear weapons are simply going to be levied from yet another source, which will be a government-imposed tax on LPG for road use. That will bring the cost of LPG up to that of petrol, and the economic advantage will be gone. Others will be left, however. LPG produces so much less pollution that even if we continue our unrestricted use of private vehicles in cities, their air is going to get a lot cleaner. Further, engines and oil last much longer on LPG. In the end, I suspect, those will prove to be the real advantages of LPG conversion.

First, basic principles. You need to connect a source of LPG to your engine. No modifications to the engine are needed. Most carburetors have what is called a butterfly choke situated at the top, below the air cleaner. When you pull the choke, a metal disc partially closes off the hole from the air cleaner, so that less air enters the carb and the mixture is richer. Just below the butterfly, the neck of the carb entrance is reduced in cross-section to form a throat called the venturi. Into this you have to drill a hole, and

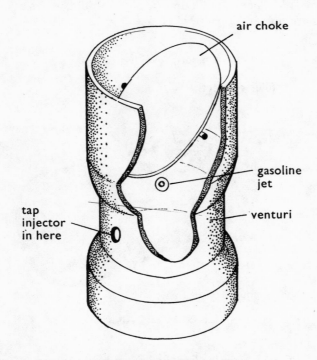

CARBURETOR CONVERSION

mount an injector through which the LPG (in gas form) will be sucked into the engine. As always, the practice involves a little – but not much – ingenuity.

First problem is the storage tank for the LPG. In the UK you can buy a 29- or 42-lb bottle of Calor gas (equivalent to $5\frac{1}{2}$ and 8 gallons of gasoline), and hook it up to the carb. It's strictly illegal in the UK, and most other places too. But there are people running round the country doing just that, and I haven't yet heard that any one's blown themselves up that way. In fact, it's no more dangerous than carrying gas and a cooking device in a camper. But apart from being illegal, it's silly because bottled gas costs a good deal more than LPG which is sold specifically for transport. To use that you must have a LPG fuel container which costs quite a lot, unless you can get a used one. With an LPG fuel container, you can drive into any LPG depot and fill up just as you would at a garage. LPG depots are not so common, of course.

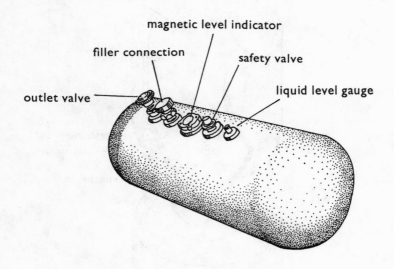

L.P.G. FUEL TANK

The LPG tank contains liquefied gas at high pressure. You can't lead that straight into the carb because, as the tank empties, your pressure falls and the amount of fuel drawn into the engine will change. So you need a converter or regulator. Calor gas supply a regulator which will control the output of their bottles in the required way, and one of these is always attached to a Calor gas bottle before the supply reaches the appliance. But there's another problem. The Calor gas regulator supplies gas at a pressure of 11 inches of water gauge (about $\frac{1}{2}$ lb per square inch) above atmospheric pressure. Your carb actually sucks in the fuel, and it needs gas at a pressure of about 6 inches of water gauge below atmospheric. One way out of this is to write to Harold Bates at Penny Rowden, Blackawton, Totnes, Devon TQ9 7DN, for instructions on how to convert the Calor gas regulator to do the necessary job in your vehicle. Bates is the man who makes much methane from chicken shit, and runs his car off it. The conversion is not difficult, but it's not wholly satisfactory.

There are two reasons. First, as your gas bottle or container heats and cools according to the weather, the pressure of the gas will change. That means the rate of tickover of your vehicle will keep altering. You can adjust it by adding a tap on your supply line, and closing off the supply a bit when idling and the weather is warm. This is tedious, and unnecessary because you can buy from Calor gas another device – called a primary regulator – which will keep the pressure from the fuel container to a constant 5 lb per square inch. But you still have another problem.

All will be fine in the summer, or at low speeds in the winter. But if you start bowling down a motorway in cold weather, you'll draw a lot of fuel through the system, and as it evaporates it will cool everything so much that the liquid will freeze. Result: total stoppage. Wait till the thing thaws out, and then continue until it happens again. By this time you'll wish you never started. The answer is to pre-heat the fuel line, which is done in water-cooled vehicles by taking a lead off the heater supply pipe, wrapping it round the fuel line just before the regulator, and returning it to the return line from the heater.

This will work fine, but of course the LPG professionals solved all these problems long ago by making a special converter. It's a one-item piece of equipment which contains a primary and secondary regulator plus channels for hot water for pre-heating. If you buy one of those you fit the fuel line on one end, the carb supply on the other, and the leads from the heater hoses at two other points. The converter may be a bit pricey, but it'll solve all those problems at the same time. Best to get one, and do it properly.

Hoses. The connection from the fuel tank to the convertor will be under high pressure. In the UK you legally must make all joints in metal to metal connections and use drawn-steel tube as the fuel line. In the US you'd use aircraft-type hose made of woven stainless steel. But if you're buying a tank and converter, whoever you buy them from will advise about the hose.

The hose from converter to carb is low pressure, and can be ordinary Calor gas tube. Finally, you need the injector for the carb. Harold Bates will sell you one, you can get one from an LPG equipment manufacturer, and some say you can bend the end of a ball-point pen casing and push it through the hole in the carb. Either way, you'll need to drill a hole in the carb at the point I've described, and if you're using a special injector, to thread the hole to receive the injector thread. Some say you should use only hand drills for this, otherwise you may damage the carb. Others manage quite well with an electric drill. The secret is great care,

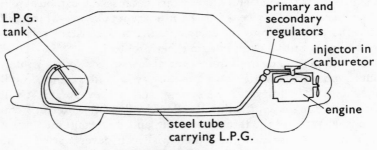

L.P.G. CONVERSION

particularly to make sure your bit doesn't burst through the carb wall and damage anything inside. When fitted, the injector should not stick more than half-way through the carb.

And that's really all there is to it. The basic system, then, is LPG tank, high pressure hose, converter (or fuel pre-heater, primary and secondary regulators), low-pressure rubber hose, hole in the carb and fuel injector sticking through the venturi. The rest is a matter of how to start and how to tune your engine to run on the new fuel.

First, you need some means of switching off the supply of gasoline. If you have an electrical gasoline pump, simply insert an on-off electrical switch in the live lead running to the pump, and mount it on the dashboard. If yours is a mechanical pump, you'll have to insert a tap or valve, which you turn off manually, anywhere between the fuel pump and the engine. In both cases, to start you first cleanse the carb of gasoline by leaving the engine running and switching off the supply of gasoline. After a time it'll splutter and die out. Then turn on the LPG tap on the fuel tank, press the starter and off you go. If you've bought a good LPG converter, you'll find it has an electrical connection which should be wired to a push button switch on the dash. With this you turn on the ignition, push the button for a couple of seconds which squirts a supply of LPG into the carb for easy starting, and then hit the starter button. In that way you'll start from cold more easily than with gasoline. If you have trouble, of course, you can always start on gasoline, warm the engine up, purge the carb of gasoline and then try LPG. It should work OK when warm. I have a tractor which runs off TVO (tractor vaporizing oil), and that has to be warmed up on gasoline in just the same way.

Next, you have to tune the engine for the new fuel. If you have a butterfly choke, it's easy. All your adjustments can be made by altering the choke position. Start with the choke full out, and then return it half-way as the engine fires. Test the vehicle out to see if you have full power. If you don't, you'll need to close the choke a little, because your mixture will be too weak. In any case, you can adjust the tickover speed by altering the choke position, but it's a good idea to take a good sniff at the exhaust when idling to make sure you're not discharging unburnt LPG.

If the choke adjustments don't give you what you want, or if you don't have a choke of the right kind, almost certainly you'll be getting too rich a mixture and you need to cut it down. The way to do this is to drill and tap a small hole in the end of the injector, and fit a small brass screw into it. The more you screw this down, the less fuel you'll admit into the carb. Tune the engine as you normally would until you get the correct idling speed when the engine is warm. After that you can run off either LPG or gasoline, as you choose, at the flick of a switch.

To do the conversion, and get the bits and pieces, you'll really need somewhat more information than I've given. The best single aid, which is designed particularly for VW owners, is an instruction manual put out by Jerry Friedberg, Arrakis Volkswagen, PO Box 531, Point Arena, California 95468. Wherever you live, it's worth getting that information from Jerry (it's called *How to convert your auto to propane*). What's more, Jerry markets a kit, complete in every detail, for the conversion at a cheaper price than you could buy it yourself. He doesn't supply the tank, because it's bulky, but he'll tell you the nearest place to find one.

Small ads in local papers and in such things as *Mother Earth News* tell you how to do a propane or LPG conversion. I've sampled three of them, and they were reasonably helpful. In any case, if you're going to convert, it's well worth spending a few dollars collecting as much information as possible to start with.

Of course there are firms which will do the conversion, lock stock and barrel, for you. Most firms are more interested in converting fleets of tankers or fork-lift trucks, but you can try them, and you can certainly get parts from them.

Prices are high, but in the UK, theoretically, 350 gallons, or say 10,000 miles later, you'll be back in pocket. In practice, it'll take a bit longer for you'll have to motor round a bit to get to the nearest LPG filling station, which will increase your mileage (depends where you live, a lot; so maybe it's best to find your nearest LPG depot before considering conversion).

Don't forget that when you come to sell your vehicle, it's very easy to unhitch your LPG fittings and transfer them to a new one. Once you've bought the stuff, in other words, it should last you through most of the rest of your vehicles.

Finally, you must check that your insurance cover is still valid after the conversion. Some insurance companies may insist on your producing a qualified engineer's report that the conversion is sound before they will renew your insurance.

Methane as transport fuel

It's not on – unless, as I mentioned earlier, we find some neat means of converting methane to methanol. The reason is very simple. Propane can be liquefied at a pressure of 250 lb per square inch. Methane needs 5,000 lb per square inch, and the amount of energy and complicated equipment needed to do that makes the fuel totally uneconomic. The New Alchemy Institute-West has worked out that a 6 hp garden cultivator could be run for only 25 minutes if its tank were filled with methane compressed to only 1,000 lb per square inch (even that is a pressure of 68 atmospheres). And the compression would use up the equivalent of more than one-fifth of the total energy in the methane thus compressed.

But it is true that many farmers, and even some buses, were run on non-compressed methane during and after the last war. The gas was simply led into huge plastic sacks on the roof, and off the drivers went, oblivious it would seem to what would happen if they had an accident and the methane formed an explosive mixture with the air as it escaped. DON'T ON ANY ACCOUNT DO IT. Apart from being highly illegal, it's very dangerous.

Which is a pity, because the LPG conversion you've done will run very well off methane. I suppose if you have copious amounts of methane and the proper compression equipment, it might be worthwhile filling a normal LPG tank with pressurized methane and operating in that way. But a tank 5 feet long and 9 inches in diameter, filled with methane to the very high pressure of 2,800 lb per square inch, will only store the equivalent of $3\frac{1}{2}$ gallons of petrol. And the compression itself will cost you at least the equivalent of a gallon of fuel.

So it doesn't seem to me that it's viable. Methane for running stationary engines, to power such things as generators, is a very different matter. Then you can use the methane at low pressure as it comes off, and use the waste heat from the generator to warm the methane digester. A nice scheme, as sewage farms have discovered to their own benefit. But for transport you'll have either to wait for the methanol conversion or plug on with propane or butane.

Chapter 13

•◦⊃◦◦⊂◦•

Food

IF you've a dozen acres and a few barns to go with it, this chapter is not for you. You need either John and Sally Seymour's *Self-sufficiency* or Richard W. Langer's *Grow it* to tell you how to turn those acres into a delicious diet with some surplus for cash income. Even if you've a large back garden, you only need a good book on how to grow vegetables to provide the bulk of your diet.

But in this benighted age most of us haven't either. A pocket handkerchief-sized backyard with a few mildewed roses, a town house, or even a high-rise apartment are not usually regarded as food production centres. They should be. And they could save their occupants quite a bit in ready cash in the process.

Not that apartment livers can be self-sufficient in food – by any means. What they can do is grow some of their food – say, salads, some vegetables, honey and fish – and change their other habits to cut food bills (and hence, incidentally, doctor's bills – see next chapter) by a half or a third. You are what you eat, the yin-yang people say. Human beings deserve better fare than canned vegetables and squashed beans made to look like pork chops.

I'm not going to get into any arguments over vegetarianism. If you find meat offensive, don't for heaven's sake eat it because there are plenty of substitutes. But it's also no good thinking you're hard done by if you can't any longer afford a 10 lb joint of beef every Sunday and meat every other day of the week except Friday. Those days are gone forever, and if you don't know why, you should. Meat takes much land, and water, at a time when we just don't have enough of either. Cereals and legumes produce far more good quality food from the same acre.

But that doesn't mean we have to forget meat altogether. We are going to need dairy products and eggs for as long as human beings live on this Earth. And as long as we have them, there'll always be some meat. Hens die, cows produce bull calves as well as milkers, farmers need something around to clean up the waste. The pig, for example, is a superb back-up system to a small holding but it should never have become an industry. From now on, it's the bits and pieces of meat that get produced as side products that we'll be eating.

And that's nothing new. In fact, it's been like that most of the time since agriculture was first invented. Only the medieval barons, and their modern imitators, could afford to guzzle their way through a brace of duck, a good helping of beef and top it off with roast swan all in the one evening. From now on it's meat once or twice a week for us, and a much more varied and healthy diet the rest of the time. The staples to that diet are likely to be bread and, finest of all vegetables, potatoes.

Cooking and eating

In the 1880s a man ate an average of 2 lb of bread a day. Now it's not often he gets through 2 lb a week. Which, in a way, is a pity because bread is very good for you. It has protein, it has energy, and a fair complement of the other bits and pieces needed for survival. Today's protein craze too often forgets that cereals have been the main, and sometimes only, source of protein for millennia. In spite of the proverb, you could live on bread alone.

It's one of the last things I'd like to give up. Good bread, that is. But that is increasingly difficult to find, unless you're lucky enough to live in a small village which still has its own bakery. As you probably aren't, and as by now you probably have a real stove in your kitchen which goes all the time, you'd better get into baking your own.

That way you'll certainly get better bread. You won't, however, get it any cheaper if you buy your flour in 5 lb bags from the supermarket. If you buy organic wholemeal flour, your bread will actually work out a great deal more expensive. You may think it's worth it. If not, you may be tempted to find a supplier who'll get you hundredweight bags. But I'm afraid you're in for a disappointment there too. It may seem much cheaper by the pound than the stuff from the supermarket but the bread you bake with your own fair hands is still not going to be much cheaper than what you buy in the shop. To get round that, you have to grind your own flour.

The first thing is to find the wheat. Don't worry as to whether it's hard or soft wheat, because you can make a very decent loaf with either. But you must buy the wheat wholesale, at a proper supplier. Now every sizeable farming township has a feed store of some sort, from which farmers buy their cattle feed, their seed grain, and their chicken food. Anyone can walk into one of those stores and buy whatever he or she wants. You'll pay agricultural prices, and you only need ordinary wheat. They won't, of course, be selling it for bread making, but for animal fodder. That's OK. If it's good enough for animals, it's good enough for you. The only thing you mustn't buy is seed wheat, which has nasty chemicals sprayed on it for agricultural reasons which will probably kill you if you make flour from it.

The store will sell you wheat at what works out at about 7¢ a lb. That's cheap – it means a 2 lb loaf is going to cost you only around 9 or 10¢, allowing for the water content. The only preferable solution is to go out into the country, knock at the nearest farm door, and ask if they've a sack of wheat to sell. If they grow wheat, they almost certainly will be delighted, because it means a few dollars in the pocket which the tax man need know nothing about. We once drove out from Paris about 5 miles, and bought 20 kilos of wheat for what was less than 5¢ a lb. This is really one of the best short circuits to the system you can ever expect to operate. You end up with cheaper and better bread, and the farmer has more money in his pocket. You can't do better than that.

To make it into flour, you need a hand mill. An electric coffee grinder will do, at a pinch, but a hand mill will actually be quicker, if much more tiring. Grinding flour by hand is hard work. Most women (though not all) find it too hard. And you won't want to do it for more than 3 or 4 minutes without a break. The ideal is to grind with someone else, taking 3 minute spells each. But don't grind more in a batch than you need for 10 days or a fortnight or it'll go mouldy.

You may be able to get a mill from your local health food shop. If you live in the States, there are plenty of models available – see, for example, the small ads in something like *Mother Earth News*.

A mill like this will have steel grinding plates, but don't listen to any nonsense you may hear about wheat having to be ground between stones because it isn't true. It is a good idea, though, to put your flour through the mill two or three times to make it as fine as possible. Incidentally, if you're near a farm which is friendly enough, you can always ask them to put your wheat through their kibbler, set as fine as possible. A kibbler is driven by belt from a

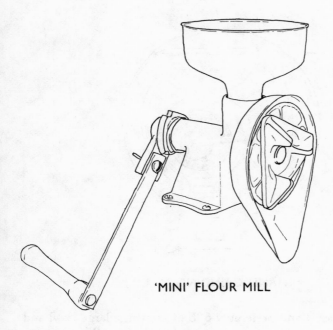

'MINI' FLOUR MILL

tractor and is used for breaking up grain for animal feed. It produces a tolerable flour, but not as fine as you'll get with a hand mill.

There's only one problem you may get with grinding. If your wheat isn't dry enough, it'll mash up in the mill and clog everything up. If it does, stop immediately because the forces that build up are sufficient to break parts inside the mill, as I know to my cost. The only thing you can do is spread the whole wheat out on a tray and dry it off in the oven a bit before you grind. That'll solve the problem.

When you've got your flour, it'll look pretty lumpy compared with the stuff featured on TV ads. Don't worry, but if you want to, sieve the result through a coarse kitchen mesh. If you've not baked before, there are countless recipes in many cookbooks. They sound interminably long, and in fact for flour as coarse as this they really are a bit on the finicky side. I don't follow any of them, and as I get good loaves every time, you may want to try my very much shortened method.

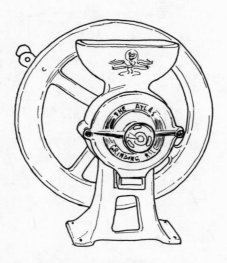

HAND GRINDING MILL

Take at least 3 and preferably 6 lb of flour in a large bowl and leave it to warm somewhere on top of the stove. When you're ready, take a couple of good teaspoonfuls of dried or fresh yeast, mash it up with the same amount of sugar or honey in a mug, and fill it three-quarters full of water which feels very warm, but not actually hot, to your finger. Leave it on the stove till it starts to foam over the top, which will take 10 to 20 minutes. Note that it doesn't matter too much how much yeast you start with. You're really making your own when the sugar solution starts its work, and the longer you leave it the more you'll end up putting in the bread.

Then dump the foaming liquid onto the flour in its bowl, to which you should by now have added two or three teaspoonfuls of salt. Experience will tell you exactly how much. Stir it all around till well mixed, and then add warm water bit by bit, mixing with a wooden paddle. When it's a bit stiffer than a cake mix – too stiff to pour but 'glistening wet' – dump it on to a floured table and start kneading.

That means spreading out the ball of dough with the heels of your hands, pushing away from you, folding it back on itself, turning it through 90 degrees and repeating. To start with, your hands will get very sticky but don't on any account try to scrape or wash the dough off. Just dip them and the dough in some more flour and carry on. Keep kneading the dough on the floured surface, picking up the extra flour with each knead. If it sticks to the table, you need more flour, and a knife to scrape the sticky bit up, other-wise it'll stick there next time too.

Most people worry a lot about when they've kneaded enough. The answer is you'll feel it in your fingers. Eventually the dough reaches a lovely malleable consistency, which is just tacky to the fingers but not sticky. Go on kneading till you've used up all the flour on the table. If you can knead some more without it sticking, and without flour on the table, it's ready.

Coat some bread tins with flour (no need to grease them as well if they're well-used tins), cut the dough up, roll into suitable lengths and gently drop each into its tin. Don't touch it any more. Leave it somewhere very warm to rise. No need for damp cloths, providing there aren't any draughts about. Your dough should fill the tin between one-third and one-half.

When the top of the dough has risen well above the top of the tin, lift the tins ever so carefully and place them very gently in the oven which should be somewhere around 350° to 400°F. This is the tricky bit, because if you jog or jar the dough, or let cold air whistle round it at this stage, it'll just flatten. You leave it in the oven until it's done, which is usually between 30 and 50 minutes. You'll know when it's done because the loaf will drop out of the tin when you tap the bottom. If it doesn't, it's not done, and don't try scraping round the edges with a knife or you'll ruin the whole thing.

When they are done, stand each loaf sideways across its tin to cool. Then eat it. And that's all there is to getting the proper foundation of your diet in good shape for a tiny cost.

That's your wheat under control. The only other grains you're likely to have much to do with are barley and oats. Barley is best made into beer, but some like to drop it into their soup to make barley broth. I loathe it, and I'd concentrate on oats every time. You can do a lot with oats and a flour mill – set coarse to give you oat meal and fine to give you oat flour. Look up oats in a good cookbook, preferably a Scots one because that northern race has made over the centuries and from necessity superb use of the oat. Just for a start, you can stuff an old chicken with it, make oat cakes, oat scones, flapjacks, oatmeal biscuits and, of course, porridge.

Why oats? Because, for one thing, they contain 12 per cent protein, compared to wheat's 9·5 per cent. For another, oats are about the easiest crop to grow in a difficult climate. At Eithin in our first year, at 800 feet up, we grew oats, wheat and barley. We got reasonable yields of all three but the quality of the wheat was poor, the barley indifferent, and the oats superb. In spite of this the UK's oat crop is now reduced to a pathetic 100,000 acres a year. When we really begin to realize for good the food fix we've got ourselves into, the oat is likely to make a big come back. In fact, cooking with grain of any kind is going to be what saves us from either bankruptcy or starvation. Start now.

The other new trick to learn is cooking with the fag-ends of meat – bacon bits, neck of lamb (why does no one eat mutton any longer?), and oxtail and pig's trotters (in other countries regarded as a delicacy). Combine these with some filling legumes, and you've a meal that'll be as tasty as it is nourishing. My favourite is an infinite number of variations of the French cassoulet – which is simply dried beans, simmered long with meat scraps. Before the French slaughter me for insulting one of their gastronomic highlights – which is meant to be prepared from special sausages and certain portions of the goose – let me remind them the cassoulet was invented in south-west France to deal with just the kind of emergency we are now in. It's a hot winter dish, using as staple the dried haricot and other beans stored from the summer's bounty. And to give them flavour, the whole thing is stewed with bits and pieces of fatty meat – the beans absorb the fattiness – which would otherwise not get eaten. Soybeans are marvellous for a dish of this kind, but any dried pulse will do. Make a lot. It'll keep several days – or months if you have a freezer – and work out pretty cheap. The most expensive thing will be the beans.

So when the oat comes back, it'll certainly be accompanied by the field legume. And a good thing too. Legumes fix nitrogen from the air, and so help fertilize the soil. When we stopped field crop rotations and their nitrogen fixing legumes, we lost control of field fertility. Now we have to add expensive artificial fertilizer, which makes the already expensive meat even more so. And, incidentally, when the oat and the legume make their return, so will the people. Much more labour will be needed on the land, and you may then be able to move to the country and by working two or three days a week on the crops, and doing the things in this book, make a good living for yourself.

Potatoes need land. Strangely, they're a really profitable side crop for the farmer, and I have plenty of dairy and beef farmer neighbours who make a tidy bit on the side by growing 2 or 3 acres of spuds every year. Yet they're also the cheapest good food you can buy. There's a real case to be made, if you've got only a tiny garden, for buying all your main crop potatoes.

But everyone, without exception, should grow a few earlies. Even if you live in the tiniest flat or apartment, you can do it just with a plastic sack full of earth and a bit of muck if you can find it. Plant a few seed earlies in the sack, keep it moist and wait. You can do it indoors, on a roof or a balcony. If you can find a barrel, that's better than a sack. This trick may not save you much money, but it'll give you several meals of a level of deliciousness so acute that next year you'll be tempted to fill your living room with potato barrels. Eat them when they're the size of golf balls.

Hens, rabbits and bees

Chances are that wherever you live you can keep some small domestic stock. The problem, these days, is feeding them. The official way, of course, is to buy your chicken food, or your rabbit pellets, and then there's no bother. It isn't worth it. You'll produce eggs or rabbit meat at only marginally below the economic rate, and it'll involve you in a fair amount of work. What you really need is some small stock that will feed either off waste, or off something that you don't have to grow. In that respect, the bee is the perfect parasite.

If you've a garden, you can – as did so many people in the last war – keep a few chickens. Six well-fed chickens will give you at least

1,200 eggs a year, which is just over 3 eggs a day, or a good meal for a family of 4 every other day. Feed them with all your scraps and leftovers, and supplement that with some bought-in lay mash. Don't give the chickens as much as recommended. You can check the right amount from the number of eggs you get in the peak laying month of May. If you get nearly an egg per chicken per day then, you're giving the birds enough food. If you're not, increase the mash.

But in a small enclosure you are going to have problems with chickens. First, they'll reduce their enclosure to a nasty, caked area of flattened mud and you must move them every other month or so, or your tiny bit of land will go permanently sour. Second, they'll probably start pecking each other, mainly in the bottom, and they'll end up looking a frightful mess. And there's not much you can do about it. If they're closely confined, they'll probably start eating their own eggs. You *can* do something about that. Break an egg, in one half mix a good dose of mustard with the yolk, and put the filled half back in the chicken run. A few pecks at that and they'll soon stop.

All of which can be avoided if you coop your hens in little cages. It's very cruel and the birds will be miserable. Don't do it.

An alternative to chickens proper is bantams, which are a really good idea for the tiny garden. They're smaller, produce tinier eggs, but eat much less. They're also easier to handle. At the other extreme, if you've a really small area, I'd buy 3 or 4 Khaki Campbell ducks in preference to chickens. They eat much the same, give you lots of beautiful big eggs, are easier to handle and don't fight. If you've a lawn, don't mow it. Buy a gosling which will grow into a plump goose acting only as a lawn-mower. Fatten it with grain for three weeks before you kill it.

Rabbit meat is something we should all eat much more of. It's delicious, goes a very long way and can be made entirely from weeds and bits of old, unwanted vegetables. Rabbits have to be kept in cages but, unlike chickens, can be made to feel happy and snug while they eat their way to the table. They do reproduce as fast as legend has it, and you'll probably end up with more than you can feed. You can control that, however, by regulating the visits of the does to the buck. Start with one buck and a couple of does. Rabbits like their cages raised at least a couple of feet off the ground and one end should be open for daytime feeding, closed

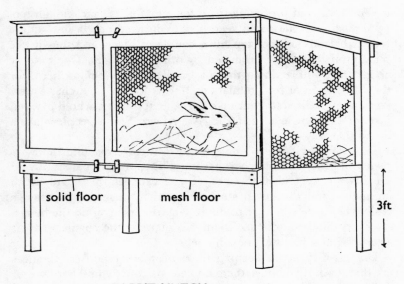

solid floor   mesh floor

3ft

RABBIT HUTCH

only with chicken wire. The other should be boarded up for nesting
and sleeping and must have a solid floor. Rabbits eat their own
droppings, and derive an essential part of their diet therefrom. If
you give them a mesh floor in the sleeping area, they'll lose their
droppings and you'll lose your rabbits.

Of course, you'll need a good book on rabbit keeping. But you
may be surprised to discover just how much a rabbit and her young
will consume. They'll keep you rushing to the nearest weedy area
to gather green stuff. If you can get it from a nearby field, your
problems are solved. Or if a friendly grocer will give you his
unwanted outer leaves. But don't keep rabbits unless you're sure
you can get enough green food for them. If you have to resort
to artificial food like rabbit pellets, the whole thing will be much
easier but quite uneconomic. It is a good idea, though, to supplement their diet with a little grain, particularly before and after
a birth.

You kill a rabbit by holding it up by its hind legs and delivering
a karate chop with the side of your hand to the back of its neck. It's
not so difficult, and much pleasanter than wringing a chicken's
neck. Don't be put off rabbits by thinking you can't do that bit of

it. You can. And preparing them for the table is easy enough too.

Almost everyone could keep bees. You need only a few square feet of balcony or roof top for a couple of hives, and they'll live mainly off the nectar produced by other gardeners. Don't worry about that; you're doing them a good turn by keeping bees, for they are essential for pollination. If you live in an orchard area, you can even hire out your hive to the fruit grower, who'll pay you just for the privilege of feeding your bees. Some people make a living that way.

Bees, of course, are a whole world in themselves, and there are plenty of good books to choose from. The expensive part is buying the hives – second-hand ones, if you can get them, are much cheaper – and the initial stock. After they've settled in, there's really very little you have to do; in fact, the less you do the better, for every time you disturb them you increase the chance of their swarming and finding a new home.

Don't worry about keeping them near other houses. Chances are that, even if you have them on your balcony, you'll hardly ever notice they're there. Bees don't plague people like wasps do, and if you've nervous neighbours, give them the first jar of honey and they'll probably be won over for life.

Bees will fly about three miles to find their food. If there are no gardens, parks, disused weedy junk heaps, or open country within that distance, don't keep bees – but nearly everyone is near enough something that will give bees the nectar they need. Even in a city there are a surprising amount of flowers about, in gardens and parks.

The two things you have to do is extract the honey and feed the bees during the winter (in the natural state they live off their own honey so if you take some of that away you have to replace it with something else). Now honey is more than $1 a lb, and a good hive will give you up to 100 lb a year – if you were foolish enough to take it. It's a good idea, though, to share the honey with the bees, which will upset them less and mean you have to provide less supplement. In the days when sugar was less expensive, you gave them a concentrated sugar solution in the winter, as much as they wanted. Now that's too costly. And the only cheap way round it is to grow a couple of rows of sugar beet, dice up the roots and boil them in water for a few hours. Give the bees the resulting sticky mess, which they'll adore. And that's a marvellous way of

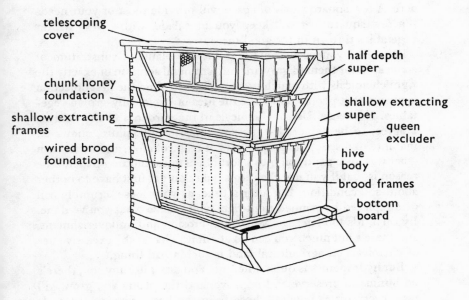

BEE HIVE

circumventing the sugar crisis, by turning a couple of rows of root crops into first-class and very expensive honey.

The honey is extracted in the autumn, and you need an extractor – a metal cylinder into which the combs fit and can be twirled round by a handle to free the honey by centrifugal force. They're expensive to buy, but if you're into bees you'll have found nearby bee keepers who'll gladly lend you their extractor, and give you a hand with it. You can extract and bottle a couple of hives quite easily in one evening. And it's one of the most delightful tasks you can do in the home. Be prepared to get a bit sticky, though.

Hydroponics

Wherever you live, even if you've no garden or yard of any kind, you can grow at least some of your own vegetables. Hydroponics is the art of growing plants without soil, either indoors or outdoors, in yields which sometimes reach the equivalent of 600 tons to the acre. A few square yards of space will provide most of your needs – a few square feet will keep you in salads, with a few winter vegetables thrown in for good measure.

Basically, you need containers for the plants, a substratum of some kind for them to grow in, and a mineral solution of exactly the right chemicals with which to nourish them. And the first objection is always that people don't like the idea of chemically-grown vegetables. Nonsense. Use of chemicals in the garden and the field is, I agree, to be deplored – it's an admission of failure, shows an inability to respect the proper laws of crop rotation, and it can turn what was once good soil into a sort of chemical blotting paper. The reason is that if you use chemicals, you don't at first have to bother about soil condition. But after a time, as your loose, crumbly soil gets replaced by panned mud-flats, you realize what you've done. By then, it's too late; you've got soil erosion and impoverishment, and there's not much you can do about it. That's why excessive use of chemicals on agricultural land is such a bad thing.

But hydroponics is quite different. You don't use any soil, there's no humus to preserve and improve, and the plants you grow will taste every bit as good as those from the best organic garden. If you don't believe it, then you must try it for yourself.

The first thing you need is containers. They've got to be waterproof, must be at least 6 inches deep, preferably a bit more, and must not contain chemicals which will either damage the plants or be subject to erosion from the chemical nutrient solution. You can use wooden boxes, and line them with plastic, making a few holes in the bottom and sides to allow for drainage. These holes must be pluggable, with wooden dowel or plasticine, or even screwed up bits of paper. The box itself is usually raised off the working level a few inches and a tray placed underneath to catch the drips. The plugs are removed from underneath when you want to wash the box and its content through with pure water, and to allow aeration of the roots.

Styrofoam window boxes are ideal, if you can get them cheaply. Old kitchen sinks, sections of barrels, big flower pots, and old tin baths are also good. But if your container is metal you must paint it with an asphalt-based paint to protect it. Creosote and similar chemicals must never be used or you'll lose all your plants.

Into this box, whatever it may be, you put the growing medium, whose job is really only to support the plant and anchor the roots.

Again you can use many different things, and the one you choose will usually be the cheapest thing you can get locally. Sand will do, for a start. But you do need coarse sand, or the bed will get water-logged. If you can mix in something slightly larger, like mixed pebbles as used for concrete mixing, that'll be fine. If you've old bricks lying around, break them up with a lump hammer till the largest bits are about ½ an inch across, and use them complete with all the brick dust you make in the process. Vermiculite (used to make lightweight concrete) is probably the best material of all, but it's not the cheapest. You can, in fact, use any inert substance which ranges in particle size from about ¼ to ½ an inch across down to dust. You must avoid anything with lime or plaster in it.

You then line your box with pebbles or broken pieces of flower pot to give you good drainage, and fill the box to within an inch of the top with your medium. Remove the plugs from the bottom and wash it all through with clean water to make the medium settle down. Firm it with the hand but don't push it down too much. The biggest problem with hydroponics is making sure the roots get enough air – and that means there must be plenty of air spaces in the medium. The plugs *must* be removed every few days to let excess moisture drain away and air flow up between the roots. Very important.

Next, you need to make up a nutrient solution. This you do either by buying the constituent chemicals from a pharmacy and mixing them yourself, or buying a proprietary brand mix direct from a supplier, which will be much more expensive.

If you make your own, the books on hydroponics will give you plenty of examples to choose from. The two most often used are BM1 and BM3.

salt	amount in ounces	
	BM 1	BM 3
Ammonium sulphate	–	10
Sodium nitrate	12½	–
Potassium sulphate	4	3½
Superphosphate	5	5
Magnesium sulphate	3½	3
Iron sulphate	enough to cover a match head	

When you have bought these chemicals, mix them up in an old

bowl with a wooden spoon and then store in an air-tight container. When you need to fuel your plants you take one-third of an ounce of the mixed salts – which in practice means one unheaped teaspoonful – and dissolve it in one gallon of water. Almost without exception, the water you use for the house will be satisfactory. There is an easy test. Put some cut flowers in a vase, add the water you intend using, and watch them for two or three days. If they stay healthy, the water is OK.

Before planting, you should wash your containers through with this water. Then plant your seed as you would in a garden, or transplant your seedlings. The only difference is that no seeds, however big, need to go more than half an inch deep. The next day take your gallon mixture, fill a watering can with it, and sprinkle it on the bed. Sprinkle enough to thoroughly moisten the medium, but not so much that any water is left standing about. Your medium must from now on be kept in this moist condition. How often you will need to feed depends on the warmth and humidity of the environment. If it's dry and hot once a day may be necessary. If it's not, twice a week will be enough.

And that's all there is to starting off on the road to hydroponics. It's best to start with just two or three containers, and growing just your salad crops, plus perhaps a few tomato plants. If all goes well, you'll certainly want to get into larger-scale hydroponics.

And if you've a large enough cellar or attic, you should be able to grow very nearly all your own vegetables (if you don't have enough daylight, you can buy daylight fluorescent lamps). As far as I know, there's nothing you grow in the garden that can't be grown in the hydroponics box. If you've room to put up that solar-heating greenhouse I recommended in chapter 7, then it may be a good idea to turn it into a hydroponic-growing area if you've no garden and hence no soil.

It's no good my telling you how much square footage you'll need to grow all your own stuff. It depends on how clever you are in inter-cropping – planting slow and fast growing crops very close so that one is pulled up and over before the next is mature. And of course, as soon as one plant is finished, you pop in the next succession as quickly as you can. That way you can get very intensive production, without exhausting the soil because you haven't got any.

But if you go big-scale, you'll probably end up with more auto-

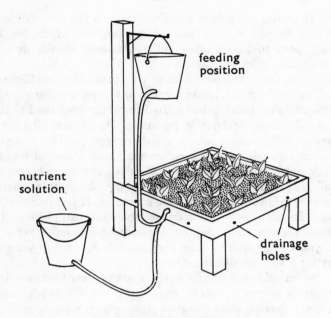

feeding
position

nutrient
solution

drainage
holes

HYDROPONIC BED

matic watering systems and possibly heating pipes running through
your medium. There are countless ways of doing all that, at very
low cost, and any good book on hydroponics will tell you how.
Happy growing.

Aquaculture

Every medieval monastery used to have its fish pond. From it it
drew a fair proportion of protein, mainly in the form of carp. Those
monasteries, in fact, have much to tell us that is relevant to contemporary problems. With vows of poverty, the monks set out to
become self-sufficient in food. They found, as will anyone who
tries hard enough to do that, that they always produced a surplus.
In the end, those accumulated surpluses made them embarrassingly
rich. Planet Earth, take note.

But not many of us now have half an acre of pond we can devote
to carp. Fish-farming is probably the most productive method in
existence of using land, giving in the Far East yields equivalent to

several thousand pounds of excellent food to the acre. With one exception, no one has yet tackled the problem of scaling fish-farming down to family size, and maintaining similar or better production.

That exception is the New Alchemy Institute-East, on Cape Cod in the United States. Thanks largely to the pioneering efforts of its director John Todd, it has started in on the long road to backyard fish-farming. In 1973 it persuaded Americans all over the country to build small pools, cover them with plastic to keep the heat in, and provided each experimenter with a pair of breeding fish. The object was to raise 500 $1\frac{1}{2}$ lb fish in an area no bigger than a small child's swimming pool during the six summer months. There were failures, and there were successes. If you join the New Alchemy Institute as an associate member, you can receive all the information gathered during that experimental period. Even if you don't, you can go quite a long way towards setting up your own fishery for a very small expenditure.

The preferred fish is tilapia, a native to the Near East and Africa which grows extremely fast in warm water, is rich in protein and has a good flavour. And the first thing you need is a pool, approximately 12–14 feet in diameter, and some 3 feet deep. You can buy such a pool from toy shops for a reasonable amount of money. Or you can make one in concrete, or dig one in the ground, lining it first with plastic to stop seepage. If you do the latter, however, you need to put insulation under the bottom and round the sides, otherwise the water will lose heat to the ground too quickly. As your pool will be emptied in the autumn, the insulation need last only six months, and bales of straw will do very well.

Over the pool you need to construct a greenhouse of some kind – or, of course, you can put the pool in an existing greenhouse. If you don't have anything suitable, the easiest, most transportable and lightest structure you can make is a dome. It needs to be between 18 and 25 feet in diameter at ground level, and you can get dome plans from many publications. Specifically, if you write to *Popular Science Magazine*, 355 Lexington Avenue, New York, NY 10017 and enclose $5 they will send you back their Sun-Dome plans, which are what the New Alchemy Institute recommends. It takes only two to three days to put the wooden structure for the dome together. And then you need to double-glaze it. As always, glass is best if you can afford it. If not, greenhouse quality transparent vinyl sheeting will last a good 5 years. Failing that, plastic will do, but don't count on it lasting for a second season. In the winter, incidentally, you can use your sun dome as a greenhouse for growing winter veg, or as a tank for growing some cold water fish.

Now tilapia will not survive in water cooler than about 60°F (15°C). Even at that temperature they won't grow at all, and will only breed and thrive when the water climbs over 80°F. Temperatures of that order are not so difficult as you might think. A double-glazed greenhouse with no ventilation will hit 90°F any time between April and September when the sun is out. And with such a large body of water in the pond, the temperature will fall only very slowly.

In the United States warm enough temperatures are obtainable simply through solar heating as far north as Cape Cod for most of the six summer months. Elsewhere it's a matter of trial and error.

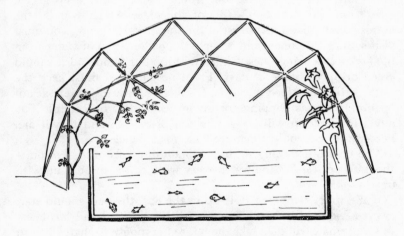

FISH POND AND DOME

Probably you'll need some additional heat source. You can put a small stove and flue in the dome, and run it off wood or coal. You can use an electric heater, which will be costly. Or you can make a small solar panel, and run the warm water from it in copper pipe through the fish tank itself.

Next fill your pool to within 6 inches of the top with water.

You'll have to use your normal supply, but if it's chlorinated allow it to stand for a couple of days and agitate it occasionally to lower the chlorine level to suit the fish. Any new tank or pond should be filled two or three times and siphoned off to leach away any contaminations. Then leave the water to stand, and get it up to the required temperature somehow or other. You should be doing this in April.

Next find your tilapia – in the US you may be able to get them from the New Alchemy people. Otherwise it's the pet shop, and they may take some tracking down. It doesn't matter greatly what species you have, but it is a good idea to order a breeding pair well in advance because they're not easy to find. Your pair will come in a plastic bag full of water. On no account just let the fish out and into your pool. You must lower the bag, complete with fish, into the pool and leave it there until the water temperature in the bag is the same as in the pool. When it is, release the pair.

By this time your pool will probably have gone deep green. That's fine. It means it's full of the algae which will be the tilapias' main food for the rest of the summer. If it's not, you must visit some local ponds, and scoop out a gallon or so of water from the greenest looking ones. Chuck that in your pond and it should green up in a couple of days. From now on you must keep the water fertilized to feed the algae. Do this by lowering in it a sack of manure, or grass clippings or green waste. But be careful. Too much fertilization will starve the fish of oxygen and they'll die. Best not to use poultry manure which is too rich.

The only other thing to do is siphon out – from the bottom – about 10 per cent of the water every week or so, and top up with fresh water.

If the water temperature is up in the 80s, the pair should start to breed straight away. The eggs will be spawned and fertilized, and the female will then take them into her mouth for hatching out after a day or two. Tilapia are mouth-breeders, and the young will live in mummy's mouth, darting out for occasional forages as they get bigger, and returning there when anything untoward occurs.

At this stage you need to provide some additional feed. Of course, you can buy fish food and throw it in, but that's expensive. You need about half a pound of meat protein per day for a growing stock of 500 fish, and perhaps the easiest way is to make an earth worm factory, and throw the worms to the fish. Any good gardening book will tell you how to grow worms in quantities which will exceed your wildest nightmares. Or you can grow maggots on rotten meat – but you run the risk of fly infestation. A hunk of meat hung over the pond is not a bad idea, for the maggots will grow quickly at that temperature and drop straight into the pond.

You don't want more than 500 fish in your pond. You'll have to gauge that by taking water samples and making rough counts. When you've got enough then hike out the breeding pair and store them in a heated aquarium for next year. A temperature in the mid-60°s will be enough to keep them ticking over.

By September or October you'll be having great difficulty in keeping your water temperature up. There's no point in keeping the fish any longer, for they won't be growing much; and if the temperature drops much lower they'll die. So drain most of the water away, using a sieve to prevent the tiniest fish escaping, and then harvest your catch. A smart blow between the eyes will kill the fish, and anything over $\frac{1}{4}$ lb is well worth eating. You may find you like to eat them smaller than that, but it will depend on how well you've done. Anything too small to eat you can give to the cat or the hens or the compost heap, or simply keep as pets.

I don't know how well you'll do – but I do know that if you get it all right you could easily end up with more than \$250 worth of really good food for the deep freeze – or even pickling. And if all the land I owned in the world was a sunny plot 20 feet square, then I'm pretty sure that's what I'd do with it. The rewards are vast. If you get 100 lb of fish from that area, you're producing at the rate of more than 10,000 lb of very good food to the acre. Say 4 tons to the acre. If you grew cereals, one of the most productive means of using land, you'd get no more than 2 tons to the acre, and those tons will have less than half the protein value. If you ran sheep, you'd do well to get more than 300 lb of lamb off each acre every year. In fact, it wouldn't take many people growing fish in their yard to solve the world food problem once and for all.

Chapter 14

 ⋯◦⋯

Health

AN amateur who writes about building, heating, or electrical wiring usually gets away with it. But anyone who writes about medicine and health without being a doctor has a much rougher passage. Everyone to whom I've talked has advised me to omit this chapter (I'm not a doctor).

My obstinate refusal to do so may have something to do with sheer stubbornness. On the other hand, I cling fiercely to the belief that there are things going wrong with our health of which our own western system of medicine has not the faintest idea. Having for many years been a science writer, I have learnt a good deal about medical research, and where it's meant to be taking us. The mortality statistics of our society are not anything of which we have reason to be proud. I've also made a study of the health of primitive peoples of the world – as far as it is known – and found some surprising anomalies. Perhaps most important, I left a relatively sedentary office job in early middle age to go to Eithin. As I watched my own waxing figure suddenly begin to wane, as I felt the return of muscles long since forgotten, and experienced the power of the human body again being used as was intended, it struck me repeatedly that the secret of good health may be no more complicated than is the business of re-learning how to build one's house and cope with one's environment. In a word, we need more common sense and a few less computers. Of which more anon.

The western way of death

Everyone dies, and whatever the pretensions of technocratic society towards what it laughingly calls 'the final conquest of human disease', I suspect that's how it will always be. But the way they die, and the age at which they do so, are constantly changing. That's a problem we think we are fast on the way to licking. Not a bit of it.

Until the early nineteenth century, and even today in some of the poorest and most exploited areas of the world, statistically a man could not expect to see his 40th birthday. Many did, of course, and some even lived to an age which we would consider old today. The Bible talks of three-score years and ten as though such longevity were not uncommon even two millennia ago. But death in infancy, childhood and even adolescence were so common that the average age of death lingered obstinately in the late 30s.

That began to change with Pasteur, and the sudden increase of knowledge we gained of the relationship between the spread of disease and insanitary conditions. When, in 1848, a Dr John Snow connected the spread of cholera to the supply of water from a pump in Soho, the way was open to environmental control of disease. Advance was rapid, and the spread of infectious disease by filth was all but halted in a few decades.

And as these great advances began to slacken, research produced the drugs which would kill infectious organisms in the body. First the sulphonamides, then penicillin, and later many more. The progress of the previous fifty years was thus enabled to continue. Life expectancy at birth continued to increase, giving an unbroken improvement record which lasted for a century.

That took us to the 1950s and 1960s. By then life expectancy at birth for a man in any advanced country was just over 60, and for women it was two or three years longer. But, and this is not much talked about, by the end of the 1960s this century-long progress had all but halted. In the first few years of this decade, some countries even began to record a small but significant decline in life expectancy at birth. It looks as though we're at the end of a long road.

Why? Because nowadays we die from what are called the hidden diseases – which means primarily a number of related conditions such as heart disease and stroke which all basically have something to do with the body's ability to pump oxygen-carrying blood around the bloodstream. The first myth is that most of us now die from cancer. Not true. Less than one-fifth of all deaths are from cancer. The real killers are these first two, which together account for more than 50 per cent of all deaths in the advanced world. You, in other words, are more likely than not to die from them.

Consequently, we put most of our research eggs in those baskets. Huge sums are spent on cancer research, and on investigations of heart complaints and arterial disease. They don't seem to make much impression on the figures. Obstinately, we continue to die from the same things – and, as often as not, somewhat before we expect to. Cancer often strikes in the 50s, arterial disease is not uncommon in the 40s, and weak hearts are found even in adolescence.

In some Calvinistic way, all this is interpreted as being the lot of civilized man. Hence the term 'the hidden diseases'. We pretend that these diseases have come up to strike us now because only we are privileged to live long enough to die from them. In previous centuries, it is assumed, men died so early that these so-called degenerative and hence hidden diseases never had time to appear. We have to grin and bear it.

Don't believe a word of it.

The primitive way of life

This myth dates from the times of Victorian anthropology. When civilized man first began to encounter uncivilized man, the latter were regarded as barbarian heathen. And, not having been endowed with the luck that we have of being born well north of the equator, it was assumed that the primitive lived in beastliness, pain and constant disease.

The fact that we are here at all today gives the lie to all this. The primitive must, after all, have survived pretty well to have given rise to such superior stock as we. Whatever his health was really like, it must have been at least reasonable, or the human species would have died off millennia ago.

Why he didn't is a long story. But some anthropologists and doctors have recently been awakened to the possibility that primitive life was not as bloody as their Victorian grandfathers would have had us believe. So they have been out to Africa, South America and a few other places where we have permitted primitive life to continue, and taken a few measurements. The results are astonishing.

For instance, longevity has been found fairly common in truly primitive societies. We all know about the Georgians and their fabulous old age, but other societies show some of the same features. In the Andes of Ecuador, for instance, there lies the valley of Vilcabamba where the oldest known inhabitant, a certain José David, has an apparently authentically recorded birth date of 1840. In that scattered community of 800 souls, more than 17 per cent are over 60 years of age. Three of them are over 120, 4 over 110, 9 over 100, 16 over 90 and 28 over 85. And these are people who drink between 2 and 4 cups of rum a day, and smoke between 40 and 60 of their own cigarettes rolled in maize leaf.

Of them, Dr David Davies, who has studied the area, writes: 'Hypertension, heart disease, and cancer are comparatively uncommon. Death is usually the result of an accident, or of catching influenza from the few outsiders who visit the place.'

The Vilcabambans may be exceptional. But other studies show that truly primitive peoples often live well over 60. And that the hidden diseases from which we suffer so acutely are all but absent. One example must suffice.

Some 3,000 miles east of Australia, almost in the middle of the Pacific, are to be found the islands of Raratonga and Pukapuka. Fate has decreed that Raratonga should follow the conventional development of the west, while progress has all but passed Pukapuka by. Life there is still mainly primitive and self-sufficient. A few export crops are grown but most inhabitants earn no more than $30 a year. On Raratonga, by contrast, the cash economy is better developed, bringing annual incomes of up to $200 a year – minute by our standards but large for a country until recently completely underdeveloped.

Dr Ian Prior, from the Wellington Hospital in New Zealand, has studied the health of these island peoples. On Raratonga heart disease was as common as in our society, and 4 per cent of the men and 25 per cent of the women were grossly overweight; 21 per cent of the men and 36 per cent of the women had high blood pressure.

On primitive Pukapuka heart disease was virtually unknown. Only 1 man and 2·2 per cent of the Pukapukan women were overweight – and only 2·2 per cent of the men and 4·4 per cent of the women had high blood pressure. I need only add that obesity is the third of the principal killers in our society, greatly increasing the risk of early death from other causes. The death rate in our society goes up 13 per cent for every 10 per cent an individual is overweight compared to the average for his build.

Two examples like these do not make a watertight case. But they are only the most impressive tips of a formidable mountain of data which has been gathered in recent anthropological research. Surveys in tribes as far apart as the Australian aboriginals, the Malayan aboriginals, the Kalahari bushmen, the Congo pygmies, the African Hadza and the Brazilian Amerindians have all shown the same thing: in all these tribes there is no, or extraordinarily little, evidence of heart disease and high blood pressure. What's more, even where traces of such diseases are found they do not, as they do in our society, become more common with old age.

The conclusion is inescapable: these are not hidden diseases. They are diseases of civilization, which somehow or other we bring on ourselves.

The way back to health

There are three main theories as to why this is. First, that the hidden diseases are caused by stress. Second, that they are caused by a faulty diet. And third, that they are caused by lack of exercise. There is some truth to each of them, but I believe that the first two are largely symptoms of the third. In other words, that sedentary man predisposes himself to the diseases of civilization, a condition which is aggravated by the stresses to which he is exposed and the kind of food which he eats.

That food alone is not the cause must be obvious. Today, a huge cult surrounds the intake of cholesterol, dairy products, eggs, even stimulants such as coffee and tea. All bad for you. Well, all food is bad for you in the sense that you eat it all your life and then die. A good statistician could show quite convincingly that the greater the volume of food eaten the greater the chance of death. We don't have to linger on such absurdities.

Of course, fatty things may well make the travel of blood through the arteries more sluggish. But look at the Eskimo, existing for much of the year almost entirely on greasy blubber. According to western medicine he ought to drop dead from arterial disease before he reaches his 20th birthday. He doesn't. Nor do the primitive pastoralists who live mainly on dairy products. And as for stimulants, we have a quaint old idea that they're somehow connected with city living. But start counting the number consumed by primitive people, either occasionally or daily, and you'll find we have few junkies even to compare to that sort of intake. The intensive use of stimulants goes back far beyond the beginnings of history.

But the one thing primitive man and civilized man do not share is hard work. By that, I mean manual work, and I mean varied manual work. I doubt very much that we would all become healthier if we became coal miners. Hard repetitive physical work, in cramped and insanitary conditions, certainly makes for early death. It is an insult to the human species. I make no defence of it.

But if you look at what a primitive did in his average day, his lot was strikingly different. Three days on foot hunting, covering perhaps 50 miles of territory. Then a week's communal work building a house for a newly married couple. Then a few days in the fields, gathering and harvesting the crops. A couple of days boat building, a couple of days rowing and fishing, an intensely active tribal dance lasting 48 hours. These are part and parcel of the primitive experience. Were they what protected him from the diseases we fall prey to? I suspect so.

In fact, lack of exercise is commonly thought of as one of the main reasons for our plight. It's not a new theory. But look at the way we try to get round it. Got a weak heart? The doctor advises us to give up using the car to the station and to walk the one mile there and back every day. Start taking exercise. Do a few press-ups. Go to a gym twice a week for half an hour a time. I submit that these are the most idiotic half-measures a society ever took to preserve its health.

For a start, they are essentially pointless activities. They form at best a boring adjunct to our lives, something to be got through in the hope of squeezing out an extra year or two of life at the far end. They are miserable palliatives.

The trouble came when we divorced the head from the hands, the body from the mind. Today you are expected to perform with one or the other, depending on your level of education, but never with both. Modern-day China has set out to eliminate this distinction between mental and physical activity. In doing so, I reckon Mao cottoned on to not only a valid political point but one of great medical importance as well.

There are many reasons for doing the things outlined in this book. Some of them I have mentioned only in passing. These are the ecological, sociological and spiritual motives for getting control of your own piece of the environment. But I've stressed the economic advantage of it all, because that is the one common language we all share in a time of inflation, falling dollar rates and increasing financial equality.

None of which, of course, means anything if you do not live to see the results. The best reason of all for any kind of technological self-sufficiency may be what it will do for your body. I know it's as good a way to health as any other for I have experienced the results myself. I suspect it's by far the best way we have of avoiding the diseases of civilization – not only the physical ones, but the sociological and psychological ones as well.

The implications of evolution

The reason for all this has basically to do with evolution. Think back a few million years, to the time when the arm-swinging anthropoids were first giving rise to human-looking apes. As the hands and the brain developed, they did so as adjuncts to a powerful, fast-moving body. They made that body the more effective, enabling what later became known as man to dominate (to a fairly sickening degree) over his fellow animals.

It continued pretty much like that until, say, 10,000 years ago, when agriculture came swinging in. With it came surplus, and some relief from the constant battle against the environment, hunger and shelter. And with surplus came profit, leisure and, in many though not all places, a class society where the top dogs were waited on by the bottom ones. Then the trouble began, because the bodies of both the top and bottom dogs were essentially the same. They had evolved to enable their contents to cope with the environment they found themselves in, and to function efficiently in it. Change the environment and the body no longer matches its functions. And, as you must count several thousand years for even a minute evolutionary change, the body has by no means caught up with the easy way of life it could now enjoy. Hence our troubles.

In a nutshell, that's why we must still use our bodies to stay healthy. They weren't designed for sitting at desks for 40 per cent of their life and, if made to do so, in the end revolt against it. But, further, there's plenty of evidence that they weren't designed to cope with the sort of food intake we now give them. Adaptable they may be, but not infinitely so.

Trying to pick one's way with reason through the mass of food fads which are today's cults is no easy matter. I wouldn't bother. Yet there is one area where it does seem that both common sense and the facts indicate a change.

The human body was not evolved to live on a high intake of refined foods. We do. We consume vast quantities of refined carbohydrates, mainly in the form of white sugar and white flour. Now any kind of sugar will make your teeth rot, but it is a fact that the digestive system needs roughage. It craves particulate matter, lumps of this and that, and will not work as it should if it doesn't get them. Is it then surprising that doctors have discovered an undeniable association between refined carbohydrates – notably white sugar and white flour – and the following diseases: obesity (and hence varicose veins and piles), dental decay, diabetes, thrombosis, peptic ulcer, constipation, diverticulosis and cancer of the bowel?

Note that these foods do not cause these diseases because, as the eco-freaks might like us to believe, they contain impurities. On the contrary, they lead to such diseases because they do not contain the impurities the body needs to work as was intended. So grind your flour, make your bread, eat a lot of it, spread it as thick with butter as you can afford, and don't worry. If you're physically active as well, there's not much more you can do, and probably very little else you need to do.

The alternative medicine

Such pragmatic advice needs situating in a broader context. Throughout this book I have been implying that there is something seriously amiss with the way we have come to use our technology – with our profligate use of energy, our shoddy building techniques, our almost total ignorance of how best to use the hidden power of the wind and the sun. Medicine is a technology as well, and the western way of moulding it to our purposes has just as many drawbacks.

At least three-quarters of our medicine is concerned with either the administration of antibiotics or surgery. The pill and the knife. Effective they undoubtedly are. But, equally, they are grossly overused. We know pretty well, for example, how dental decay could be virtually eliminated by changing dietary habits. We do nothing about it – and instead employ a veritable army of dentists to drill their way through rotting teeth and fill the holes with cement. An environmental approach to that problem would save a small fortune and much anguish. So it is with other diseases. We concentrate on a cure, where prevention would be better.

But, for the diseases of civilization, prevention involves doing something about civilization – something which, on the surface, looks suspiciously like a return to less civilized conditions. Why it should be less civilized to do something which lessens the incidence of heart disease, cancer, stroke and digestive complaints has always puzzled me. But you can choose. A sedentary life, refined carbohydrates, obesity and heart attack – or an active one, and a greatly increased chance of longevity, with fewer minor troubles on the way.

But so spectacular have been the triumphs of western medicine, that all other systems of healing have been thrown out. I cannot accept that the thousands of herbs used by the human race for millennia to improve health have all been useless. Or that the Chinese system of acupuncture, for which so much is now claimed outside the developed world, is a sinister oriental fabrication. Or even that today's more mystical cults, which draw their inspiration from the relationship between diet, mind and body, are the nonsense most western doctors would claim them to be. In all these areas, and perhaps many more, lie some remarkable alternatives to the western way of life – and death.

But, of course, I can't tell you which to espouse. No one has yet produced the definite guide to this maze of new ideas which has suddenly invaded the western world. Doubtless they soon will. Meanwhile, you can do no better than follow your instincts.

Chapter 15

This and that

Electrical wiring

WIRING a house for electricity is so easy that it doesn't merit a whole chapter of this book. There is no need ever to have an electrician visit your house. Though it's potentially much the most dangerous of all the jobs you may do, common sense, a good book on wiring, and a test meter are all the equipment you need.

The common sense bit is only a matter of remembering to turn off the current before you start to fiddle. You can either turn off the supply to the whole house at the main switch, or remove the fuse to the circuit you are working on. Always test that circuit with an appliance like a table lamp which you know works reliably before touching any wires. The trouble may come when you've been at it for a bit. Your first bit of re-wiring will be done with great care, and you'll be meticulous about checking that the current is off. It's after you've got the hang of it, and got thoroughly used to handling the ends of cables which would normally be live, that the danger comes. When you've got used to the idea of touching 'live' cable ends, you must get on your guard again, because it's very easy to forget about switching the juice off. Be *very* careful.

Don't start any wiring of any kind, or buy any new fittings, until you've bought, or looked at in the library, a standard electrical guide (I've listed three recent titles on page 289). They take you through all the rules and regulations, all the wiring diagrams, all the appliances you can use. If you follow the instructions, you can't go wrong.

The one addition you do need is a good test meter. You can buy small ones for around $10 now, and it'll be one of the best investments you ever made. All test meters measure voltage. You must make sure that yours will also measure resistance, for that's what you mainly need it for. Except *in extremis*, don't use the meter to test for live voltage – you can, of course, but there's always the danger your hand may slip and touch a live lead. You can do all the tests you need with the current turned off.

First, select for measuring resistance. The needle on the gauge will sit at 'nought', until you touch the two leads from the meter together. There is then virtually no resistance between them, and the needle should swing right over to the other side. That tells you you have a circuit flowing.

To get the hang of it, now test a few of your appliances. First touch one lead from the meter to the ground pin of a plug connected to something like a table lamp, and the other lead to the live pin. There should be no reading. If there is, the appliance is faulty, as current is flowing from the live terminal through the ground. Overhaul it before re-connecting it. A test meter is worth having just for this trick.

Now if your appliance has an on/off switch, as does a table lamp, put the test leads across the two pins of the plug. When the appliance switch is off, there should be no reading. When you turn the switch on, you should get a high reading, showing that current is now flowing round the circuit. If you don't, again there's something wrong, and your appliance won't work.

Next, suppose you have just installed a new ring main in your house. A ring main starts with one cable coming from the fuse in your consumer unit, leads to the first power point, and is then linked by another cable to the next power point, and so on until the cable returns to the distribution box. You normally install one ring main for each floor of your house. And you end up with two cables to fit in the distribution box. The two live (red) leads go into the fuseway (30 amps for a ring circuit), the two neutrals into the neutral terminal block, and the two grounds into the ground terminal block. But before you connect them, think. If you've made a mistake in the wiring somewhere, when you turn on after connecting, the fuse is going to blow straight away. You'll then wish you'd never started because finding the fault can be very tedious.

But you can check all this with a meter. As its name implies, a ring circuit is a ring of current, and there should be a continuous circuit between the two ends of the live leads, the neutral leads and the ground leads. So connect your meter to the two live leads, and check that you get a high reading. If you don't, you don't have a ring circuit. Do the same for the neutral and the ground leads.

Next you need also to check that you haven't anywhere got a neutral wire touching a live one, or a live one touching a ground. So use the test meter to link the live lead to the ground. There should be no current. Then check the neutral against the live. Again there should be no current. Finally, check the neutral against the ground.

The first time I tried this, I found I had a high reading between neutral and live, and thought I'd have to re-check the whole circuit. Then I remembered I'd left a clock plugged in, and the reading was simply due to the current flowing through the circuit and round the clock as intended. So all these tests must be made with all appliances either unplugged or turned off. But once you've done them, and got all the right readings, you know for sure you can connect to the distribution panel, turn on, and all will work according to plan.

You'll then be able to devise your own tests for the lighting circuit. Contrary to what most people think, a lighting circuit is considerably more complicated than a power ring main (and, incidentally, every bit as dangerous). But with your meter you'll soon be able to discover where your faults lie, and rectify them easily.

Last time I re-wired a house, I found only two faults on testing. As they were both caused by the same thing, it may be worth describing a common amateur error. Every light switch, ceiling rose and power circuit is fitted in basically the same way. The cable or cables come in and are stripped of their outer PVC sheath, leaving three wires exposed. The ground is already bare, but the other two are covered in black and red plastic. The end of this plastic must be stripped off, and the bared copper pushed into the appropriate hole in the socket, and held there by tightening up a brass screw.

Now you want to bare just enough of these two wires so that when pushed in and tightened up, there is bare copper inside the hole, and the red or black plastic runs up as far as the entry to the hole. It is not a good idea to have exposed copper visible outside the hole (except in the case of the ground wire). This is common sense. But many amateur electricians are over cautious, bare too little of the wire, push it in, and then (although they don't realize it) tighten the brass screw down, not over the copper, but over the plastic sheath. That way, you don't have a proper connection, and when you switch on the current will be flowing, if at all, through the plastic sheath. You probably won't get any result at all when you switch on. If the fault is in a lighting circuit, you may find the bulb does light but only dimly, because the current is flowing through the very high resistance plastic. So check that all your brass screws are actually tightening down over bare copper.

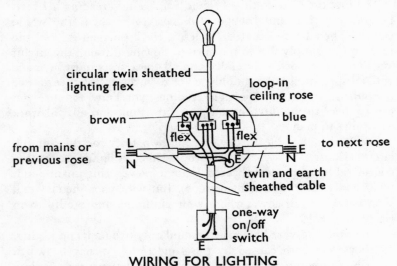

WIRING FOR LIGHTING

If you are wiring a house for the first time, you will have to have the electricity supply people in to make the final connection. But if you are re-wiring, or extending an older wiring system, there is no need for that expensive operation unless you have to move the fuse box or distribution panel to a new place, or unless you plan to use so much more juice that your supply has to be up-rated. If you find you can't bring your new leads into the fusebox or distribution panel because of the way it's constructed, you'll have to disconnect all the old leads, label them with great care so you know how to reconnect them, take down the consumer unit, thread in your new leads, and connect it all up again. Probably you'll buy a new distribution panel to allow for the extra circuits you're adding.

While doing all this, of course, the main switches near the meters must be turned off. And when you fit the new consumer unit make sure you put it somewhere where the supply 'tails' from the meter will reach. You can't lengthen those tails yourself, although you can shorten them, or disconnect and reconnect them to the consumer unit.

Finally, if any of your existing wiring is rubber, it must be replaced with PVC cable as it will be beginning to perish. If it's PVC, you're OK because that will last indefinitely.

Heat pumps

A heat pump is a refrigerator working in reverse. When you put food in a refrigerator, the cooling mechanism takes heat from the food and throws it out of the back through the coils you'll find there. If you could measure it, you would find that the heat ejected is considerably more than the work put in by the refrigerator motor. That is because you are collecting the heat from the food as well as the motor.

Now consider the refrigerator, not as a cooling mechanism, but as a heater. If you had a large refrigerator you could, for instance, cool a whole larder or cold store room with it, and use the heat collected to warm at least part of your house. The key to the idea is that you can collect, say, 3 kWh of heat by putting in only 1 kWh of energy. You're not, of course, actually getting something for nothing – you're taking heat from one place and transferring it to another: hence the name heat pump.

In 1852 Lord Kelvin first suggested using this idea to heat houses. Unfortunately, not much progress has been made since then, except in the United States where most houses have air conditioners. These are essentially heat pumps, and they can be used either way – to cool the house in summer, or warm it in winter. If you live in a place where summer cooling is really essential, a heat pump may well be worth the expense and trouble it involves.

But people are now making much noise about heat pumps again. Most of it is ill-considered, and my purpose really is to show why heat pumps are not, in general, worth investigating – with one or two exceptions. First, the basics.

A heat pump must get its heat from somewhere. The one thing

everyone has plenty of is air – and you can indeed extract heat from the air outside your house, and use it to warm the inside. But the trouble is that in a moist climate the heat collector outside the house, which will operate much below freezing point, soon gets covered in frost – as do the coils in a fridge. And when that happens, the heat collection efficiency of the device will drop rapidly.

You can also collect heat from running water – if you're lucky enough to have a stream flowing through your garden. Or you can bury pipes underground in your garden and take heat from the sub-soil. All these methods have been tried and found to work. But you need a lot of pipe and a lot of digging for a soil heat collector; and not many of us have running water to filch our heat from. Someone once did it by collecting from a permanently running tap, but if we all did that we'd soon run out of water. Anyway, the Water Board wouldn't like it. So the first problem is where to get the heat from.

The second problem is that to buy a heat pump is costly, and to make one difficult, though not impossible. You need a compressor, an evaporator, a condenser, an expansion valve, and an odd assortment of pressure dials and temperature recorders. The whole thing must be connected together using copper pipe and silver brazing for the joints so that the vibrations caused by the compressor don't start a leak going. The system must then be filled with a refrigerant liquid, usually Freon 12, which can only be done by a specialist refrigeration engineer. The refrigerant is expensive, and it's very likely you'll lose the lot unless all your joints have been made with super-human care. Upkeep and maintenance of this lot is quite troublesome.

Thirdly, you must consider what you're going to get out of it. Most of the heat pumps actually built so far have not produced more than 3·5 kWh of heat for every 1 kWh of work put in. At Eithin we originally thought this gain well worthwhile. We designed quite a large heat pump because we were lucky enough to have a stream flowing down by the side of the house. We planned to take 15 kW out of the stream which, though small, would be lowered only one or two degrees Centigrade in the process. We reckoned that for this amount of output we would have to put in only some 3 kW of energy. We bought a 3 kW compressor second-hand for £165 and would then have had to buy at least £50 worth of motor to run it. With a heating system like that you need to be able to turn the motor on and off by thermostat which means starting quite a large electric motor automatically, which in turn demands some complicated equipment and a large flick in the lights every time it goes on and off. We were going to make our own evaporator, and to buy a second-hand condenser.

Then we hit the fourth problem. To get the biggest gain from a heat pump you must have the smallest possible temperature difference between the heat collected and the heat output. We thought we had this one licked, because the temperature of the water was on average some 41°F, and we planned to convert the heat into warmed air at about 85°F. A pretty small temperature difference, which should give a good gain. The gain drops rapidly if you want a heat output to power hot radiators at, say, 158°F. But the trouble with our well-insulated timber frame house was that it had no heat capacity. For that you need water somewhere in the system which will cool and warm much more slowly, so that the heat pump turns on and off only a few times a day. With our warm air system, the thing would have been constantly 'hunting', switching on and off every few minutes trying to maintain the thermostat temperature. We therefore decided to use the heat pump to warm a large volume of water, instead of air, and then of course the gain we would have expected would drop from say 5 to 1 to 3 to 1, or even 2 to 1.

At about this time, I left Eithin – before any real practical work had started on the heat pump. In the year since I left the project has not progressed any further, and now I doubt that it will. Only after I left did I discover another obvious drawback.

Nearly all heat pumps are run directly from an electrical motor powered off the mains. All right: we hoped to get at least 3 kWh out for every 1 we put in. But then electricity generation and transmission is only about 20 per cent efficient. So 5 kWh of coal were being fed into a power station somewhere, to provide us with 1 kWh of electricity, which we would then use to make 3 kWh of heat. Five in, 3 out, over-all efficiency 60 per cent. Now you can buy a coal-fired or even oil-fired boiler which will work at 65 per cent efficiency, and which will cost perhaps one-tenth as much as the heat pump we were planning. Also: less work, less main-tenance, and less hassle.

For these reasons I doubt that anyone should seriously consider building a heat pump.

Exceptions: one I've already mentioned in chapter 7, which is to use a solar roof as the heat source for a heat pump. All the objections I've just mentioned still apply, but you are now increasing the efficiency of your solar collector so much it might be worthwhile. It might, but I doubt it, unless you happen to be a refrigeration engineer.

Second, if you could drive your compressor by wind power, you would certainly be onto a good thing. Now a small compressor will take quite a lot of wind power, and the whole thing would be much simpler if you could link the wind power drive direct to the compressor, and power it without converting first into electricity and then back again into mechanical power. This is really one for the labs, because no one has ever built a variable speed compressor-driven heat pump, which is what a windpowered device would be (no need to govern the windmill, incidentally, because the compressor will do that for you). An interesting but very complicated project for someone. Probably not you.

Thirdly, there may be a future for a different type of refrigerator or heat pump. The one I've described so far, consisting of electric motor and compressor, operates on what's called the vapour compression cycle. But gas refrigerators, for example, operate on a vapour absorption cycle. The energy is put in in the form of heat, usually a gas flame, and there is no compressor or motor. The details are not important, except that the gain from such a system is smaller than in the compression cycle, and there's no point in wasting precious natural gas for such a small gain as a method of house-heating.

But if you are a King Methane Producer, that could be your best way of utilizing it. Of course, you'd need quite a lot of methane, and that means that probably you'd have to be a farmer of some kind, almost certainly the intensive kind who keeps his animals in sheds and has easy access to their muck. You might get very cheap house-heating that way, but maintenance of the heat pump and methane plant would be considerable.

If, in spite of all this, you persist in having a heat pump, there is only one further piece of advice I can offer. You must splash out about $15 and buy *Modern refrigeration and air conditioning* by Althouse, Turnquist and Bracciano. It's available from Goodheart-Willcox Co., South Holland, Ill. 60473. This has absolutely everything in it you could need to know.

Yoghourt

From heat pumps to yoghourt is the sublime to the ridiculous. But my gloom about heat pumps is vastly exceeded by my enthusiasm for yoghourt. And that's because it is so easy to make, and the result is so much cheaper than shop-bought yoghourt. You can make 3 pints of yoghourt for what it would cost you for less than half a pint from the shop.

Here's how. Boil 3 pints of milk. Then let it cool till it's finger-warm, and stir in the smallest pot of shop-bought yoghourt you can buy. There is some nonsense abroad that you can use only what is called 'live' yoghourt, and that that is difficult to buy. As far as I know all yoghourt is live, and certainly all the stuff I've bought can be used to make your own.

When you've stirred it up in a big bowl, put a plate on top and put it in the airing cupboard overnight. Or anywhere that's really warm, say 85°F. In the morning it'll be yoghourt, although the curds will have separated from the whey. Just stir it all in with a fork, put it in the refrigerator and it's ready to eat. Add your own flavouring, if you want; my favourite is brown sugar (don't, of course, start your brew with a flavoured yoghourt: you must buy a plain one). If you haven't a warm place, then wrap the yoghourt in a sleeping bag. Don't have any truck with rip-off electric yoghourt-makers.

When it's nearly finished (which in our house takes about two days) haul the kids off before they scrape the bowl. Keep back just the amount you needed to start it off with, and use that as the starter for your next batch. You can go on like that for dozens of batches, but when it begins to get very thin, it's time to lash out and buy another yoghourt for starter.

Candles

And I don't mean those arty-crafty coloured and sculpted jobs that cost more than $2 each and are good only as Christmas presents for people you can't think what to buy. People always used to make their own candles, and there's no reason why you shouldn't. If you want to go into it as a trade, then you'll be buying paraffin wax and moulds and selling the product. That's your affair.

Mine is what you do with old unwanted fat – either what you have left over in the house, or what you can beg from the butcher. He may know it as tallow, and as he doesn't any longer have any use for it, you can probably get all you want from him for nothing. When you've got it, melt it in the oven and skim off the bits and pieces. Keep it hot.

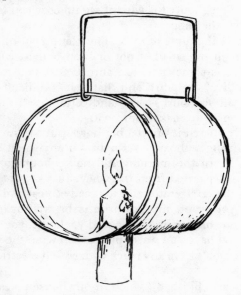

CANDLE TORCH OR 'BUG'

You now need some thick cotton thread and a stick, plus some old washers. Tie one end of the thread to the stick, and the other end to a washer (or some similar small weight), until you have a line of weighted threads hanging from the stick. Then pour your hot fat into small plastic containers, and place them under the stick, so that the cotton hangs down into the centre of the fat, with the washer not quite touching the bottom. Let it cool and you have candles. If they won't come out when they're cold, just warm them slightly in front of the fire.

People say tallow candles smell horrible. It depends on the fat, but most of the ones we have made have been perfectly acceptable. They do burn a little differently from paraffin wax candles, though. They give a little less light, the light is whiter and less yellow, and they tend to sputter somewhat. But then they aren't costing you anything, and you're putting waste material to good use.

Don't bother making candles if you're going to stand them up in saucers and then carry them about. It's not worth saving a few pence when the fire you'll inevitably have in the house will cost you several thousand dollars. If you use candles, you must put them in the proper thing. The old glass lanterns were superb, but are now difficult to get. Almost as good are old-fashioned enamelled candlesticks, with a loop of metal for a finger hold. They're difficult to find new, but you can pick them up in junk shops. And if you want a directional light, or something you can take outside, make a 'bug'.

For this you need an old can, about 1 lb size or bigger, with the top and bottom removed. Then cut a cross with a sharp knife in the middle of the side, and push your candle up through the centre of the cross until the wick lies almost exactly in the centre of the can. Make two small holes in the top and fit a wire handle. A bug gives something like a lantern beam, and only the strongest of winds out-doors will ever blow it out. One of them can save you a lot in flashlight batteries when you go out to put the hens to bed.

Soap

Soap I have never made, but I keep reading about how to do it and forgetting to try myself.

First thing you need is a barrel without a bottom. Place it on a board, slightly tilted so that liquid will run down it and collect in a vessel at the bottom. Then line the bottom with straw (to filter impurities), add about four large mugfuls of lime (from a builder's supplier or agricultural store) and fill the rest of the barrel with wood ashes. Empty slowly a bucketful of water into the top, and then some more until it's good and wet. According to a recipe in *The Whole Earth Catalog* you should then add more water, at intervals of 3 to 4 hours, on the first, third and fifth days. In other words, keep the water going, and by the end of a week what you have collected in the vessel at the bottom is a strong alkali called lye.

Don't put lye into aluminium pans or it'll eat its way through them – use enamelware or iron pots. When the lye is strong enough to float an egg on, it's ready for soap making. Stir into 15 gallons of lye about 11 lb of tallow or grease heated to boiling point.

The tallow you can get from the butcher, or you can keep your own meat scraps and render them down, carefully taking off all bits and pieces before adding it to the lye. Traditionally, only goat tallow was used in soap-making, and that's about as good a use for

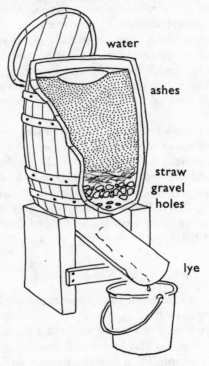

water

ashes

straw
gravel
holes

lye

LYE MAKING FOR SOAP

goats as I can think of (though John and Sally Seymour also recommend curried goat meat – a good combination with soap-making). Stir in the tallow, and stir for 5 minutes every day. If you don't have something very like soap inside a week, add a pail of rainwater.

Soap needs to be hardened off by ageing, and if you've got your proportions wrong in some way, you can add a salt solution and stir it all round. Impurities will dissolve in the brine, and you collect the solid bits by filtering, which will harden off to make soap.

If it sounds like a lot of work, remember 15 gallons of lye and 11 lb of tallow will make a lot of soap. And technological self-sufficiency, however rewarding and economic it may be, is certainly a dirty occupation.

Chapter 16

Community

To all of which there is only one other piece of economic advice which I ought to give: if you really want to save money, join or found a community.

I've already said we lived pretty well at Eithin on £2 per head a week. We pooled most, though not all, our income. And though the income savings seemed colossal enough, the capital savings were very much greater. First of all, we bought, in 1972, a 43-acre hill farm with an uninhabited stone cottage and farm buildings for £10,000. We then spent another £12,500 – of which £12,000 went on the new house for 16 people, and £500 on stock and equipment for the farm. We ended up, in other words, with a very substantial house, complete with dairy, workshops, food store, kitchen, 40 foot long dining room, two sitting rooms, two conservatories, eight double bedrooms, two bathrooms and a 43-acre farm. Which meant that individually we were well housed, provided nearly all our own energy for heating, and could count on nearly 3 acres per head. All this cost us just over £1,400 a head. That was at 1973 prices. Today the exercise would cost at least £2,500 a head, maybe more.

Even that is less than the average family spends on a home. Our money paid for a home, most of our heat, nearly all food, and provided some income from the farm. All for a labour input of what should have been at most 2 days each per week, which would have left us 3 days to use in local jobs or money-making hobbies.

But . . . the advice to join or found a community is not so easily given. For months I dreamt of all the obstacles to the project . . . failure to get planning permission, difficulties with building inspectors, the impossibility of finding the right farm to buy in the first place, the difficulty of finding members, the even greater difficulties of finding members with capital to spend, our lack of expertise, a disaster with the building project, complete failure to learn the craft of simple farming . . . yet none in the end proved any problem. The building sailed up, officials were helpful, the farm was soon productive, and we even had luck with the first hay harvest.

The one obstacle which I was confident of overcoming proved our undoing: we failed to make it as a community. Not all the time, in that I and many others there almost certainly spent some of the best moments of our lives at Eithin. But, in the end, after the first year, those at first intangible differences between us rose up and smote us most mightily. We lost the impetus we had in the first nine months about the time when our ebullient carpenter moved on to a job in the west country. And thereafter we never seemed to regain our *joie de vivre*. Risings became later. Members retreated to their bedrooms earlier. The food took a turn for the worse. And the pleas to hold more discussion meetings, at which no one said what they felt, became more frequent.

Where there had been happiness and sunshine, there rose up a feeling of leaden skies, of hens picking their way in desultory manner through untended barns, of fields returning to their natural state of tangled undergrowth. The smell of stale wood ash lingered permanently in the house. The dust from the unfinished concrete floors covered all with a layer of gritty gloom. The mud from the farm seemed to engulf us.

It might well have been simply our first winter in the hills: but the coming of spring seemed to make little difference. There was little enough argument, and what there was was mainly between those who wanted more visitors to liven the place up, and those who found visitors an unnecessary encumbrance at a time of obvious internal dissent. There were those of us who thought psychiatry, or group behaviour sessions, would solve the problem. Others preferred the Tarot pack, or the I Ching. Others had trouble with their partners. Most of us were miserable. The house remained unfinished.

I can't remember what decided us to go, but we were the first to do so. And, once decided, the decision seemed so obvious, the fate of the community so inevitable. We tried to tell those others to whom we were closest of what would happen, but they were not ready. The experiment had to run its course, and it did. But, seven months later, only four of the 14 people who had at one time or another been permanent members were left. Within a year the farm and the house were up for sale.

With such a history, it may seem strange to urge anyone to join a community. Yet I believe it is a sensible way to live . . . if you can do it. I am quite sure that everyone should try it at least once in their life. And I doubt very much that anyone who does will ever regard it as a failed experiment.

I certainly don't – nor, I think, does anyone else who was at Eithin. Hardly anyone goes into a community and comes out quite the same, for it is what the contemporary American sages would call 'a fairly total experience'. Regardless of how you plan it. Most communities, of course, fail in the end through lack of competence, lack of money, or both. That we seemed to have both these problems licked makes our own failures if anything more significant. We didn't have those hard economic facts forever draining away our morale. We were just unable to live with one another as human beings with any enjoyment. It was as simple as that.

So, if you are planning to do it, what advice could I offer? First, perhaps, never join a community because you want to live in a community, or think you do. Do so only if you discover a group of people, or even one or two, with whom you positively think a shared life would be a turn for the better. I've met a good few such people – and some of them were at Eithin. Some of them visited Eithin but left before they decided to join. Those people are the only reason for living in a community. The economic ones, or whatever other justifications you care to discover for yourself, are secondary. They are the spin-offs, the trade-ins which pay you their interest for sharing your life.

But never make the mistake of thinking them to be the reason. All such communities are bound to fail.

And, second, how do you know whether you really want to live in a community with someone? I'm quite sure there's no easy answer – in the positive sense. But there is one negative test, in which I'd put quite a lot of faith. Take your prospective communard, and get stoned, or drunk, or whatever your thing is, with him for a whole evening. If the evening's a success, it just might work. If it isn't, it certainly won't.

Appendix

⟢⟜⟣

Units

TECHNOLOGICAL self-sufficiency means a lot of sums, and plenty of switching from metric to older units, or vice versa. The table below shows you how to convert almost anything you're likely to need. In addition you'll want either a slide rule (cheaper) or, better and quicker, a pocket electronic calculator. These are now almost as cheap as a good slide rule and much more accurate.

MULTIPLY	BY	TO OBTAIN
atmospheres	76	cm mercury (Hg)
,,	1,033	cm water (H_2O)
,,	33·9	ft of water
,,	29·92	in of mercury
,,	14·7	lb/in^2
Btu	252	calories
,,	777·6	foot-pounds
,,	1,054	joules (watt-seconds)
,,	0·000293	kiloWatt-hours (kWh)
Btu/h	4·2	cal/min
,,	777·6	foot-pounds/h
,,	0·000393	horsepower
,,	0·000293	kW
Btu/ft^2	0·271	cal/cm^2 (langleys)
,,	0·293	watts (joules/sec)
$Btu/ft^2 h$	$3·15 \times 10^{-7}$	kW/m^2
,,	$4·51 \times 10^{-3}$	$cal/cm^2/min$
,,	$3·15 \times 10^{-8}$	$watts/cm^2$

MULTIPLY	BY	TO OBTAIN
Btu/ft² h °F (U-value)	5·67	W/m² °C
Btu in/ft² h °F (k-value)	0·144	W/m °C
calories	0·00397	Btu
,,	3·086	foot-pounds
,,	1·559	horsepower-hours
,,	4·184	joules
,,	1·162	kWh
cal/min	0·00397	Btu/min
,,	0·0697	watts
cal/cm²	3·687	Btu/ft²
cal/cm² min	796,300	Btu/ft² h
,,	251	W/cm²
centimetres	0·0328	ft
,,	0·394	in
,,	0·01	m
cm Hg	0·0132	atmospheres
,,	0·446	ft water
,,	0·1934	lb/in²
cm H₂O	0·00097	atmospheres
,,	0·014	lb/in²
cubic cm (cm³)	0·00948	ft³
,,	0·061	in³
,,	10⁻⁶	m³
,,	0·001	litres
cubic feet (ft³)	0·028	m³
,,	7·488	gallons
,,	28·32	litres
cubic feet of water	62·37	pounds of water
cubic feet/min	471·9	cm³/sec
cubic inches	16·39	cm³
,,	0·000579	ft³
,,	0·00432	gallons

MULTIPLY	BY	TO OBTAIN
cubic metres	10^6	cm^3
,,	35·3	ft^3
,,	264	gallons (US)
,,	1,000	litres
cubic yards	0·76	m^3
,,	222·2	gallons
,,	27	ft^3
degrees C	9/5 and add 32	degrees F
degrees F	subtract 32, × 5/9	degrees C
feet	30·48	cm
,,	0·00019	miles
feet of H$_2$O	0·029	atmospheres
,,	2·24	cm Hg
,,	0·43	lb/in^2
ft/min	0·51	cm/sec
,,	0·018	km/h
,,	0·011	miles/h
foot-pounds	0·0013	Btu
,,	0·32	calories
,,	$5·05 \times 10^{-7}$	horsepower-hours
,,	$3·77 \times 10^{-7}$	kWh
gallons (imperial)	1·2	gallons (US)
gallons (US)	5·460	cm^3
,,	0·194	ft^3
,,	332	in^3
,,	0·00545	m^3
,,	5·45	litres
horsepower	42·44	Btu/min
,,	550	ft lb/sec
,,	745·7	watts
horsepower-hours	2,546	Btu
,,	641,600	calories
,,	$1·98 \times 10^6$	ft-lb
,,	0·746	kWh
inches	2·54	cm

MULTIPLY	BY	TO OBTAIN
inches Hg	0·033	atmospheres
,,	1·13	ft of water
,,	0·49	lb/in²
inches of water	0·00246	atmospheres
,,	0·074	in of Hg
,,	0·0361	lb/in²
joules	0·000949	Btu
,,	0·738	ft-lb
,,	0·000278	watt-hours
,,	1	watt-second
kilograms	2·205	pounds
kilometres	1,000	metres
,,	0·621	miles
km/h	54·68	ft/min
kW	3,414	Btu/h
,,	737·6	ft-lb/sec
,,	1·341	horsepower
kWh	3,414	Btu
,,	1·341	horsepower-hours
litres	1,000	cm³
,,	0·0353	ft³
,,	0·264	gallons
litres/min	0·035	ft³min
,,	0·264	gallons/min
metres	3·281	feet
,,	39·37	inches
,,	1·094	yards
miles	5,280	feet
,,	1·609	km
,,	1,760	yards
miles/hour	0·447	m/sec
,,	88	ft/min
,,	1·609	km/hour

MULTIPLY	BY	TO OBTAIN
pounds	0·4536	kilograms
,,	16	ounces
pounds of water	0·016	ft³ of water
,,	0·12	gallons
pounds/in²	0·068	atmospheres
,,	5·171	cm of Hg
,,	27·69	in of H_2O
square cm (cm³)	0·001076	ft²
,,	0·155	in²
square feet (ft²)	$2·296 \times 10^{-5}$	acres
,,	0·0929	m²
square inches (in²)	6·452	cm²
,,	0·00694	ft²
square kilometres (km²)	247·1	acres
,,	$1·076 \times 10^{7}$	ft²
,,	0·3861	square miles
square metres (m²)	10·76	ft²
,,	1·196	yd²
square miles	640	acres
,,	$2·787 \times 10^{7}$	ft²
,,	2·59	km²
square yards (yd²)	9	ft²
,,	0·8361	m²
watts	3·414	Btu/h
,,	0·0569	Btu/min
,,	14·34	cal/min
,,	0·001341	horsepower
,,	1	joule/sec
watts/cm²	3,172	Btu/ft² h
W/m °C (k-value)	6·94	Btu in/ft² h °F
W/m² °C (U-value)	0·176	Btu/ft² h °F

MULTIPLY	BY	TO OBTAIN
watt-hours	3·414	Btu
,,	860·4	cal
,,	0·001341	horsepower-hours
yards	3	feet
,,	0·9144	metres

Table adapted from *Energy Primer* (Portola Institute, 558 Santa Cruz Avenue, Menlo Park, California 94025).

Books

ANYONE embarking on the sorts of things I've described in this book needs other books – and plenty of them. The best way to learn anything, of course, is to work with someone who knows more than you. But, time and again, you'll find that a master craftsman is not on your doorstep when you need him. There is nothing worse than having to tackle a job not knowing how to do it. Before you start any job, make sure you have sufficient information on hand to finish it. Our generation may have lost the ancient crafts that used to be handed down from father to son, but we have something almost as good: printed information.

Tools, materials and building

I could fill another book with a list of all the stuff published on building, but I've only ever used two books. The first, perhaps surprisingly, is the *Reader's Digest Complete Do-it-yourself Manual*. I don't like everything in it, particularly in the Projects Section, but the Techniques Section is superb, mainly on tools and how to use them. Also good for joinery. Well worth having, although its approach is sometimes a bit dainty – it fights shy, for instance, of big concreting jobs.

A good building book is Ken Kern's *The Owner Built Home* (Owner-Built Publications, Box 550, Oakhurst, California 93644). More conventional but nevertheless useful is *Building Construction Illustrated* by Francis D. K. Ching (Van Nostrand Reinhold, 1975). If you're building in rammed earth or soil-cement blocks, then you must try to get a copy of *Building in Cob, Pisé and Stabilized Earth* by C. Williams-Ellis and J. and E. Eastwickfield (published by Country Life, London, 2nd edition, 1947).

Heating and Insulation

I've dealt with insulation in more detail than you'll find in most books. And sources on heating are mainly restricted to the 1950s and 1960s, when gas and oil-fired central heating were all the rage. But there's a good section on heating with wood in *Energy Primer*: Advice on chimneys and flues is best obtained from *The Book of Successful Fireplaces* by R. J. and M. J. Lytle (Structures Publishing Co., 1972) and *How to Plan and Build Fireplaces* (Sunset Books, 1973). Finally, *The Woodburner's Handbook* by David Havens ($2.50 from Media House, Box 1770, Portland, Maine) is essential for timber burners.

Solar, wind and methane energy

First, there are a number of general books covering most aspects of alternative energy. The most professional is Brenda and Robert Vale's *The Autonomous House* (Universe Books, New York, 1975). Second is *Energy Primer* (see above). Third, try *The Mother Earth News Handbook of Homemade Power* (Mother Earth News, PO Box 70, Hendersonville, NC 28739).

Solar energy

The classic, but really for background information, is *Direct Use of the Sun's Energy* by Farrington Daniels (Ballantine Books, 1964). More recent, and in similar vein (but don't let it discourage you), is B. J. Brinkworth's *Solar Energy for Man* (Halsted Press, 1973). More specifically, the BRAD plans from Conservation Tools and Technology Ltd, 143 Maple Road, Surbiton, Surrey, are well worth having, and are also described in *New Scientist* ('Sun on the roof' by Philip Brachi, 19 September 1974). These sources list most of the other, pre-1970 solar literature but no one has yet written a good account of the masses of novel ideas which have been tried out in the past 5 years – perhaps because 1970 was really the year solar energy left the hands of the specialists and went public. But a useful recent compilation is *Low-Cost, Energy-Efficient Shelter for the Owner and Builder* edited by Eugene Eccli (Rodale Press, 1976).

Wind power

Again recent data is not adequately covered in one volume. The classic is *The Generation of Electricity by Wind Power* by E. W.

Golding (Spon and Philosophical Library, Inc., 1955) now also obtainable from Conservation Tools and Technology Ltd. Much shorter, more recent, and excellent value is Henry Clews' *Electric Power from the Wind* ($2 from Solar Wind Company, PO Box 7, East Holden, Maine 04429). And you must have *The Journal of the New Alchemists*, no. 2 ($6 from PO Box 432, Woods Hole, Mass. 02543). Glean extra information from *The Mother Earth News* – best take out a subscription and buy all the back numbers. If you can't afford it, sample vol. 17, p. 60; vol. 5, p. 42; vol. 6, p. 60; vol. 18, p. 25; vol. 20, p. 32; and vol. 24, pp. 52, 67 and 82. Also consult nos. 8, 10 and 12 of *Alternative Sources of Energy* (from Rt. 1, Box 36-B, Minong, Wisconsin 53859). Below are the addresses of the main firms manufacturing aerogenerators:

Aerowatt S.A., 37 Rue Chanzy, Paris 11ᵉ, France

Bucknell Engineering, 10717 Rush Street, So. El Monte, California 91733

Winco Dynatech Inc., PO Box 3263, Sioux City, Iowa 51102

Dunlite Electrical Co., 21 Frome Street, Adelaide 5000, Australia

Elektro GmbH, St Gallerstrasse 27, Winterthur, Switzerland

Enag, S.A., Rue de Pont-l'Abbé, Quimper, Finistère, France

Lübing Maschinenfrabrik, Ludwig Bening, 2847 Barstorf, PO Box 171, West Germany

Domenico Sperandio and Ager, Via Cimarosa 13–21, 58022 Folloncia, Italy

Methane

Plenty of good material to choose from here. Start with L. John Fry and Richard Merrill *Methane Digesters for Fuel and Fertilizer* ($3 from NAI-West, PO Box 376, Pescadero, California 94060). Most of this information, and more, is also to be found in Fry's *Practical Building of Methane Power Plants* ($12 from Fry, 1223 N. Nopal, Santa Barbara, California 93102).

There are two interesting publications in the UK. *Methane: Planning a Digester* by Peter-John Meynell (Prism Press, 1976) is a detailed account of the production and uses of methane gas and its by-products. *Methane* by Steve Sampson and edited by A. MacKillop (from Wadebridge Ecological Centre, 73 Molesworth St, Wadebridge, Cornwall, UK) is best treated as a source of inspiration. If you really want to build, there is nothing to beat two

287

publications by the Indian, Ram Bux Singh: *Bio-gas plants: generating methane from organic waste* and *Bio-gas plants: designs with specifications* from Gobar Gas Research Station, Ajitmal, Etawah (U.P.), India. See also occasional articles in *The Mother Earth News*.

Water, plumbing, waste and compost

No need for anything especially detailed here. Use the first two books cited in 'Tools, materials and building' above, and you can't go far wrong.

Transport

Write to Philip Brachi, 23 Meadow Road, Beeston, Notts., for his elegant essay on the bicycle as transport system. Don't forget, for lighter reading, Daniel Behrman's *The Man who Loved Bicycles*, (Harper's Magazine Press, 1973). You'll learn a lot about France as a pay-off. For LPG conversion there is nothing to beat *How to Convert your Auto to Propane* by Jerry Friedberg (Arrakis Volkswagen, PO Box 531, Point Arena, California 95468). But write also to Harold Bates, who's always doing new things, at Penny Rowden, Blackawton, Totnes, Devon, UK.

Food

No one should do anything about food until they've read Frances Moore Lappe's *Diet for a Small Planet* (Friends of the Earth and Ballantine, 1971). This not only spells out what the problem is in no uncertain terms, but tells you how to cook to provide a solution. A must. Bees and rabbits are best kept not from a book but from experience – join your local producer's association and seek fellow growers. Introductory books on poultry are published by Garden Way in Charlotte, Vermont, and by Prism Press in England. For hydroponics there's plenty to choose from; my choice would be *A Beginner's Guide to Hydroponics* by James Sholto Douglas (Drake, 1973). Backyard aquaculture is now almost the exclusive property of NAI-East, Box 432, Woods Hole, Mass. 02543. Write to them.

This and that

To sort out any electrical wiring problem, look at *Basic House Wiring* by Monte Burch (Popular Science, 1975); *Practical Electrical Wiring* by H. P. Richter (10th edition, McGraw-Hill, 1976); and *The Encyclopedia of Home Wiring & Electricity* by Martin Clifford (Drake, 1974). *Do-it-yourself Plumbing* by Max Alth (Popular Science, 1975) tells you almost everything you need to know to be your own plumber. Heat pumps are briefly described in *Energy Primer* (see above) but the real thing is *Modern Refrigeration and Air Conditioning* by Althouse, Turnquist and Bracciano (Goodheart-Willcox Company, South Holland, Ill. 60473). You don't need a book to make yoghourt, candles and soap.

Index

NOTES FOR THE FUTURE

An Alternative History of the Past Decade

Edited by Robin Clarke

"A compendium of much of the best committed writing of the past decade that is intended to alert us to the world resource crisis, the need for population control, proposals to subordinate science and technology to human desires and emotions, and the triumphs and heartaches of the new alternative culture. This is a brilliant collection by Clarke, an editor committed both in writing and action to research on alternative technology and self-sufficiency. . . . Highly recommended."

—Choice

"A compelling set of views on survival in the postindustrial age."

—Science Teacher

"This brilliant collection by many writers represents some of the best thinking of the past decade. . . . Contributors such as Barry Commoner, Paul Ehrlich, Murray Bookchin, Theodore Roszak, George Wald . . . sustain the high level of this multiperspective anthology."

—Publishers Weekly

$10.00 (cloth) $4.95 (paper)

THE AUTONOMOUS HOUSE

Design and Planning for Self-Sufficiency

Brenda and Robert Vale

"An 'autonomous' house is a shelter that operates on the energy income of its immediate environment. Thus, with the idea that one working experiment is worth more than a shelf full of theoretical reports, the Vales (both architects) unveil their own award-winning design of such a house. . . . And though the book is not long, its concise explication of the idiosyncrasies of heat pumps, fuel cells, recycled wastes, etc. has been braced with more than 100 diagrams and tables, plumbed by apposite and plentiful references, and founded on a functional index. Strongly recommended."

—Library Journal

"Two architects offer practical solutions for building a house that is not linked to utility lines, but instead uses the energy of sun, wind and rain to service itself and process its waste."

—Science News

$10.00

THE SURVIVALISTS

Patrick Rivers

"According to [Patrick] Rivers, the counterculture in Britain and the U.S. has evolved into an effort to live nondestructively in our delicate biosphere. The people involved in this effort, the survivalists, believe that our culture needs to be radically changed if it is to survive, and they have responded to this challenge by establishing small, nearly self-sufficient, usually agricultural communities. . . . Interesting and even inspiring."

—Library Journal

To track down the people who have felt constrained to *do* rather than talk about what should be done, Patrick Rivers traveled from Great Britain across North America, seeking them in the countryside and in the cities: people like Steve Baer, Robert Reines, John Todd, and Brenda and Robert Vale, who are experimenting in alternative technologies to produce nonpolluting forms of energy; those like Robin Clarke, who are trying to achieve a form of rural self-sufficiency; those who are publishing media for change, like *Mother Earth News*; those who have started free schools and psychiatric services. What binds them is their shared conviction that *living* differently is the only cure for our sick society. Patrick Rivers seeks to acquaint people who are still "inside the system" with that part of the alternative society which recognizes the importance of awareness and action. His up-to-date guide to reading materials and organization will be particularly useful to readers who want to find out more or want to become active.

$8.50 (cloth) $4.95 (paper)

OTHER UNIVERSE BOOKS ON
SURVIVAL AND SELF-SUFFICIENCY